Foucault's Aesthetics of Existence and Shusterman's Somaesthetics

Also Available from Bloomsbury

On the Politics of the Living, Federico Testa
The Late Foucault, ed. by Marta Faustino and Gianfranco Ferraro
The Ethics of Epicurus and Its Relation to Contemporary Doctrines,
Jean-Marie Guyau
Hegel's Political Aesthetics, Stefan Bird-Pollan and Vladimir Marchenkov

Foucault's Aesthetics of Existence and Shusterman's Somaesthetics

Ethics, Politics, and the Art of Living

Edited by
Valentina Antoniol and Stefano Marino

BLOOMSBURY ACADEMIC
LONDON • NEW YORK • OXFORD • NEW DELHI • SYDNEY

BLOOMSBURY ACADEMIC
Bloomsbury Publishing Plc, 50 Bedford Square, London, WC1B 3DP, UK
Bloomsbury Publishing Inc, 1359 Broadway, 12th Floor, New York, NY 10018, USA
Bloomsbury Publishing Ireland, 29 Earlsfort Terrace, Dublin 2, D02 AY28, Ireland

BLOOMSBURY, BLOOMSBURY ACADEMIC and the Diana logo are
trademarks of Bloomsbury Publishing Plc

First published in Great Britain 2024
This paperback edition published 2026

Copyright © Valentina Antoniol, Stefano Marino, and Contributors, 2024

Valentina Antoniol and Stefano Marino have asserted their right under the Copyright,
Designs and Patents Act, 1988, to be identified as Editors of this work.

Cover design by Charlotte Daniels
Cover images: Michel Foucault, 1979 (© Bettmann / Getty Images);
Richard Shusterman (Photo courtesy of R. Shusterman)

All rights reserved. No part of this publication may be: i) reproduced or transmitted in any form, electronic or mechanical, including photocopying, recording or by means of any information storage or retrieval system without prior permission in writing from the publishers; or ii) used or reproduced in any way for the training, development or operation of artificial intelligence (AI) technologies, including generative AI technologies. The rights holders expressly reserve this publication from the text and data mining exception as per Article 4(3) of the Digital Single Market Directive (EU) 2019/790

Bloomsbury Publishing Plc does not have any control over, or responsibility for,
any third-party websites referred to or in this book. All internet addresses given in
this book were correct at the time of going to press. The author and publisher regret
any inconvenience caused if addresses have changed or sites have ceased to exist,
but can accept no responsibility for any such changes.

A catalogue record for this book is available from the British Library.

Library of Congress Cataloging-in-Publication Data
Names: Antoniol, Valentina, editor. | Marino, Stefano, 1976- editor.
Title: Foucault's aesthetics of existence and Shusterman's somaesthetics :
ethics, politics, and the art of living / edited by Valentina Antoniol and Stefano Marino.
Description: 1. | London : Bloomsbury Academic, 2024. | Includes bibliographical references and index. |
Summary: "This volume provides the first critical comparison of Michel Foucault's aesthetics of
existence and Richard Shusterman's somaesthetics. Introduced by a comprehensive overview of the
concepts by the editors, the ensuing chapters build on the interdisciplinary character of both ideas, beyond
a narrow focus on art and beauty, exploring a wide range of topics ranging from politics to the philosophy
of sexuality. This volume reveals not only the important role Foucault's philosophy has played in
Shusterman's work, but also how recent developments in somaesthetics and somapower present a
complement, or even alternative, to Foucault's notions of biopower and biopolitics"– Provided by publisher.
Identifiers: LCCN 2024004749 (print) | LCCN 2024004750 (ebook) | ISBN 9781350384804 (hardback) |
ISBN 9781350384835 (paperback) | ISBN 9781350384828 (epub) | ISBN 9781350384811 (ebook)
Subjects: LCSH: Foucault, Michel, 1926-1984. | Shusterman, Richard. | Human body (Philosophy) | Biopolitics.
Classification: LCC B2430.F724 F735 2024 (print) | LCC B2430.F724 (ebook) |
DDC 128/.6–dc23/eng/20240508
LC record available at https://lccn.loc.gov/2024004749
LC ebook record available at https://lccn.loc.gov/2024004750

ISBN: HB: 978-1-3503-8480-4
PB: 978-1-3503-8483-5
ePDF: 978-1-3503-8481-1
eBook: 978-1-3503-8482-8

Typeset by Integra Software Services Pvt. Ltd.

For product safety related questions contact productsafety@bloomsbury.com

To find out more about our authors and books visit www.bloomsbury.com
and sign up for our newsletters.

Contents

List of Contributors   vi

Introduction. Foucault's Aesthetics of Existence and Shusterman's Somaesthetics: Ethics, Politics, and the Art of Living   *Valentina Antoniol and Stefano Marino*   1

1. Aesthetics of Existence: From Foucault to Stirner, via Baudelaire   *Philippe Sabot*   27
2. The Body at the Limits of Subjectivity. For a Philosophy-Performance as Political Aesthetics through the Thought of Michel Foucault   *Arianna Sforzini*   43
3. Pleasure, Scandal, and the Body: Foucault on Somatic Askesis   *Daniele Lorenzini*   63
4. *Leib, Körper*, and the Body Politic   *Martin Jay*   77
5. Care of the Social Self as Embodied   *Vincent M. Colapietro*   101
6. Somaesthetics and the Philosophical Life   *Richard Shusterman*   121
7. Somaesthetics, Foucauldian Aesthetics of Existence, and Living Ethically as White   *Chris Voparil*   145
8. *Aphrodisia, Eros, Charis*: Holistic Bodies and the Stylistic of Reciprocity   *Barbara Formis*   165
9. The Body Must Be Defended: Somapower and the Women's Strike in Poland   *Leszek Koczanowicz*   183

Index   193

List of Contributors

Valentina Antoniol is a Researcher in Political Philosophy at the University of Bari "Aldo Moro." She was Visiting Research Fellow at Brown University and at Cuny and held postdoctoral positions at the University of Bologna, where she obtained her PhD in joint supervision with the École des Hautes Études en Sciences Sociales (EHESS) of Paris. Her reseach focuses mainly on Michel Foucault's thought and, more generally, on political theory and contemporary continental philosophy. She is the author of *Foucault et la guerre. À partir de Schmitt, contre Schmitt* (Éditions Mimésis, 2023) and *Foucault critico di Schmitt. Genealogie e guerra* (Rubbettino, 2024).

Vincent M. Colapietro is a Liberal Arts Research Professor Emeritus, in Philosophy & African American Studies, at Pennsylvania State University, while now formally associated with the Center for the Humanities at the University of Rhode Island. His books include *Peirce's Approach to the Self* (1989), *A Glossary of Semiotics* (1993), *Fateful Shapes of Human Freedom* (2003), and *Acción, socialibidad ye drama: Un retrato pragmatista del animal humano* (2020). He is the author of numerous articles, including "Practicing Freedom and Emancipating Practices: Foucault's Pragmatism and Dewey's Genealogies" (Part I) and "Foucault's Pragmatism and Dewey's Genealogies: Mapping Our Historical Situations and Locating Our Historical Maps" (Part II), both in *Cognitio*, vol. 13 (n. 1 and n. 2). His writings have been translated into over ten languages. While his principal focus of historical research is pragmatism, he, like the pragmatists to whom he has devoted himself, is a comparativist.

Barbara Formis is Senior Lecturer in Aesthetics and Philosophy of Art at the School of the Arts, Sorbonne University, Paris 1, ACTE Institute. She obtained her PhD in philosophy from the Sorbonne University. Mainly influenced by pragmatism, she works in the interdisciplinary field between philosophy and performance. She is a founding member of EVA network (Everyday Aesthetics Network) and Pragmata (French association on pragmatist studies). She is co-director of Ressorts Esthétiques, a book collection of aesthetics at the Sorbonne Publishing House, and co-director of the Laboratoire du Geste, a platform that promotes research, publication, and experimental research in performance studies. She has published *Esthétique de la vie ordinaire* (PUF, 2010) and edited two anthologies: *Gestes à l'oeuvre* (2008, 2015) and *Penser en Corps. Somaesthetique, art et philosophie* (2009). She has been a dancer and has also worked as a dramaturge.

Martin Jay is Sidney Hellman Ehrman Professor Emeritus of History at the University of California, Berkeley. Among his works are *The Dialectical Imagination* (1973 and 1996); *Marxism and Totality* (1984); *Adorno* (1984); *Permanent Exiles* (1985); *Fin-de-Siècle Socialism* (1989); *Force Fields* (1993); *Downcast Eyes* (1993); *Cultural Semantics* (1998); *Refractions of Violence* (2003); *La Crisis de la experiencia en la era postsubjetiva*, ed. Eduardo Sabrovsky (2003); *Songs of Experience* (2004); *The Virtues of Mendacity* (2010), *Essays from the Edge* (2011); *Kracauer l'exilé* (2014); *Reason after Its Eclipse* (2016); *Splinters in Your Eye* (2020); *Trois études sur Adorno* (2021); *Genesis and Validity* (2021); and *Immanent Critiques* (2023).

Leszek Koczanowicz is Professor of Cultural Studies and Political Science at the Department of Cultural Studies at the SWPS University (Poland). He specializes in theory of culture, social theory, and cultural aspects of politics. His previous appointments include inter alia Wroclaw University, SUNY/Buffalo, Columbia University, and SUNY/Geneseo Helsinki Collegium for Advanced Studies. Leszek Koczanowicz is the author and editor of twelve books and numerous articles in Polish and English, including *Politics of Time: Dynamics of Identity in Post-Communist Poland, Politics of Dialogue. Non-Consensual Democracy and Critical Community, Anxiety and Lucidity: Reflections on Culture in Times of Unrest*, and recently *Emancipatory Power of the Body in Everyday Life: Niches of Liberation*.

Daniele Lorenzini is Associate Professor of Philosophy at the University of Pennsylvania. He is the author, most recently, of *The Force of Truth: Critique, Genealogy, and Truth-Telling in Michel Foucault* (University of Chicago Press, 2023), as well as *Éthique et politique de soi: Foucault, Hadot, Cavell et les techniques de l'ordinaire* (Vrin, 2015). He is also a co-editor of *Foucault Studies* and of two book series: *Philosophie du présent* (Vrin) and *The Chicago Foucault Project* (University of Chicago Press).

Stefano Marino is Professor of Aesthetics at the University of Bologna. His main research interests and research fields are hermeneutics, critical theory, neo-pragmatism and somaesthetics, philosophy of music, and aesthetics of fashion. He has authored several books, among which are: *Verità e non-verità del popular* (2021), *La filosofia dei Radiohead* (2021), *Le verità del non-vero* (2019), *Aesthetics, Metaphysics, Language: Essays on Heidegger and Gadamer* (2015), *La filosofia di Frank Zappa* (2014), and *Gadamer and the Limits of the Modern Techno-Scientific Civilization* (2011). He has co-edited several volumes and special issues of philosophical journals, among which are: *Varieties of the Lifeworld* (2022), *Pearl Jam and Philosophy* (2021), *The "Aging" of Adorno's Aesthetic Theory* (2021), *Kant's "Critique of Aesthetic Judgment" in the 20th Century* (2020), *Adorno and Popular Music* (2019), and *Philosophical Perspectives on Fashion* (2017). He has translated books of Th.W. Adorno and H.-G. Gadamer from German into Italian, and books of C. Korsmeyer and R. Shusterman from English into Italian.

Philippe Sabot is Full Professor of Philosophy at the University of Lille (UMR 8163 Savoirs, Textes, Langage). He is President of the Centre Michel Foucault since 2017. His research interests focus on Foucault's thought and his legacy in contemporary philosophy. He has published *Lire Les Mots et les choses* (2014) and *Le Même et l'Ordre. Michel Foucault et le savoir à l'âge classique* (2015), and has contributed to the edition of the works of Michel Foucault in the *Bibliothèque de la Pléiade* (2015). He recently edited *Phénoménologie et psychologie* (2021) and directed a book on *Michel Foucault. Discours et politiques de l'identité* (2022).

Arianna Sforzini is an Associate Professor (maîtresse de conferences) in contemporary philosophy and aesthetics at the University of Paris-Est Créteil. Her research focuses on Michel Foucault's thought and contemporary continental philosophy, particularly in its relationship to the arts and the performances of the body. She held postdoctoral positions at Sciences-po, the University of Fribourg, and the ICI Berlin. She is the author of *Les Scènes de la vérité. Michel Foucault et le théâtre* (Le Bord de l'eau, 2017) and *Michel Foucault. Une pensée du corps* (PUF, 2014), and the editor of *Michel Foucault, La question anthropologique. Cours. 1954–1955* (Seuil/Gallimard, 2022).

Richard Shusterman is the Dorothy F. Schmidt Eminent Scholar in Humanities and Professor of Philosophy at Florida Atlantic University, where he directs the Center for Body, Mind, and Culture. His primary research areas are philosophy of culture, aesthetics, ethics, and somaesthetics, a field he pioneered in the late 1990s. His books include *Body Consciousness* (2008), *Thinking through the*

Body (2012), *Ars Erotica* (2021), *Philosophy and the Art of Writing* (2022), and *Pragmatist Aesthetics* (1992/2000) which has been translated into fourteen languages. The French government awarded him the title of Chevalier des Palmes Académiques for his philosophical and cultural work.

Chris Voparil is Associate Professor of Philosophy at Lynn University. He is the author of *Reconstructing Pragmatism: Richard Rorty and the Classical Pragmatists* (2022) and *Richard Rorty: Politics and Vision* (2006), and co-editor of *Pragmatism and Justice* (2017) and several collections of Rorty's work, including *What Can We Hope For? Essays on Politics* (2022), *On Philosophers and Philosophy: Unpublished Papers, 1960–2000* (2020), and *The Rorty Reader* (2010), in addition to numerous articles on pragmatism.

Introduction. Foucault's Aesthetics of Existence and Shusterman's Somaesthetics: Ethics, Politics, and the Art of Living

Valentina Antoniol and Stefano Marino

Foucault and Shusterman: Philosophy as a "Way of Life"

Michel Foucault's aesthetics of existence and Richard Shusterman's somaesthetics can be probably considered as two of the most important and most influential philosophical conceptions of the late twentieth century and early twenty-first century. Thanks to their openness, their interdisciplinary character, their strong focus on the central role played by the body in human experience, and also their capacity to overcome the sad narrowness of certain academic limitations (and, vice versa, their capacity to profitably intersect different concepts and fields), both Foucauldian aesthetics of existence and Shustermanian somaesthetics have proved to be able to offer a complex and stimulating framework for the investigation of various philosophical topics, ranging from aesthetic questions to existential, ethical, social, and political problems. The present collection aims to inquire into both the affinities and differences between Foucault's and Shusterman's philosophical approaches. In particular, the essays from various authors collected here will try to show how the critical confrontation with Foucault's influential theories played an important role in the development of Shusterman's path of thinking and in many of his works. At the same time, what will emerge is also that, precisely due to a serious confrontation with Foucauldian aesthetics of existence, certain recent developments in the field of somaesthetics

---

The first and the third sections of this Introduction were written by Stefano Marino, while Valentina Antoniol authored the second and the fourth sections. The general structure and contents of the text, however, were planned, discussed, and conceived collaboratively by both authors.

can be understood as aimed to provide a notion of somatic power that presents a complement to (or, for some, an alternative to) Foucault's notions of biopower and biopolitics.

In this context, given the presence of the term "aesthetic" in both expressions (and thus also the strategic function of this term in the title itself of our book), it can be useful to immediately point out that both Foucault's aesthetics of existence and Shusterman's somaesthetics are characterized by a tendency to break aesthetics out of its narrow focus on the high fine arts and various concepts that have been traditionally associated to them (art, beauty, the sublime, genius, taste, autonomy, formalism, etc.). Rather, both Foucault and Shusterman have originally insisted on the fundamental somatic but also ethical, social, and political dimension of the aesthetics of life, thus arriving to extend aesthetics deeply into (but not only) the realm of sexuality and disclosing new paths for thinking, sometimes in surprising and unprecedented ways—especially in the case of Foucault, one of the most influential authors of the second half of the twentieth century, whose intellectual legacy forty years after his untimely death (1984–2024) will be the specific object of another collection.[1]

The notion itself of "aesthetics of existence"—as will be explained in a more detailed way in the second section of this Introduction—was not coined by Foucault in the context of a traditional aesthetics as philosophical theory of art,[2] but rather appeared first and foremost in the context of "a series of studies on 'the arts of oneself,' that is, on … the government of oneself and of others" (Foucault 1997c: 207). Foucault thus conceptualized the aesthetics of existence in terms of an ethical and political practice of production of subjectivity through processes of subjection and practices of subjectification that determine the relationship of the self with itself, with its *actualité*, and with others. In turn, Shusterman's somaesthetics, although originally deriving from a development of pragmatist aesthetics—as will be explained in a clearer way in the third section—consists of "the critical study and meliorative cultivation of the body as the site not only of experienced subjectivity and sensory appreciation (aesthesis) that guides our action and performance but also of our creative self-fashioning through the ways we use, groom, and adorn our physical bodies to express our values and stylize ourselves" (Shusterman 2019: 15). On this basis, it is not surprising that, in recent times, somaesthetic inquiry—in accordance with the long-lasting influence of Foucault's aesthetics of existence, outlined also in his *History of Sexuality*—has found in the dimension of lovemaking another fertile and stimulating field of investigation, as especially testified by Shusterman's treatise *Ars Erotica* (2021).

This courageous attempt to broaden the field of aesthetics beyond the traditional limits that have been assigned to this academic discipline in the modern age—an attempt that, as we said, can be found, although not exactly in the same form, in both aesthetics of existence and somaesthetics— can be associated, in Foucault's and Shusterman's thinking, to a more general aim: the aim to reconcile philosophical reflection with life. This leads to discover (or better, rediscover) an idea of philosophy as a "way of life" and an "art of living" that had been partly forgotten or neglected by modern philosophy, which had often favored a narrower and more delimited conception of philosophy as a merely academic discipline: a discipline strictly focused on certain epistemological, ontological, or ethical problems, typically considered as "philosophical," and hence somehow disconnected from a critical understanding of real life as it is actually lived by human beings. From this point of view, it is not surprising that both Foucault's aesthetics of existence and Shusterman's somaesthetics have offered stimulating insights on many fundamental dimensions of human existence, originally intersecting questions and fields that have been usually considered distant or different in standard scholarly research and considerably influencing the development of new researches on different topics that include, besides aesthetics, also politics, society, bodily experiences, human nature, sexuality, power relations, and human emancipation. With regard to this, although recognizing various elements of difference and sometimes also of distance between his approach and Foucault's, Shusterman has always been very clear about the great relevance of Foucault's intellectual legacy and its specific influence on somaesthetics; for example, when he observes in *Body Consciousness* that:

> Among the many reasons that made Michel Foucault a remarkable philosopher was a doubly bold initiative: to renew the ancient idea of philosophy as a special way of life and to insist on its distinctly somatic and aesthetic expression. This double dimension of Foucault's later work ... is pointedly expressed through his central ideas of the "aesthetics of existence," the stylizing "technologies of the self," and the cultivation of "bodies and pleasures." ... [H]is somaesthetics confronts us (even affronts us) with the crucial issue: conceived as an art of living, philosophy should attend more closely to cultivating the sentient body through which we live. (Shusterman 2008: 15, 48)

Foucault's Aesthetics of Existence

Before getting to the heart of the investigation of the comparison—in terms of proximity or distance—between Foucault's and Shusterman's philosophies, as well as on the fruitful possibilities of their joint employment, it is appropriate to start with a quick look at the French philosopher. This involves focusing on the theme of the aesthetics of existence, identifying some of the main traces that define the framework for understanding this concept, as well as its lines of provenance and emergence. If we were to go so far as to use the Foucauldian genealogical terminology of the early 1970s, we could even say that, *mutatis mutandis*, it is a matter of grasping the *Herkunft* and *Entstehung* of the question (see Foucault 1977: 139–64), which, in turn, will be adequately interrogated and tested by some of the authors of the essays collected in this volume.

When we speak of aesthetics of existence in Foucault's thinking, what we mean is a set of criteria—rules, opinions, advice—applied to practices of the self. These criteria establish the modes of relating to oneself and to others, through which subjectivities are transformed, constituted, and recognized as subjects. In this way, lines of connection are established between the subject, the truth, and the experience, the constitution of which is to be understood precisely as the "correlation between fields of knowledge, types of normativity, and forms of subjectivity in a particular culture" (Foucault 1990: 4). Going even more specifically, it is particularly useful to cite the definition provided by Foucault himself in the second volume of the *History of Sexuality*: "the arts of existence" are those "intentional and voluntary actions by which men not only set themselves rules of conduct, but also seek to transform themselves, to change themselves in their singular being, and to make their life into an *œuvre* that carries certain stylistic criteria" (Foucault 1990: 10–1).

Foucault also points out that, although these arts and technologies of existence have lost some of their autonomy since the Christian era, and although they have undergone a series of modifications and diversifications over the centuries, they nevertheless show a non-secondary relevance within a long-lasting history. As Foucault points out, Burckhardt himself had highlighted their importance in relation to the Renaissance era, and this theme was also present in Benjamin's essay on Baudelaire (see Foucault 1990: 11). Not only that, again with reference to Baudelaire, a key example is represented by his pages devoted to the "asceticism of the dandy who makes of his body, his behavior, his feelings and passions, his very existence, a work of art" (Foucault 1997a: 310). More generally, Foucault states that, although "in our society this idea is almost never remembered"

(Foucault 1994: 624), it is the history of nineteenth-century thought, or at least a layer of it, that should be taken up in this perspective. Indeed, in addition to Baudelaire and dandyism, one can also consider in this context the role of Stirner, Schopenhauer, Nietzsche, and anarchist thought; these are "attempts that are, of course, very different from each other, but which are all more or less obsessed by the question: Is it possible to constitute, or reconstitute, an aesthetics of the self?" (Foucault 2005: 251).

However, beyond these indications, which allow us to frame the relevance of the topic also from a temporal and historical point of view, we cannot fail to recognize how the notion of aesthetics of existence is elaborated by Foucault—in terms, admittedly, far from systematic—primarily within a series of broader reflections centered on the period of Greco-Roman antiquity and the early Christian age. These reflections and analyses were developed from the early 1980s and continued until the author's death in 1984. These researches are extraordinarily wide-ranging, that is, very rich in insights and depth, and extremely fruitful from the point of view of the possibilities of reworking, which find their main exposition in the lecture courses of Foucault's last years at the Collège de France, in a number of interviews and short speeches, and in the final volumes of the *History of Sexuality*. In particular, the Foucauldian production of this period turns out to be marked by investigations and researches devoted to the formation of a hermeneutics of the self, the government of self and others, and the emergence of a problematization of sexual behavior as the object of a moral concern: all investigations that, in turn, show the centrality of the theme of "care of the self." It is this theme and its arrival at what Foucault calls "a veritable culture of the self" (Foucault 2005: 205) that constitute, in fact, what we can understand as a premise for the development and understanding of analyses devoted to the aesthetics of existence. Indeed, the continuity and connection that exists between these researches makes it difficult to establish precise boundaries and areas of application, although there is no lack of specification and differentiation.[3] It is therefore a matter of framing the relevance of these reflections.

In *The Hermeneutics of the Subject*, Foucault observes that the Greek notion of *epimeleia heautou* ("care of the self")—which spans, modifying and expanding, almost a thousand years of history, from ancient Greek philosophy to Christian asceticism, from the fifth century BC to the fourth/fifth century AD—constitutes a privileged lens to investigate the relations between subject and truth in Western culture, with particular reference to the period named as Antiquity. More precisely, although this notion has been historically neglected in favor of that of *gnothi seauton* ("know yourself"), it is a matter of recognizing that subjectivities are precisely constituted and modified by the "form of reflexivity specific to this or that type of care of the self" (Foucault 2005: 462). Indeed, the care of the self has to do with spirituality, which involves the necessary transformation of the subject by the subject itself in order to have access to truth.

Foucault also points out a distinction: while in the Socratic-Platonic era the notion of care of the self was linked to the exercise of power—that is, in order to govern others well it was necessary to take care of oneself—what we see in later times is different. Referring to the Cynic, Epicurean, and Stoic philosophies, as well as to the developments of these traditions in the first/second century AD, Foucault shows that, in this context, the care of the self no longer appears as a precept to which it is necessary to devote oneself at a specific time of life, in the transition from adolescence to adulthood, but becomes co-extensive with life itself. So, it is possible to observe a change in the goals of the care of the self: the goal is no longer (properly or exclusively) that of learning the skills of governing others—an instrumental care of the self with respect to care of others—but is directed toward the development of a full relationship with oneself: namely, the constitution of self as an accomplished subject who has dominance over external events. In this sense, the care of the self also makes possible the care of others and may have, as in the case of the Cynics, the goal of "a change in the general configuration of the world" (Foucault 2011: 313). In fact, from this point on, what we can see is the development of a culture of the self—the maximum extent of which is observed in the first two centuries of the imperial age—that establishes an increasing degree of identification between care of the self and *tekhne tou biou*, "that is to say, the art, the reflected method for conducting one's life, the technique of life" (Foucault 2005: 177–8). More precisely, the art of living—also referred to as the "aesthetics of existence" (Foucault 1990: 11)—is guided "by the principle that says one must 'take care of oneself'. It is this principle of the care of the self that establishes its necessity, presides over its development, and organizes its practice" (Foucault 1986: 47). Ultimately, in the modification and expansion of the theme of self-care, which acquires the forms of a culture of the self, it becomes a principle of general scope that:

> It also took the form of an attitude, a mode of behavior; it became instilled in ways of living; it evolved into procedures, practices, and formulas that people reflected on, developed, perfected, and taught. It thus came to constitute a social practice, giving rise to relationships between individuals, to exchanges and communications, and at times even to institutions. And it gave rise, finally, to a certain mode of knowledge and to the elaboration of a science. (Foucault 1986: 45)

It is especially to this model that Foucault turns his attention when he raises the question—not only philosophical, but also ethical and political—of the reworking of the subject's relationship with himself/herself, with others and with the world, through an aesthetics of existence. The crux for Foucault, then, is to address an issue that has a character he defines as "remarkable": making (one's) life an object of *tekhne*, a work of art (see Foucault 1994: 615). It is remarkable because the importance of the issue stems from the fact that, especially in our present, "for us there is a work of art only when something escapes the mortality of its creator" (Foucault 1994; see also Foucault 2011: 162), that is, when we speak of objects, texts, fortunes, inventions, and institutions. On the contrary— and here we can find the Nietzschean roots of Foucault's work (see Nègre 1996: 57–62)—the aesthetics of existence is about stylizing one's life and understanding existence as art. Or, again, it is about arguing that "art is capable of giving a form to existence which breaks with every other form" (Foucault 2011: 187). It is art, in fact, that lays existence bare. The relationship with the self, mediated by art (which has nothing to do with the contemporary cult of the self), must therefore "be describable in terms of a multiplicity of forms, of which 'authenticity' is only one ... [I]t must be structured as a practice that can have its models, its conformities, its variations, but also its creations" (Foucault 1994: 617).

In the wake of these analyses, it is therefore a question of getting to the heart of the matter and recognizing the centrality of the problem of the self in the art of existence. As Foucault notes, theoretical knowledge is not enough in order to establish an adequate relationship with the self. Again, a key example can be found in the care of the self in the Hellenistic and Roman periods, on the basis of which what can be observed is not only an attitude of readiness for self-modification, but also the need to resort to a set of techniques and practices of the self.[4] The latter consists of a set of daily prescriptions and exercises, aimed at the body, soul, thoughts, and conduct; and traceable in moral, philosophical, and medical texts. In fact, with reference to classical antiquity, Foucault stresses the recognized need to develop an *askesis*,[5] that is, an asceticism, understood as an exercise of the self on self, which poses the question "of the subject in the realm of practice" (Foucault 2005: 318) and leads to recognize the centrality of the body as an object of care and concern. Of fundamental importance, in this regard, is the difference between asceticism in Hellenistic and Roman times, on the one hand, and Christian asceticism, on the other. If the goal of the Christian pastoral was to bring the individual—through progressive stages—to a renunciation of the self, it is only by turning to Greco-Roman antiquity that we obtain, on the contrary, the valorization of an antithetical goal, namely that of the constitution of the self. More precisely, what we see here is a return of the self—a theme that, as Foucault makes explicit, will also become recurrent within "modern" culture, allowing one to find in this culture an ethics and an aesthetics of the self "which refers explicitly ... to what is found in the Greek and Latin authors" (Foucault 2005: 251).

What follows from this is that Hellenistic-Roman asceticism should in no case be understood as the effect of subjecting the individual to an imposed law, which would decree what the latter can or cannot do. Otherwise, it is a principle of intensifying subjectivation. To put it another way: it is not a reduction, but an endowment, a *paraskeue* ("equipment," "preparation"), which enables the subject to cope with unforeseen events that may befall him or her (Foucault 2005: 315–29). It is in this way, through such practices of the self, that the subject is allowed to grow in terms of independence and autonomy, with respect to himself/herself, but also with respect to others. Thus, while it is true that the same types of exercises practiced in the earlier period can be also observed with reference to the Christian era, it is equally true that in the Hellenistic and Roman epoch one never finds a rigid definition of these exercises. In fact, the subject's questioning of his or her own conduct is accompanied by the relationship to the rules of that conduct, which need not be understood in terms of inflexible codifications of behavior but can in fact be thought of, and identified as, practices of the self.[6]

For Foucault, it is fundamental to emphasize that the possibility of freedom of the subject, who makes his/her own choices regarding the practices of the self, is inescapable within the framework of the *tekhne tou biou*, which has little to do with the *Christian regula*. In fact, Hellenistic-Roman culture presents a clear ethical orientation, whereby this term—derived from *ethos*, that is, what was an individual's mode of existence and behavior for the Greeks—is meant the way in which subjects seek, through the elaboration of a relationship with themselves, to transform themselves into the moral subjects of their own conduct, not having as an end the fact of bringing their behavior into compliance with a given rule (see Foucault 1990: 27). It is "[a] history—as Foucault says—not of the moral law, but of the moral subject" (Foucault 1994: 621–2). From all this we can better understand what Foucault argued in an interview from 1984, during which he asserted that ethics is nothing more than the reflected practice of freedom (Foucault 1997b: 284). And it is within this ethical reflection that the aesthetics of existence is inscribed, masterfully exemplified by Greco-Roman culture (see Foucault 2015: 143). In fact, there is no codification of acts in the moral reflection of classical antiquity, but rather what Foucault calls an aesthetics of existence—which counts precisely as ethics—understood as the "purposeful art of a freedom" (Foucault 1990: 253) that takes the form of self-mastery and implies the (creative) capacity to modify oneself.

It is crucial to draw two orders of questions from these reflections. On the one hand, it must be noted that Foucault outlines a close articulation between ethics and aesthetics. It is ethics, understood as the practice of freedom, that enables the forging of one's existence as a work of art. On the other hand, it must also be recognized that the intertwining of ethics and aesthetics is composed of a third element, which is political. As we have seen, the practices and techniques of the self—which are central to understand the aesthetics of existence—define the modes of subjectification, that is, the ways in which subjects construct themselves as such. What emerges from these analyses, then, is the possibility of elaborating practices of freedom through a work on the self, for a free constitution of the subject other than the imposed one. As Foucault notes with particular reference to the Cynics, the production of the self, mediated by art, implies "a polemical relationship of reduction, refusal, and aggression to culture, social norms, values, and aesthetic canons" (Foucault 2011: 188).

It is thus understood that, based on these reflections, a connection between forms of subjectification and forms of power cannot but be established—a theme, the latter, that had already been fully defined by Foucault since his analyses on critical attitude (centered on the Kantian concept of *Aufklärung*: see Revel 2015), elaborated in the late 1970s and further developed by him until his untimely death. More precisely, what deserves to be emphasized here is the fact that it is precisely through the accentuation of the subject's possibilities for action within power relations that the Foucauldian researches of the 1980s (and, specifically, the analyses of the aesthetics of existence) are developed. In fact, for much of the 1970s Foucault had been concerned with the mechanisms of subjugation, with specific reference to the French classical age—during which the subject "was reflected as the objective product of systems of knowledge and power, the alienated correlate of these apparatuses of power-knowledge from which the individual drew and exhausted an imposed, external identity beyond which the only salvation was madness, crime, or literature" (Gros 2005: 513). Differently, his main interests in the 1980s, in relation to Antiquity, are related precisely to the attempt to bring out the existence of different mechanisms of configuration of subjectivity. Foucault, in fact, focuses his attention on specific techniques and practices of the self, the operation of which was not traceable either in the study of disciplinary and biopolitical mechanisms or in the research on pastoral power, related to the origins of governmentality.

However, misleading inferences should not be drawn from the above. Approaching the conclusions of this section of our introduction specifically centered on Foucault, it is essential to emphasize at least two issues that are eminently political. First, it must be stressed that the fact of referring to the active possibilities of subjectivation in relation to the aesthetics of existence is not at all equivalent to an endorsement of the hypothesis of a return to an essentialized or sovereign subject. On the contrary, Foucault argues: "I think that the subject is constituted through practices of subjection or, more autonomously, through practices of liberation, of freedom, as in antiquity, on the basis, of course, of a certain number of rules, styles and conventions present in the cultural environment" (Foucault 1994: 733). Thus, the creative and inventive practices of the self, related to the aesthetics of existence (which find in the history of cynicism one of the most striking examples), are opposed to the inevitable processes of subjugation that similarly define the ways in which subjects are constructed. That is, there are no totally active or passive subjects; instead, there are processes of the self that involve for the subject both practices of conduction and spaces of freedom available to him or her. The aesthetics of existence thus designates a field of analysis and reflection that is eminently political or, more precisely, ethico-political, where ethics and politics are inseparable in the gesture—again, political—of producing a subjectivity, which may be the bearer, as precisely in the case of the Cynics, of an outrageous and subversive way of life.

Second, it should be noted that Foucault's focus on the practices of the self and the aesthetics of existence, promoted particularly during Hellenistic and Roman antiquity, does not reside at all in the belief that we can reproduce the same model centuries later. On the contrary, it implies recognizing that a recourse to such distant epochs allows Foucault (but also us, as scholars and/or readers of Foucault's work) to critically rethink our *actualité* and our positioning within it. Ultimately, this operation allows us to demonstrate, in the face of a necessity of the present, a precise historical possibility. As Foucault states, "We do not have to choose between our world and the Greek world. But since we can see that some of the great principles of our morality were once linked to an aesthetics of existence, I think this kind of historical analysis can be useful" (Foucault 1994: 616–7).

Having arrived at this point, the question is therefore the following (and it is the same question posed by Foucault): Is it possible to constitute, or reconstitute, an aesthetics of the self? It would be too easy, but also misleading, to simply answer in positive or negative terms. However, what we can certainly recognize, with respect to the possibility of an aesthetics of existence, is its necessity. That is, the necessity, for each and every one, of an attention directed toward "a beautiful, striking, and memorable existence" (Foucault 2011: 163), bearing not only a potentially subversive impact against conventions, habits, and cultural and social values ("as form of life in the scandal of truth" [Foucault 2011: 180]), but also a transformative capacity of the world, measured from what we can call an "aesthetic politicization" of our existence. Once again, for each and every one.

Shusterman's Somaesthetics

After the brief outline of the main themes and directions of Foucault's aesthetics of existence, let us now shift our attention to Shusterman's somaesthetics. As has been recently noted by Jerold J. Abrams (2022: 1–13) in a contribution on the overall development of Shusterman's path of thinking throughout the decades, the latter can be divided into three main phases: corresponding to (1) Shusterman's early work in the field of analytic aesthetics, then (2) his turn to pragmatist aesthetics, and finally (3) his "baptize" of somaesthetics, a new disciplinary proposal strongly rooted in the pragmatist tradition but also open to other approaches, and specifically dedicated to the philosophical investigation of the soma.[7]

The concept of soma was introduced by Shusterman in the late 1990s to designate "the sentient purposive body," conceived as "both subject and object in the world," both *Körperhaben* and *Leibsein*, breeding the insight that "[o]ur experience and behavior are far less genetically hardwired than in other animals" and revealing that "human nature is always more than merely natural but instead deeply shaped by culture" (Shusterman 2019: 14–5). For Shusterman, the soma thus expresses "our ambivalent condition between power and frailty, dignity and brutishness, knowledge and ignorance," proving to be "a single, systematic unity that however contains a multiplicity of very different elements (including diverse organs) that have their own needs, ailments, and subsystems" (Shusterman 2019: 16–7). Starting from his 1996 book *Von der Interpretation* (a revised German translation of one of his books, originally published in French in 1994: *Sous l'interprétation*), his 1997 article "Somaesthetics and the Body/Media Issue" (later included in the collection *Performing Live* from 2000) and, above all, his 1999 essay "Somaesthetics: A Disciplinary Proposal" (later republished in the second, revised edition of *Pragmatist Aesthetics* from 2000), in which the concept itself of somaesthetics was introduced for the first time, Shusterman has progressively specified in greater detail the breadth, complexity, and significance of his original philosophical proposal.[8]

Ever since the introduction of somaesthetics—"an interdisciplinary field of research, rooted in philosophical theory, but offering an integrative conceptual framework and a menu of methodologies not only for better understanding our somatic experience, but also for improving the quality of our bodily perception, performance, and presentation"—Shusterman has always suggested to distinguish three main branches of somaesthetics ("that overlap to some extent," though): analytic, pragmatic, and practical somaesthetics (Shusterman 2017: 101–2). At the same time, "[a]long with the three branches of somaesthetics," for Shusterman it is also important to differentiate "three dimensions" of it: representational, experiential, and performative somaesthetics, where this differentiation is basically connected to the fact that "[s]omatic disciplines or practices can be classified as to whether their major orientation is toward external appearance or inner experience" (Shusterman 2017: 102–3). On the basis of a broad and pluralistic concept of art and aesthetic experience, Shusterman's somaesthetics has suggested to overcome the "dominant aesthetic ideology [that] identifies art with the institution of high fine art" (Shusterman 2000: 140) and, rather, to embrace a wide group of different activities, experiences, or techniques that can be philosophically stimulating at the level of both theoretical analysis and practical everyday life: eating, cooking, dancing, clothing, sport, urban life, performing in various forms and at various levels, etc.

"An ameliorative discipline of both theory and practice" (Shusterman 2000: 101), somaesthetics has deep historical and genealogical roots in Deweyan pragmatism and, to some extent, can be understood as a coherent and logical development of pragmatist aesthetics: not by chance, the first systematic presentation of this new disciplinary proposal can be found in the tenth chapter of a book precisely entitled *Pragmatist Aesthetics*, as a chapter added to the second, revised edition of Shusterman's most famous book. At the same time, due to its dialogical openness, its interdisciplinary nature, and its theoretical curiosity originally combined with its practical orientation, somaesthetics also has historical and genealogical roots that can be found elsewhere, that is, outside of the modern tradition of American pragmatism; for example, in the "ancient Greek practice of philosophy" and in "ancient Asian wisdom [that] privileges embodiment" (Kremer 2022: 50). Besides this, a crucial role in the birth and development of somaesthetics has also been played by Shusterman's critical confrontation with other traditions in modern and contemporary philosophy. In this context, especially the potential intersections between, on the one hand, a coherently Deweyan pragmatist approach and, on the other hand, hermeneutical thinking (Gadamer, Derrida), critical theory of society (Benjamin, Adorno, Marcuse) and the philosophies of French thinkers like Merleau-Ponty, de Beauvoir, and Foucault have proved to be very stimulating and fruitful to fuel a further advancement of Shusterman's somaesthetic thought.[9]

Apropos of the influence of Foucault's aesthetics of existence (and, more in general, of his theory of power) on somaesthetics, Shusterman has observed that, for example, "Foucault is exemplary for working in all three dimensions of somaesthetics" and that "the exemplary value of Foucault's ... contributions to somaesthetics" also lies, for instance, in "his seminal theories of biopower, gender construction, and somatically based social domination" (Shusterman 2008: 29, 31). According to Shusterman, "[m]odern philosophy too often displays [a] sad somatic neglect," but "contemporary philosophers [like] John Dewey and Michel Foucault," notwithstanding all the divergences, in theory and practice, that surely characterize their respective philosophies, nonetheless "differently exemplify [the] idea of somaesthetics, though without properly thematizing or articulating this field as such" (2000: 263). In particular, in the case of Foucault, Shusterman observes that, "[a]dvocating the body as an especially vital site for self-knowledge and self-transformation, Foucault argues that self-fashioning is not only a matter of externally stylizing oneself through one's bodily appearance but of transfiguring one's inner sense of self (and thereby one's attitude, character, or ethos) through transformative experiences" (Shusterman 2008: 9). So, in the final chapter of the second edition of *Pragmatist Aesthetics*, specifically dedicated to the introduction of the new disciplinary proposal of somaesthetics, Shusterman explicitly praises

> Foucault's seminal vision of the body as a docile, malleable site for inscribing social power [that] reveals the crucial role somatics can play for political philosophy. It offers a way of understanding how complex hierarchies of power can be widely exercised and reproduced without any need to make them explicit in laws or to officially enforce them. Entire ideologies of domination can thus be covertly materialized and preserved by encoding them in somatic norms that, as bodily habits, typically get taken for granted and therefore escape critical consciousness ... However, if oppressive power relations can impose onerous identities that get encoded and sustained in our bodies, these oppressive relations can themselves be challenged by alternative somatic practices. (Shusterman 2000: 270)

These quotations from some relevant passages of Shusterman's fundamental works *Pragmatist Aesthetics* (1992[1]; 2000[2]) and *Body Consciousness* (2008) clearly show that his critical confrontation with Foucault's stimulating thinking played a significant role in his process of transition from pragmatist aesthetics to somaesthetics and, in particular, in his definition of the main ramifications, contents, and aims of somesthetics itself, as "a discipline of theory and practice" (Shusterman 2000: 271). However, the influence of Foucault on Shusterman's thinking—also in terms of a critical dialogue with Foucault's theory: namely, a dialogue in which not only convergences and agreements but also divergences and disagreements clearly emerge—is not limited to that phase of Shusterman's path of thinking: that is, the phase in which the new philosophical discipline of somaesthetics was first defined and proposed. As a matter of fact, also Shusterman's aforementioned systematic exploration of the somaesthetics of sexuality in his research monograph *Ars Erotica*[10] bears clear traces of the influence of Foucault's aesthetics of existence.

The connection of sexuality to a "transformation into discourse" and a "technology of power" plays a central role in Foucault's original project of an aesthetics of existence, as part of his general approach to the history of sexuality. With his seminal contribution to a historical-philosophical interpretation of sexuality—understood by him as "*un dispositif historique*, a historical *device*" or, depending on the English translation, "a historical *construct*" (Kelly 2013: 78)— Foucault apparently aimed to inscribe his analysis of this phenomenon into a more general context centered on elements and dimensions such as "instances of discursive production," the "production of power," and the "propagation of knowledge." From a certain point of view, Shusterman's *Ars Erotica* can be understood as an extension of Foucault's approach to this topic, presented in his seminal and ambitious *Histoire de la sexualité* in four volumes (*La volonté de savoir* from 1976, *L'usage des plaisirs* from 1984, *Le souci de soi* from 1984, and *Les aveux de la chair* from 2018, reconstructed from Foucault's manuscripts).[11] More precisely, as an extension but, at the same time, also as a complement and a critique, especially with regard to certain specific issues. In fact, in Shusterman's intentions, a serious consideration of the theories of sexuality developed in non-Western cultures (while Foucault notoriously limited his attention to ancient Greco-Latin and early Christian culture), and an equally serious consideration of the experience of women in the historical development of various practices of lovemaking throughout the centuries and in different contexts, represent a way to broaden the framework of a historical-philosophical investigation of sexuality beyond certain limits that, for Shusterman, characterized Foucault's project. As Shusterman observes in the Preface to *Ars Erotica*:

> My book on *ars erotica* owes a deep debt to Foucault's ideas, though I diverge from them in important ways ... [I]n our age of progressively transcultural globalization, it is important to look beyond Foucault's focus on the West and its ancient thought ... [T]his book presents a somewhat different perspective than Foucault's, but one that hopes to complement rather than replace his impressive work. (Shusterman 2021a: XI–XII)

In particular, apropos of the sharp distinction—introduced by Foucault in his *History of Sexuality* and in some of his interviews—between the notions of Asian *ars erotica* and Western *scientia sexualis*, Shusterman expresses some perplexities and disagreements, claiming that:

> [D]espite his enthusiastic interest in Chinese sexology, Foucault has gravely misunderstood it ... Looking for a contrasting culture to challenge the dour sexual science of the West and highlight erotic artistry as a key element in his project of a self-styling "aesthetics of existence" grounded in pleasures, Foucault projects this theoretical desire onto Chinese sexology by exoticizing it as that radical other, erecting it as a pleasure-seeking, aesthetic *ars erotica* to contrast to *scientia sexualis*. Fixated on sexual pleasure, he failed to see that Chinese erotic arts were primarily designed for health, procreation, and the harmonious management of a polygynous household. This blindness was surely intensified by Foucault's inattention to the philosophical, social, and cultural background in which Chinese erotic theory was embedded and functioned ... If one construes Foucault's notion of *ars erotica* as implying an emphasis on the aesthetic pleasures and artfulness of lovemaking in contrast to a *scientia sexualis* that focused on truth and health (whether physical, mental, or spiritual), then Indian erotic theory provides a better paradigm for such art. While China's sexual theory drew most heavily on medical texts and derived its concern for pleasure from the key medical aims of health and progeny, Indian erotology drew most heavily on the fine arts and their sensuous aesthetic pleasures ... Nonetheless, Indian sexual theory cannot fully support Foucault's sharp distinction between esoteric *ars erotica* and *scientia sexualis*, because it defines itself in essentially scientific terms as providing knowledge about empirical matters based on observation. (Shusterman 2021a: 150, 157, 202)

Of course, such divergences and partial disagreements must *not* lead to neglect or undervalue the relevance of the convergences and agreements that are also present in Shusterman's relation to Foucault's thinking. Precisely the articulation of such a complex and stimulating dialectics of proximity and resemblance, on the one hand, and distance and difference, on the other hand, is at the center of Shusterman's own contribution included in the present collection. A contribution in which Shusterman clearly acknowledges the importance of Foucault as one of the "most influential contemporary advocates of philosophy as an art of living" and arrives to define Foucault as "a crucial exemplar, indeed a hero, for [him] and for somaesthetics."

Comparisons, Challenges, Critiques: An Overview

The book that we are happy and honored to introduce here to our readers, *Foucault's Aesthetics of Existence and Shusterman's Somaesthetics: Ethics, Politics, and the Art of Living*, is the first study specifically devoted to the development of rigorous critical comparisons between the theories and works of these two important contemporary philosophers. The present volume aims to fill a gap in the existing international literature, and it is in this direction that the essays presented here have been developed, confronting the thoughts of Foucault and Shusterman and offering innovative possibilities for the development and deepening of the themes investigated.

All the authors of the contributions collected in this book are leading experts in the field. Among them is Richard Shusterman himself, who, from his peculiar somaesthetic perspective, has authored an original essay that constitutes—and probably it could not be otherwise—a sort of barycenter within the book, among the texts of the various authors. Investigating Foucault's work, Shusterman in fact clearly recognizes the inescapable influence of the French philosopher's thought on his own philosophy and, more generally, on philosophy understood as an "art of living." More specifically, in this new contribution, entitled *Somaesthetics and the Philosophical Life*, Shusterman traces the lines of elaboration of somaesthetics, which, by recognizing the centrality of the body (soma)—"our tool of tools"—in its ameliorative sense of a care of the self, allows for the presentation of a specific model of philosophical life. It is precisely from this position that, while holding both Foucault's and Hadot's perspectives in high regard, Shusterman at the same time distances himself from both these thinkers and stands on a kind of intermediate road between the two. In particular, Shusterman's contribution develops a critique of both Hadot's notion of a philosophical life, which, for him, neglects the body by focusing only on spiritual exercises, and Foucault's all-too-modernist advocacy of radical novelty in his vision of life as a work of art.

While Shusterman's essay, as we said, can be understood as the barycentric node of this volume, its starting point is represented by Philippe Sabot's contribution, entitled *Aesthetics of Existence: From Foucault to Stirner, via Baudelaire*. Sabot's text develops an in-depth and accurate investigation of the notion of aesthetics of existence in Foucault and its connection to the concept of dandyism. The aim of this chapter is to investigate, starting from the analysis of some works of Baudelaire, what Foucault himself, in the pages devoted to the "cursed poet," calls the "attitude of modernity." In particular, Sabot shows that the interpretation of dandyism promoted by Foucault is intended to detach itself from the one developed by Sartre in his 1975 introduction to Baudelaire's *Intimate Writings* which, more generally, was also devoted to the relationship between self and the self. Baudelairean dandyism cannot be reduced to an aesthetic question (in a narrow sense of this concept); it is also an ethical and political concern. It is thus on the basis of this basic understanding that Foucault recontextualizes Baudelaire and the figure of the dandy within a framework of transhistoricity that, in turn, allows Sabot to explore the parallels between dandyism and "anarchism," especially through the prism of Stirner's philosophy. Ultimately, Sabot's essay shows how one, moving from these reflections, can certainly argue that Foucault's aesthetics and ethics of the self cannot unfold in a truly political dimension.

The theme of the body is one of the subjects that are central to the reflections developed in this entire volume; hence it is a node of interest that, although in different ways and various degress, cuts across all the content proposed. This theme acquires a position of absolute centrality especially in some of the essays collected here, such as, the one authored by Arianna Sforzini. In her contribution, *The Body at the Limits of Subjectivity: For a Philosophy-Performance as Political Aesthetics through the Thought of Michel Foucault*, Sforzini precisely and deeply explores the presence and role of the body in Foucault's philosophy and, from these analyses, examines the paradox of a philosophical body that is often despised, objectified, and reduced to the pre-given materiality of natural existence, and yet still required in any form of embodied experience of thought. The body, in fact, should not be understood as the limit of our finitude (the prison of the soul, the trap of thought, the aporia of the mind), but rather as a critical weapon that counters and makes impossible any fundamental claim of philosophy that is aimed to support the universality of its discourse. Moreover, making specific reference to the importance of the body in Foucauldian analyses of subjectivities and practices of subjectivation, Sforzini pays a special attention to an important notion in the contemporary philosophical and political landscape, that of "agency." In this regard, and especially on the basis of the (posthumous) dialogue between Foucault and Butler, Sforzini shows how current philosophical debates have placed the body at the center of new interrogations and struggles based on the development of situated disciplines (Gender Studies, Queer Studies, Theoretical Feminism), as if identities and subjective agencies were now decided on the basis of the body.

Ascetic techniques of the body are the focus of Daniele Lorenzini's chapter, entitled *Pleasure, Scandal, and the Body: Foucault on Somatic* Askesis. In this text, Lorenzini investigates Foucault's project of an aesthetics of existence on the basis of a rigorous analysis of two different types of somatic *askesis*: on the one hand, the Greco-Roman techniques of the self that target the body in order to develop an appropriate "use of pleasures"; on the other hand, the Cynic practices of the self aimed at producing a scandalous "stripping of existence." Lorenzini's investigation aims to show that, although these two ascetic techniques of the body (which play a crucial role in Foucault's lectures and writings of the 1980s) have several features in common, they are actually strikingly different in their function and their ultimate ethico-political significance. Unlike other ancient philosophies, the aesthetic and ethical shaping of the Cynic's body, as well as his life, become in fact—according to Lorenzini's interesting conclusion—an immediately political stake because of their being inscribed in the public space.

In the essay Leib, Körper, *and the Body Politic*, Martin Jay provides a very rich analysis on a new way of conceptualizing the body politic, starting from the non-hierarchical distinction between the *Leib*, that is, the body as subjectively experienced (implicitly the "lived body"), and the *Körper*, that is, the lived body as an extended object in the world (related to the "dead body"): a distinction that, as is well known, has been especially developed in the twentieth century by philosophical anthropologists and phenomenologists. According to Jay, this perspective prevents assuming that the aesthetic ideal of organic holism and harmony can be the model of political health or identifying popular sovereignty with transcendental vitalism. Instead, it introduces a new appreciation of the role of mortality in conceptualizing politics, which goes beyond the problematic role played by death in other theories, such as Kantorowicz's notion of the king's two bodies, Hegel's sacrificial sublation of the negativity of death, and the critique of thanatopolitics and necropolitics in the work of Mbembe, Esposito, and Agamben. In contrast, Jay shows how Walter Benjamin's anti-vitalist anthropological materialism acknowledges the value of the disunited body, which oscillates between subjectivity and objectivity, as an allegory of the distinction between a people and a population. Insofar as we are all destined to die, this helps those who are included in the former category to make common cause with those who are abjected from the demos or ethnos—migrants, the homeless, the disenfranchised, the occupied—and excluded from a vitalist image of popular sovereignty.

In the essay *Care of the Social Self as Embodied*, Vincent M. Colapietro delves into the theme of experience, noting the centrality of this issue in both Foucault's work on the aesthetics of existence and Shusterman's work on somaesthetics. In this way, the two authors are fruitfully investigated jointly. In particular, the starting point of Colapietro's analysis is the observation that very often these two philosophers have been unfairly criticized for (exclusively or simply) focusing on the individual self, in isolation from other human beings. On the contrary, for Colapietro a charitable reading of their respective projects discloses that neither forgets nor ignores human selves as social, embodied actors who nonetheless have the capacity to twist free, to some extent, from the nexus of relationships in which these selves are inextricably enmeshed, in order to care in a focused, intense, and imaginative manner on the self.

The comparison between Foucault's work on the aesthetics of existence and Shusterman's work on somaesthetics is also the main focus of Chris Voparil's essay, entitled *Somaesthetics, Foucauldian Aesthetics of Existence, and Living Ethically as White*. Voparil uses these philosophical perspectives as a starting point for addressing the ethical and epistemic challenges associated with living and being in the world as white. In particular, Voparil argues that Foucault's and Shusterman's insights into ethical-aesthetic self-transformation suggest ways to move beyond and transform the ethically compromised white subjectivity that is sustained and perpetuated by white privilege and white ignorance. In Foucault's distinctive sense of ethics, white people need to develop a new relationship to themselves—a new *rapport à soi*—as normalized white subjects, and it is toward this end that, according to Voparil, the critical and ameliorative emphases of somaesthetics offer practices and habits of somatic normativity that circumvent reliance on increased self-knowledge, which white ignorance often renders unavailable. By approaching whiteness as something that we do—a somatic style—we can, according to Voparil, foster a Foucauldian ethics oriented to alternative forms of aesthetic self-stylization and develop a positive program of cultivating new ethical practices of white subjectivity and, ultimately, reconstructing whiteness. Precisely on this basis, Voparil's analyses suggest that our best hope for promoting ethically improved white self-transformation resides in conceiving of whiteness as a style of existence and developing practices and habits of alternative embodied styles of living and being as white people.

The theme of aesthetics as a way to think, imagine, and inhabit the world is the focus of Barbara Formis' essay, entitled Aphrodisia, Eros, Charis: *Holistic Bodies and the Stylistic of Reciprocity*. Formis notes that pragmatist aesthetics, in general, and somaesthetics, in particular, have insisted on the idea of aesthetics as a field of sensitive faculties that are not restricted to the realm of the arts. Formis then focuses on the very ancient idea of "desire," showing its usefulness for the purpose of understanding "eros" in relation to "*holos*," as an entanglement proper to pragmatist aesthetics as a discipline that interrogates affects and intentions in a community of interactions. It is thus on the basis of these analyses that Formis draws some interesting lines of inquiry that make use of the philosophical input offered by both Shusterman's recent book *Ars Erotica. Sex and Somaesthetics in the Classical Arts of Love* (2021) and the third volume of Foucault's *History of Sexuality, The Care of the Self* (1984). Finally, Formis suggests a feminist reading of these texts.

Leszek Koczanowicz's essay, entitled *The Body Must Be Defended: Somapower and the Women's Strike in Poland*, closes the list of contributions collected in the present volume by directly addressing our *actualité* and, once again, placing a specific investigation of the body—based on the work of both Foucault and Shusterman—at the center of the analysis. The starting point of Koczanowicz's text concerns an October 2020 decision of the Constitutional Tribunal of Poland that drastically reduced the availability of legal abortion in this country. As Koczanowicz accurately reconstructs, under communism, abortion was legally accepted and widely practiced in Poland for social reasons, despite the predominantly Catholic orientation of the country. After the fall of communism, the Sejm, under strong pressure from the Catholic Church, limited the possibility of abortion only to three cases: crime (incest, rape), serious threat to the life or health of the pregnant woman, and severe damage to the fetus; however, the 2020 ordinance practically excluded the latter case. As a consequence, a wave of mass demonstrations and performances against this decision swept through Poland in October and November 2020. The main philosophical point of Koczanowicz's analysis concerns precisely the fact that these political demonstrations had a twofold corporeal character: on the one hand, they were centered on women's rights to use the body, while, on the other hand, the body was also the main instrument of protest and resistance. On the basis of these reflections, Koczanowicz then interprets these events through the category of somapower, understood as an extension of Shusterman's notion of somaesthetics to the realm of politics, which is useful in delineating the political significance of the Women's Strike in Poland. Indeed, for Koczanowicz somapower denotes the emancipatory potential of the body in resisting an oppressive regime and, as such, is the opposite of biopower, which is primarily concerned with the way in which the body is shaped and controlled by power.

In conclusion, all the contributions included in this volume do not limit themselves to "simply" pay tribute to the great value of Foucault's and Shusterman's thought in the field of contemporary philosophy, through the adoption of a historical and reconstructive perspective. This was not (or, at least, not only) the goal of this work. In fact, ever since we began planning and then developing this project, the common aim of the editors and the authors has undoubtedly been more ambitious. All the essays that compose *Foucault's Aesthetics of Existence and Shusterman's Somaesthetics* intend above all to highlight the potentialities of the comparison between these two authors and the relevance, even with respect to our *actualité*, of their ideas and theories, through the adoption of radical interpretive perspectives and approaches that do not hesitate to elaborate the "aesthetics of existence" and "somaesthetics" in terms of comparisons, challenges, and critiques (as highlighted by the subtitle of our Introduction). It is precisely from this purpose that several lines of inquiry and analysis have been drawn by all the authors who generously contributed to our volume (whom we, as editors of this book, would like to thank for their commitment to our project); in our view, the meticulousness of their investigations is matched only by their originality. In presenting this volume, we thus leave to our readers the pleasure of reading and the task of judging this work.

Notes

The multilingual collection of authors have sometimes used their own translations of the cited works (of Foucault or other thinkers), when there was no English translation or sometimes where there is but the authors have prefered their own translation.

1. We allow ourselves to remind here our readers of the planned collection of essays *Foucault's Legacy in Contemporary Thinking: Forty Years Later (1984–2024)*, edited by Valentina Antoniol and Stefano Marino, special issue of *Foucault Studies*, n. 1, 2024 (https://rauli.cbs.dk/index.php/foucault-studies/announcement/view/32).
2. On Foucault's aesthetics, understood as a philosophy of art, see Tanke 2009.
3. For a partially different position from the one proposed here, tending mainly to mark some aspects of distance between the culture of the self and the aesthetics of existence, see Mees 2021.

4   In this regard, consider the following definition of techniques of the self: "techniques which permit individuals to effect, by their own means, a certain number of operations on their own bodies, on their own souls, on their own thoughts, on their own conduct, and this in a manner so as to transform themselves, modify themselves, and to attain a certain state of perfection, of happiness, of purity, of supernatural power, and so on. Let's call this kind of techniques a technique or technology of the self" (Foucault 1993: 203).

5   As is well known, Foucault was largely influenced by Pierre Hadot's studies on spiritual exercises (see Hadot 1987; see also Cremonesi 2015).

6   Regarding the practices of the self, a particularly important reference is that to the *aphrodisia* (especially, but not only, with respect to Greek antiquity), that is, those "acts, gestures and contacts that produce a certain form of pleasure" (Foucault 1990: 40), which "situated in an agonistic field of forces difficult to control" and which required "in order to take the form of a conduct that was rationally and morally admissible … a strategy," and "this strategy aimed at an exact self-mastery … whereby the subject would be 'stronger than himself' even in the power he exercises over others" (Foucault 1990: 250).

7   For a thorough account and interpretation of Shusterman's concept of soma, regarding the influence of the notions of *Körper*, *Leib*, and body-mind (and the corresponding influence of philosophers such as Merleau-Ponty, Plessner, Dewey, and Foucault) on the shaping of the somaesthetic conception of the body, see Snævarr 2022.

8   The publication of a journal specifically dedicated to the development of this field of research, *The Journal of Somaesthetics*, and a book series animated by analogous ambitions and aims, "Studies in Somaesthetics" (published by Brill), has surely contributed to further strengthen and enhance this new philosophical discipline at an international level, also favoring comparisons and debates with other philosophical traditions and approaches.

9   On Shusterman's relation to hermeneutics and, more generally, questions concerning interpretation, see, for example, his essays "Organic Unity: Analysis and Deconstruction," "Pragmatism and Interpretation," and "Beneath Interpretation" (Shusterman 2000: 62–135), and, more recently, also his work "Pragmatism and Interpretation: Radical, Relativistic, but not Unruly" (Shusterman 2022a). On Shusterman's relation, as a pragmatist philosopher, with some aesthetic theories developed in the context of Frankfurt critical theory, see his recent contribution "Pragmatist Aesthetics and Critical Theory: A Personal Perspective on a Continuing Dialogue" (Shusterman 2022b). The first three chapters of Shusterman's book *Body Consciousness: A Philosophy of Mindfulness and Somaesthetics*, respectively entitled "Somaesthetics and Care of the Self: The Case of Foucault," "The Silent, Limping Body of Philosophy: Somatic Attention Deficit in Merleau-Ponty," and "Somatic Subjectivities and Somatic Subjugation: Simone de Beauvoir

on Gender and Aging," are specifically dedicated to his relation with these eminent French thinkers (Shusterman 2008: 15–111).

10   Apropos of the concept itself of *ars erotica* in Shusterman's somaesthetics and its significance today, we can say that, for him, *ars erotica* "deserves serious critical and theoretical attention so that we can reconstruct our sexual attitudes, practices, and techniques to free them from flaws resulting from eroticism's long association with evils of predatory patriarchy and injustice ... Old taboos on philosophizing frankly about sex may have faded, but philosophical discomfort and moral reluctance to write candidly about lovemaking and erotic experience still haunt our pragmatist tradition today ... However, without forthright, concrete theorizing about sexual matters, we risk perpetuating mistaken assumptions and inadequate or harmful practices that result in experiences of painful disappointment instead of rewarding pleasure. Excited but still confused and uncertain about the promising pluralism of LGBTQ+ options, our culture needs more critical, yet positively reconstructive, thinking about sexuality and eroticism. This seems a worthy task for progressive pragmatist theory, if not also for other philosophical approaches" (Shusterman 2021b: 21, 25).

11   To be precise, as noted also by Shusterman, Foucault "devoted his final years of research to an extensive study of sexuality in Western culture, but died before completing the project. Initially, Foucault planned a six-volume project entitled *The History of Sexuality*, with the first introductory volume published in 1976, together with a list of the five planned subsequent book titles. None of those titles, however, ever appeared, because of the difficulties he faced in pursuing this initial project. The research was incredibly demanding, and it required moving in unanticipated directions. Finally, eight years later, shortly before his death in 1984, Foucault published two other volumes of *The History of Sexuality* (*The Use of Pleasures* and *Care of the Self*), together with a revised and abridged program of only four volumes for the entire work. The final volume, *Les aveux de la chair*, was posthumously published only in 2018, reconstructed from manuscripts" (Shusterman 2021a: XI).

Bibliography

Abrams, J. J. (2022), "Introduction," in *Shusterman's Somaesthetics: From Hip Hop Philosophy to Politics and Performance Art*, ed. J. J. Abrams, 1–19, Leiden: Brill.

Cremonesi, L. (2015), "Pierre Hadot and Michel Foucault on Spiritual Exercises: Transforming the Self, Transforming the Present," in *Foucault and the History of Our Present*, eds. S. Fuggle, Y. Lanci, and M. Tazzioli, 195–209, New York: Palgrave Macmillan.

Foucault, M. (1977), "Nietzsche, Genealogy, History" [1971], trans. D. F. Brouchard and S. Simon, in *Language, Counter-Memory, Practice: Selected Essays and Interviews by Michel Foucault*, ed. D. F. Bouchard, 139–64, Ithaca: Cornell University Press.

Foucault, M. (1986), *The History of Sexuality. Vol. 3: The Care of the Self* [1984], trans. R. Hurley, New York: Vintage Books.

Foucault, M. (1990), *The History of Sexuality. Vol. 2: The Use of Pleasure* [1984], trans. R. Hurley, New York: Vintage Books.

Foucault, M. (1993), "About the Beginning of the Hermeneutics of the Self: Two Lectures at Dartmouth," *Political Theory*, 21 (2): 198–227.

Foucault, M. (1994), "À propos de la généalogie de l'éthique: un aperçu du travail en cours" [1984], in *Dits et écrits. Vol. IV*, eds. D. Defert and F. Ewald, 609–31, Paris: Gallimard.

Foucault, M. (1997a), "What Is Enlightenment?" [1984], in *The Essential Works 1954-1984. Vol. I: Ethics. Subjectivity and Truth*, ed. P. Rabinow, 303–19, New York: New Press.

Foucault, M. (1997b), "The Ethic of the Concern of the Self as a Practice of Freedom" [1984], in *The Essential Works 1954-1984. Vol. I: Ethics. Subjectivity and Truth*, ed. P. Rabinow, 281–301, New York: New Press.

Foucault, M. (1997c), *The Essential Works 1954-1984. Vol. II: Aesthetics, Method, and Epistemology*, ed. J. D. Faubion, New York: New Press.

Foucault, M. (2005), *The Hermeneutics of the Subject. Lectures at the Collège de France 1981-1982* [2001], ed. F. Gros, trans. G. Burchell, New York: Palgrave MacMillan.

Foucault, M. (2011), *The Courage of Truth: The Government of Self and Others II. Lectures at the Collège de France 1983-1984* [2009], ed. F. Gros, trans. G. Burchell, New York: Palgrave MacMillan.

Foucault, M. (2015), "La culture de soi" [1983], in *Qu'est-ce que la critique? Suivi de La culture de soi*, eds. H. P. Fruchaud and D. Lorenzini, 81–109, Paris: Vrin.

Gros, F. (2005), "Course Context," in M. Foucault, *The Hermeneutics of the Subject. Lectures at the Collège de France 1981-1982* [2001], ed. F. Gros, trans. G. Burchell, 507–50, New York: Palgrave MacMillan.

Hadot, P. (1987), *Exercices spirituels et philosophie antique*, Paris: Études augustiniennes.

Kelly, M. G. E. (2013), *Foucault's History of Sexuality Volume I, The Will to Knowledge*, Edinburgh: Edinburgh University Press.

Kremer, A. (2022), "From Pragmatism to Somaesthetics as Philosophy," in *Shusterman's Somaesthetics: From Hip Hop Philosophy to Politics and Performance Art*, ed. J. J. Abrams, 44–60, Leiden: Brill.

Mees, M. (2021), "La vie comme œuvre d'art? Actualité de l'esthétique de l'existence chez Foucault," *Nouvelle revue d'esthétique*, 28: 61–8.

Nègre, F. (1996), "L'esthétique de l'existence dans le dernier Foucault," *Raison présente*, 120: 47–71.

Revel, J. (2015), "'What Are We at the Present Time?' Foucault and the Question of the Present," in *Foucault and the History of Our Present*, eds. S. Fuggle, Y. Lanci, and M. Tazzioli, 13–25, New York: Palgrave Macmillan.

Shusterman, R. (2000), *Pragmatist Aesthetics: Living Beauty, Rethinking Art* [1992], Lanham/Boulder/New York/Oxford: Rowman & Littlefield.

Shusterman, R. (2008), *Body Consciousness: A Philosophy of Mindfulness and Somaesthetics*, Cambridge: Cambridge University Press.

Shusterman, R. (2017), "Fits of Fashion: The Somaesthetics of Style," in *Philosophical Perspectives on Fashion*, eds. G. Matteucci and S. Marino, 92–106, London/New York: Bloomsbury.

Shusterman, R. (2019), "Bodies in the Streets: The Soma, the City, and the Art of Living," in *Bodies in the Streets: The Somaesthetics of City Life*, ed. R. Shusterman, 13–37. Leiden: Brill.

Shusterman, R. (2021a), *Ars Erotica: Sex and Somaesthetics in the Classical Arts of Love*, Cambridge: Cambridge University Press.

Shusterman, R. (2021b), "Pragmatism and Sex: An Unfulfilled Connection," *Transactions of the Charles S. Peirce Society*, 57 (1): 1–31.

Shusterman, R. (2022a), "Pragmatism and Interpretation: Radical, Relativistic, but Not Unruly," *Contemporary Pragmatism*, 19 (2): 91–112.

Shusterman, R. (2022b), "Pragmatist Aesthetics and Critical Theory: A Personal Perspective on a Continuing Dialogue," *Scenari*, 16 (1): 197–217. Available online: https://mimesisjournals.com/ojs/index.php/scenari/article/view/1874 (accessed September 6, 2023).

Snævarr, S. (2022), "Shusterman's Pragmatist Philosophy," in *Shusterman's Somaesthetics: From Hip Hop Philosophy to Politics and Performance Art*, ed. J. J. Abrams, 23–43, Leiden: Brill.

Tanke, J. J. (2009), *Foucault's Philosophy of Art: A Genealogy of Modernity*, New York: Continuum.

1

Aesthetics of Existence: From Foucault to Stirner, via Baudelaire

Philippe Sabot

Life as a Work of Art: A Transhistorical Issue?

The topic of the aesthetics of existence, as developed by Foucault from the 1980s, has been the subject of numerous and varied comments for over thirty years, which testify to both the stimulating nature of this topic and the questions it has raised with regard to the evolution of Foucault's thought. In the French-speaking field, I will mention only, in addition to the well-known comments by Pierre Hadot (1989),[1] a very comprehensive article by Fabien Nègre on "The Aesthetics of Existence in the Last Foucault" (1996) where the Nietzschean stakes of Foucault's aesthetics of existence were highlighted, as well as the incorporation of studies of ancient ethics, particularly cynicism, into the broader framework of a politics of truth, or the more recent article of Martin Mees, "La vie comme œuvre d'art? Actualité de l'esthétique de l'existence chez Foucault" (2021). Mees rightly recalls the criticisms that have been formulated against this notion, which in reality operates a double crossing: the crossing of aesthetics and ethics first of all, with the question of how to articulate them or how to justify the shift from one to the other. That is to say, how does a technique of the self rooted in the aesthetic dimension acquire an ethical value—and what value?[2] But the aesthetics of existence also unfolds at the intersection of several genealogies, with at least two being clearly identifiable. First, the genealogy of the subject of desire, proposed by the *History of Sexuality* and ultimately oriented toward the transformation of ancient techniques of the self within the framework of the emergence of a Christian morality establishing a completely different relationship with the self. Then there is another genealogy, which links the development of the aesthetics of existence to another long-term historical sequence, from the Renaissance to the nineteenth century and perhaps beyond—as Martin Mees suggests based on his reading of the lecture on *The Culture of the Self* (Foucault 2015). In this lecture, the aesthetics of existence does indeed echo forms of life and modes of stylization of existence that can have a subversive and critical impact in relation to the truth games and power relations in which certain lives—those of the "infamous men" (Foucault 1999)—may have been taken and subjected (Mees 2021: 68).³

In the English-speaking field, it is mainly the philosophical and "pragmatic" significance that Richard Shusterman gives to Foucault's proposition of life as a work of art that will be retained in this contribution. In the first chapter of *Practicing Philosophy*, Shusterman suggests that some singular lives reactivate a relationship between *bios* and *philosophia* that were at the heart of the practices of thought that originated in antiquity (most notably that embodied by Socrates). Shusterman also notes that the actualization of this *bios philosophikos* in Foucault's terms of the aesthetics of existence reveals a series of productive tensions: tension, aesthetically, between the respect for certain universal values defining the work of art (harmony, beauty, and moderation) and the temptation for radical creative transgression aimed at novelty in the invention of the self; tension, in relation to the body, between somatic discipline (up to asceticism) and anarchic somatic explosion (up to the dissolution of the bodily self); and finally, tension, politically, between the potentially elitist objectives of self-improvement and the promotion of a more egalitarian democratic society. Shusterman also shows that these tensions are not the expression of a schematic opposition between an ancient ethics and a modern ethics, but rather that they nourish the notion of aesthetics of existence from within, as Foucault elaborates it in the context of a genealogical and critical approach that is rooted in antiquity but also aims to shed light on the field of practices of the self since modernity.

This contribution aims to both continue the work of these previous studies and approach the questions they raise in a slightly unconventional way. On the one hand, it is a matter of returning to one of the major and explicit figures of the aesthetics of existence, which is dandyism, and specifically the place and importance that Foucault accorded to it in "What Is Enlightenment?" when defining, from some excerpts of Baudelaire, what he calls the "attitude of modernity" (Foucault 1997c: 310). But, on the other hand, it is also a matter of expanding the analysis of this figure of dandyism in directions that are sometimes only hinted at by Foucault, but that precisely allow us to explore the tensions highlighted by Shusterman in *Practicing Philosophy*. The first of these lines of study thus makes it possible to highlight the gap that Foucault clearly seeks to create in relation to Sartre's interpretation of dandyism, and more broadly of the relationship to oneself, proposed in his long introduction to Baudelaire's "intimate writings" (Sartre 1950). But Baudelaire's dandyism is obviously not just a hermeneutic issue between Foucault and Sartre. It is also a major ethical and political issue that leads Foucault (and this is the second expansion I propose) to reinsert Baudelaire and the figure of the dandy in this crossing of genealogies that I mentioned earlier and which amounts to situating the aesthetics of existence in a form of historical transversality, of transhistoricity (as Foucault suggests with regard to cynicism) (Foucault 2011: 174, 179) deserving to be questioned in terms of the connections it might suggest between cynicism and dandyism, for example, or between dandyism and "anarchism"[4]—starting from the figure of Stirner in particular, as it is mobilized in this surprising (and rarely commented upon) passage from *The Hermeneutics of the Subject*:

> [A] whole section of nineteenth-century thought can be reread as a difficult attempt, a series of difficult attempts, to reconstitute an ethics and an aesthetics of the self. If you take, for example, Stirner, Schopenhauer, Nietzsche, dandyism, Baudelaire, anarchy, anarchist thought, etcetera, then you have a series of attempts that are, of course, very different from each other, but which are all more or less obsessed by the question: Is it possible to constitute, or reconstitute, an aesthetics of the self? At what cost and under what conditions? (Foucault 2005: 251)[5]

It will therefore be necessary to ask what kind of relationship between ethics and aesthetics of existence is carried by the series of figures evoked by Foucault in this excerpt, and particularly by those that, within this series itself, open aesthetics and ethics of the self to a purely political dimension. My contribution therefore proposes a double exploration through the spaces of thought and forms of life opened by the aesthetics of existence. This exploration will first go from Foucault to Baudelaire, passing through Sartre; then from Baudelaire to Stirner, passing through Foucault.

From Foucault to Baudelaire, through Sartre

To introduce my remarks, it is necessary to briefly revisit the place that Foucault gives to Baudelaire and, particularly, to dandyism in "What Is Enlightenment?" In what way is dandyism a relevant figure to qualify the aesthetics of existence? How does it define what Foucault calls, in *The Hermeneutics of the Subject*, "an ethics and an aesthetics of the self" (Foucault 2005: 251)?

These questions invite us to take a closer look at the few pages where Foucault seeks to define the "attitude of modernity" by referring to the essay on *Le Peintre de la vie moderne* and the fate that Baudelaire reserves for what he calls, "according to the vocabulary of the time, dandyism" (Foucault 1997c: 311). It is possible to note in passing that this kind of concession to the "vocabulary of the time" already allows us to consider that "dandyism" is only the modern (and, in this sense, conjunctural or transitional) name for an attitude, an *êthos* that circulates in history under other names and other forms but that is connected to the same etho-poietic operation: "to take oneself as object of a complex and difficult elaboration" (Foucault 1997c). This etho-poietic operation corresponds to the overcoming of the Aristotelian divide between *poiesis* and *praxis* which, according to Shusterman, contributed to sharply separating art and philosophy (in its ethical aim). It is precisely to the revision and overflowing of this divide that the (modern) injunction to make one's life a work of art responds.

In general, the reference to the attitude of modernity is itself clarified through the connection between historical and aesthetic experience, which reflect each other through Kant's mirror of criticism. Being modern is not just about taking "consciousness of the discontinuity of time" (Foucault 1997c: 310) but also about discernment, at the heart of this experience of discontinuity, what constitutes the very form of a critical relationship with the present, conceived as the gap between the contingency of the present and the necessity proper to the era. The whole art of the poet or painter of modern life then consists in taking the measure of such a gap, in making the modernity of fashion (and modernity itself) visible or audible, so that not only the snapshots of a particular era, but also the "permanent reactivation" of a modern attitude are manifested in singular works. This attitude is a "permanent critique of our historical being" (Foucault 1997c: 312). Baudelaire can thus be assimilated to a thinker of modernity as crisis, which finds a crucial relay in Foucault's reformulation of the Kantian theme of criticism, in relation to the ethical requirement of "work on our limits" (Foucault 1997c: 319), itself founded on an untimely, inactual, relationship to the present as such.

It is still necessary to understand how dandyism embodies this "work on our limits" in the form of self-improvement. To better understand this and the context of Foucault's discussion of Baudelaire in "What Is Enlightenment?," it may be helpful to consider it in the context of a hidden confrontation with Sartre and the way in which he seeks to characterize Baudelaire's *êthos* as an attitude of "countermodernity" (Foucault 1997c: 310). In Sartre's view, dandyism represents the most obvious manifestation of this attitude and deserves the strongest condemnation for its inauthenticity toward the self.

This confrontation is systematically developed in relation to the three main points that Foucault addresses successively regarding Baudelaire in his 1984 lecture. It is interesting to note that these three points tend to reclaim certain fundamental elements of Sartrean conceptuality (choice, freedom, and existence) while significantly shifting their stakes. However, it seems that this shift ultimately allows us to clarify the ethical *and political* stakes of an aesthetics of existence as embodied by dandyism, in contrast to the persistent but common criticism (developed to the point of caricature by Sartre) of a pure aesthetics of the self as being cowardly and gratuitous, and without a grasp on the present (on Sartre's *Baudelaire*, see my study "Lectures de Baudelaire: Benjamin, Sartre, Foucault": Sabot 2008).

Foucault begins by analyzing Baudelaire's attitude of modernity (which could be associated with that of the dandy) as it relates to "a voluntary choice made by certain people" (Sabot 2008: 309) toward the present. This conscious choice, which forms the very condition of the lucidity of the artist, is in contrast to all forms of passive acceptance of change that lead to idolizing fashion and being mesmerized by the spectacle of the contingent. The "heroism" of modern life, on the contrary, consists of overcoming this passivity without denying the ephemeral nature of daily reality, but rather subjecting it to an effort of aesthetization—albeit an ironic aesthetization, since the abstract and indefinable beauty of the classics is now replaced by a "bizarre," irregular beauty that reflects the irregularity of reality itself.

This highlights how the theme of ironic heroization of the present—which identifies the possibility of a gap between the current and the non-current, between the historical and the poetic, within the present itself—diverges from Sartre's pathetic description of the poet as "a man bending over himself" (Sartre 1950: 22) who, through his unreflective choice of himself, seems to have condemned himself to endure his destiny as an existent, despite believing he is inventing it. According to Sartre's analysis of Baudelaire's case, the choice to be a poet is completely a default choice, imposed on him by circumstances and with which he tries to cope—being a poet is also a way of avoiding taking responsibility for this choice by fleeing from the real world and submitting this reality to the transfiguring work of imagination. For Foucault, on the other hand, the choice to be a poet or a painter of modern life, or a dandy, testifies less to a disposition of consciousness toward oneself than to a voluntary, concrete engagement at the heart of a present reality, simultaneously experienced as both a constraining mode of belonging and a transformative and creative task.

This leads us then to the second topic of Foucault's intervention, which concerns the modalities of this poetic or artistic engagement in and for modernity: "For the attitude of modernity, the high value of the present is indissociable from a desperate eagerness to imagine it, to imagine it otherwise than it is, and to transform it not by destroying it but by grasping it in what it is" (Foucault 1997c: 311). Imagination thus becomes the privileged vector for transfiguring the real, seeking to reveal its essence rather than destroy it, to bring out what is essential or absolute within its relativity. Imagining the present, then, is a way of being able to detach oneself from it without ceasing to belong to it, and being able to "grasp" it differently than it initially appears (as sordid), in order to capture, obliquely, its "highest value" (its poetic use value). According to Foucault, this creative imagination, which is integral to the movement of poeticization of the fleeting characteristic of Baudelaire's modernity, is the result of a "difficult interplay between the truth of what is real and the exercise of freedom" (Foucault 1994: 311), and this interplay takes the form of an immanent transformation of reality into beauty. We find ourselves again at the farthest remove from Sartre's problematic, which tends to present the work of imagination not as a transformative practice but rather as an activity of the transcendence of consciousness that negates the given. According to Sartre, the specific characteristic of the poet, and his limit, precisely lies in the fact that he makes the choice of the unreal rather than the real and that he incarnates up to the bad faith (*mauvaise foi*) the negating function of image-forming consciousness. Foucault takes care to distinguish the work of imagination and the exercise of freedom from any form of negativity that could associate the poetics of modernity with a "taste of nothingness" (*goût du néant*) (Baudelaire 1972: 203–4) seen as the symptom of an unhealthy consciousness, tendentially disconnected from reality due to self-indulgence in sterile self-contemplation. In contrast to Sartre's theme of nihilism, Foucault therefore proposes the theme of an interplay between reality and freedom. The artist, like the dandy who embodies the artistic life, uses reality to reveal its transformative potentialities.

This is where the reference to dandyism appears explicitly in Foucault's argument. The immanent power of transformation and contestation that is inherent in the transfigurative activity of imagination not only affects the relationship with the present, but also the relationship with oneself. There is indeed an exercise of freedom that the artists can undertake on themselves, making "their body, behavior, feelings and passions, and even their very existence, a work of art" (Foucault 1997c: 312). The figure of the dandy, which overlaps with that of the poet, therefore completes the picture outlined by Foucault, giving the aesthetic attitude of modernity its specifically ethical meaning, based on a set of ascetic practices aimed at a rigorous and continuous self-transformation by oneself. Here, the modern dandy joins the ancient figures of self-mastery and self-control. However, as Shusterman rightly points out, this model of the aesthetic stylization of oneself is not contradictory with the more transgressive dimension attributed to it by Foucault. On the contrary, the "experimental dissolution of a repressive body-set can be a necessary first step for the disciplined reconstruction of a better one" (Shusterman 1997: 36). According to Foucault, the transformative work on oneself is indeed a positive invention (one could say imagination) of oneself in the perspective of a difference from the norm of individual and social behaviors. Significantly, Foucault carefully distinguishes this figure of the dandy from the one stigmatized by Sartre in his essay. Sartre indeed devotes a long analysis to Baudelaire's "dandyism" (Sartre 1950: 133–61), reduced to a behavior characterized by bad faith. To grasp the tone and content of his argument, we will only quote one significant excerpt:

> Through obligations which were constantly renewed, he concealed his own inner gulf from himself. He was a dandy first and foremost because he was afraid of himself ... It will be seen that by its gratuitousness, by the free creation of values and obligations, dandyism resembled the choice of a moral system. It seems that at this level, Baudelaire satisfied the transcendental element in himself of which he had been aware from the first. But it was a spurious satisfaction. Dandyism was only the pale image of the absolute choice of unconditional Values. (Sartre 1950: 133–4)

In short, for Sartre, the aesthetics of existence is likely to be nothing more than a deception, or even an artificial trickery of the real issues of responsible existence. It is only the amplified reflection of man's ontological impotence: "Man is a useless passion" (Sartre 1950: 615). Dandyism characterizes and embodies the failing conduct of the poet, unable to exist on the mode of being and fleeing this failure in bad faith and the delusion of poetic imagination. However, according to Foucault, this pathological retreat into oneself is the complete opposite of the attitude of modernity he seeks to define. He writes in "What Is Enlightenment?": "Modern man, for Baudelaire, is not the man who goes off to discover himself, his secrets and his hidden truth; he is the man who tries to invent himself. This modernity does not 'liberate man in his own being'; it compels him to face the task of producing himself" (Foucault 1997c: 312). We see the reversal: what Sartre considered to be the pathological principle of the poet's attitude and of an artistic life, excessively preoccupied with itself and its ultimate truth (to be conquered in the idealized form of a coincidence with itself), becomes for Foucault the accomplishment of aesthetic modernity, its possible transformation into an ethics of modernity. Being modern indeed, if we follow this latter path, means being able to play with the current forms of one's existence (corporeal, personal, but also social) in order to transform one's relationship to the present: being able to think differently by transforming one's relationship to oneself.

By emphasizing the dynamic of transformation and self-transformation inherent in the aesthetics of existence, Foucault therefore departs from Sartre's morality of authenticity, which primarily signifies the ideal of self-adequacy and evaluates each of our actions according to the norm of "one must be oneself": as we see with Baudelaire, "Sartre refers the work of creation," that of the poet but also that of the dandy, "to a certain relation to oneself ... which has the form of authenticity or inauthenticity" (Foucault 1997b: 262)—and, in this case, it is the inauthenticity which prevails, for what concerns the poet, unable to find himself since he only tries to flee himself and to flee a reality that he cannot face. Instead, Foucault proposes to reverse the relationship between self-practice and creation by defining the former in terms of the latter, and not in terms of a fixed and pre-given model of subjectivity (to which one should strive to adhere, lest one's life be a failure, or be inauthentic): "I would like to say exactly the opposite: we should not have to refer the creative activity of somebody to the kind of relation he has to himself, but should relate the kind of relation one has to oneself to a creative activity" (Foucault 1997b). This means that, instead of evaluating creation (of an artistic work, of oneself, or of oneself as a work of art) based on a normative understanding of the self as identical to itself, we should evaluate the creative potential of the self and the self-practices they involve in terms of their ability to form a dynamic relationship with oneself and a critical relationship with the moral and social values that usually dictate what is considered a legitimate existence. These values often condemn "deviant" or "bizarre" forms of self-expression in the name of the "morality of authenticity" and the forms of life or art it allows. According to Foucault, the creative aspect of the relationship with oneself allows for an aesthetic of existence to have an ethical purpose. This aesthetic is a disciplined and austere effort to break free from the forms of individualization and ways of being that have been imposed upon us from external sources, such as nature or society. This detachment from oneself and others is a form of asceticism that the poet and dandy embody through their aesthetic creation, which coincides with their own lives.

However, it is worth noting that Foucault does not completely reject the concept of authenticity. In the French version of the interview with Dreyfus and Rabinow, he criticizes the "morality of authenticity" that Sartre uses as a standard to evaluate the success or failure of a life and work, but he also adds:

> Il me semble que le rapport à soi doit pouvoir être décrit selon les multiplicités de formes dont l'"authenticité" n'est qu'une des modalités possibles. Il faut concevoir que le rapport à soi est structuré comme une pratique qui peut avoir ses modèles, ses conformités, ses variantes mais aussi ses créations. La pratique de soi est un domaine complexe et multiple. (Foucault 1994: 617)[6]

Therefore, Foucault does not reject authenticity outright (presumably because it shapes the relationship between the subject and truth in ancient times), but rather distances himself from the idea of a pre-constituted universal subject that one should try to resemble. Authenticity remains one of the possible ways of relating to oneself, and this relationship can be based on a certain regime of truth or agreement between a subject and their own life. This agreement can only be achieved through effort, possibly through asceticism, and through working on oneself. This is not to access one's ultimate, metaphysical truth, but rather to define an ethics of true life by placing the demand for truth at the center of existence, experience, and creation.[7]

By requalifying authenticity from existence itself rather than from a universal moral norm, Baudelaire and the attitude of modernity that he embodies and that is also manifested in the experience of dandyism can be seen at the intersection or even convergence of two genealogical series that allow for a transhistorical dandyism. On the one hand, there are certain techniques of the self developed in ancient Greece and Rome: we think in particular of cynicism, cynical *parrhesia* as presented in *The Courage of Truth*. Cynicism is presented there as "an historical category which, in various forms and with diverse objectives, runs through the whole of Western history" (Foucault 2011: 174). On the other hand, there is this other critical aspect of culture of the self in nineteenth-century German thought, as seen in philosophers like Stirner, Nietzsche, Schopenhauer, and anarchism. One could consider the possible meaning of a "transhistorical" dandyism that could be detected in ancient cynicism as well as in nineteenth-century anarchism but in different forms, changing the regimes of truth and authenticity that self-practices must follow in order to deepen the aesthetic dimension of existence in the pursuit of an ethics of the self.

From Baudelaire to Stirner, through Foucault

Rather, I will focus on a different line of questioning. As previously mentioned, it is unusual to see Stirner mentioned alongside Baudelaire as a key reference point in a genealogy of the ethics and aesthetics of the self. What does it mean to include Stirner among these "difficult attempts to reconstitute an ethics and an aesthetics of the self" (Foucault 2005: 251)? How does this inclusion help to understand the ethical and political significance that Foucault ascribes to the aesthetics of existence in the early 1980s, whether based on ancient ethics or Baudelaire's aesthetics?

To address these questions, it may be helpful to briefly recall the singular profile of Stirner's thought in order to understand what it might have to do with the issues involved by Foucault's aesthetics of existence. In his book *The Ego and Its Own*, Stirner conducts a radical critique of all the figures and institutions that stand in the way of the recognition of the value of the individual sphere, in a displayed and claimed break with the idols of Christianity and Feuerbachian humanism. Stirner aims to expose the exploitation of the self by the "human" (which he sees as a continuation of the alienation of the individual self from a transcendent idea of Humanity, depriving the individual of a direct link to his own unique and incomparable reality and reducing him to the community of Humanity or any other established human community). The rejection of the transcendence of the "human," as well as the unconditional affirmation of the self, naturally leads to a rejection of the transcendence of society, which is also supposed to instill in the self norms of behavior and collective life that conflict with the preservation and affirmation of individual independence.

Stirner's critique therefore aims to consider the conditions for a liberation that allows the self to reclaim and assert itself as its own self, against all forms of dependence that constantly threaten to alienate its power, in the sense of its ability to be and act. By outlining the conditions for a radical self-relationship that is derived from a critique of universal figures, perceived as figures of alienation, Stirner proposes an ethics of independence. This ethics involves a profound transformation of the usual relationship with oneself, which is distorted by false representations of the Ego, its abilities, and its *Eigenheit*.[8] One might reasonably question the "aesthetic" aspect of this radical ethics, which primarily aims to liberate the "I" from all subjections that threaten its integrity or authenticity. In this sense, Stirner's *Einzige* pits the authenticity of the relationship to oneself against moralities of authenticity that impose transcendent values and inappropriate (*uneigen*) and distorted ways of being and living, imposed from the outside to uphold and sustain the social body based on a collective illusion. Nietzsche agrees with Stirner on this point.

The characteristics of eccentricity and exclusivity in the relationship to oneself found in Stirner's philosophy bear some resemblance to Baudelaire's dandyism and to this attitude of modernity that is based on "a voluntary choice made by certain people" (as Foucault states) to diverge from modes of being imposed in the name of universal or transcendent values and prescribed forms of individualization by social and cultural norms. By pushing to the limit the historical connections that Foucault establishes around the theme of the aesthetics of existence, one could even argue that Stirner's egoism embodies a form of "cynicism," perhaps cynical dandyism, characterized by a strict discipline of self-control and requiring the self "to the task of elaborating itself," of inventing itself, of proclaiming, in a truthful, provocative, and disturbing manner, the value of destitution and the difficult journey toward breaking with dominant social conventions and moral norms. If Stirner's egoism indeed represents a profound transformation of the self, one could argue that it also falls under Pierre Hadot's criticism of Foucault for promoting harmful individualism (Hadot 1989: 261–8; 2001: 217), since the self-relationship is liberated from any dependence on the universal or even on the perspective of a transcendence (cosmic, divine, or supra-individual, as represented by the concept of "Man")—which is the mark of its philosophical anarchism. One could also ask, following Richard Shusterman, if this pursuit of extreme originality (symbolized by the assertion of the self as *Einzige* or unique) does not lead the self into an exclusive self-relationship that risks excluding any shared understanding of a solitary and esoteric way of life. Is this "attitude" compatible with the perspective of a care of the self that is open to the care of others, as Foucault develops it, particularly through the figure of Socrates?

Therefore, it seems necessary to examine this issue more closely and consider the possibility of finding, within Stirner's anarchism, the motivation for a potential political expression of his ethics of the Unique. The Stirnerian *Einzige* does not deny the existence of others and cannot imagine ceasing to have relationships with them. Rather, Stirner simply asks that these relationships cease to be exclusively perceived in the artificial and dangerous form of "social bond"—which is a paradoxically dissolving and potentially alienating link as it compels the Unique to renounce itself (its *Eigenheit*) in order to relate to others on the basis of equality and a shared interest. What is the new form of sociality that emerges through Stirner's repeated criticisms of the "social"? Is there a way to overcome the tension between "Self and society," which Richard

Shusterman identifies as a central aspect of contemporary philosophical lives (Shusterman 1997: 50–60)?

To answer these questions, it is important to note that Stirner tends to distinguish between "society (*Gesellschaft*)," which refers to a factual gathering of individuals, and what he calls "real intercourse" between individuals—dynamic and contingent relations that are "independent of society" (Stirner 1995: 193) in the sense that they are not subject to a predetermined institutional framework or the authority of a third (transcendent) party, but rather only truly involve the "I" in spontaneous exchanges where each individual is the self-sufficient and creative source. Unlike established society, which is founded on a social contract that is in reality nothing more than a market of dupes, social relations ("intercourse") as Stirner envisions them are "mutuality, the action, the commercium, of individuals" (Stirner 1995: 194). Such social relationships are truly a work of creation that is less a reciprocal creation (which would imply mutual limitations of individuals within the institutional or legal framework of a social contract) than a creation of reciprocity, this reciprocity being based primarily on concrete, potentially antagonistic, but expressive interaction, even in this antagonism, of a form of independence toward any central power (serving as a regulatory "third party"). Stirner here outlines what we now refer to as "social networks." Such networks can only be created and sustained by the initiative of separate individuals who seek less to form organized and stable communities through contact with each other than to freely associate with other individuals who also seek freedom through this association. For Stirner, the egoist therefore advocates for the free creation of such an "association (*Verein*)," which is simply another way of freely creating relationships with others, without feeling constrained by the typical and oppressive forms of "society" established as a third party.

This way of linking the self-relationship to creative activity (to use Foucault's terms) allows the Stirnerian *Einzige* to avoid the dizzying solipsism that also threatens the dandy (strongly criticized by Sartre). It is noteworthy that this type of free association, in which the self-relationship flourishes and even finds its preferred milieu of expression, resembles (with necessary adjustments) what Foucault has discussed regarding friendship as a "way of life" (Foucault 1997a).

The starting point is of course quite different, and the nature of the friendship networks in question is also quite distinct: it concerns experiences lived in homosexual milieux where, on the basis of a kind of desexualization of pleasure, friendly relations can be established, where identity and the relationship to oneself are reinvented, to say the least. In this context, identity, instead of being predetermined and shaping our way of being, is itself put back into play in the movement of relationships that are created during improvised encounters, and whose justification is above all the pleasure produced by bodies in contact. Identity is literally played out in these relationships that carry it beyond itself by pluralizing it in its expressions. The focus here is on a relational ethics based on the playing and moving of bodies in relationships of pleasure, on encounter and friendship as a "way of life," in contrast to a universal ethics that evaluates each act according to its conformity to a pre-established law. Foucault outlines in this way the contours of an alternative relationship between individuals and their identity, and between identity and power: a relationship in which the mobile play of identities can serve as a point of resistance to the prescriptions and exclusions that are carried out in the name of the law; a relationship in which networks of friendship (homosexual) can contain or mitigate the effects of vulnerability produced by the statement of a universal rule of sexual identity.

In conclusion, it should be noted that Stirner's *Verein* and Foucault's friendship do not overlap. While Stirner seeks to account for a *being-with* that does not compromise the uniqueness of the self, Foucault primarily seeks to dissolve the forms of identity attached to our sexuality and defined as alienating modes of being. However, both offer a political outlet for the ethical transformation of the self and therefore contribute to defining a "common" aesthetics of existence (or an aesthetics of *being-with*), which ultimately consists in making the life we share with others (in a potentially conflictual manner—Stirner—or spontaneous attachment—Foucault) a kind of work of art, as fragile as it is heroic.

Whether at the strictly individual level or at the level of the communities it makes possible, the aesthetics of existence, in the different figures that give it form, clearly and fundamentally refers to practices of freedom. Its main characteristic is to short-circuit relations of domination, seek to take power, or powers, out of the game, and open up spaces of creativity to bring about new forms of existence and new relationships with oneself and others.

Notes

1   The colloquium dedicated to *Michel Foucault philosophe* was also the occasion of an important contribution (in French) by Rainer Rochlitz: "Esthétique de l'existence. Morale postconventionnelle et théorie du pouvoir chez Michel Foucault" (Rochlitz 1989).

2. This major question is thoroughly examined in Daniele Lorenzini's book, *Éthique et politique de soi. Foucault, Hadot, Cavell et les techniques de l'ordinaire* (2015), in particular in the third part of this work ("Esthétique de l'existence, stoïcisme universel ou perfectionnisme moral?") where the perspectives developed by Foucault, Hadot, and Cavell on this set of practices of the self, through which individuals are invited to give shape to their lives, transform their relationship to themselves, others, and the world, are rigorously compared to one another.

3. Over the last forty years, many studies have been produced on the place of the aesthetics of existence in what has been referred to as the "last Foucault." For example, Edouard Delruelle's study "Faire de sa vie une œuvre d'art?" recalls the "Californian" context of Foucault's ideas about the stylization of existence. Delruelle shows how Foucault sought to take the opposite side of a culture of self-fulfillment and sexual liberation, emphasizing the crucial ethical alternative represented by the aesthetics of existence as a counterpoint to Christian morality and to secularized forms of confession (Delruelle 2006). Along the same lines, Pierre Macherey identified in 1988 the link between the genealogy of the modern subject that leads Foucault to study the Greek world as a historical and cultural crucible of the aesthetics of existence, and the attempt to promote new forms of subjectivity by "seeing if certain 'folds' (Deleuze) are forming within the cultural system to which we belong" (which is marked by the reference to Christianity), "that can be opened and expanded to allow for forms of constitutive singularity of the existence of subjects" (Macherey 1988: 98; my translation).

4. In Chapter 1 of *Practicing Philosophy*, Shusterman is quite sensitive to the dimension of anarchy that is expressed in Foucault's forms of experimentation accompanying the promotion of a non-disciplinary eroticism or transgressive aesthetics, aimed primarily at dissolving traditional hierarchies (social, moral, and sexual).

5. The inventory of modern figures of the aesthetics of existence, as Foucault presents it in this excerpt, resonates with certain figures of the "révolte métaphysique (*metaphysical revolt*)" explored by Albert Camus in *L'Homme révolté*, published in 1952. In particular, this register of metaphysical revolt includes a discussion of the "révolte des dandys" (Camus 1965: 458–4) and the successive evocation of Stirner ("L'Unique") and Nietzsche ("Nietzsche et le nihilisme") (Camus 1965: 472–89).

6. "It seems to me that the relationship to oneself must be able to be described according to the multiplicity of forms of which 'authenticity' is only one of the possible modalities. It is necessary to conceive that the relation to oneself is structured as a practice that can have its models, its conformities, its variants but also its creations. The practice of oneself is a complex and multiple field" (my translation).

7   The reconstruction of the ancient *parrhesia*, from Socrates to the Cynics, is worth, for Foucault, as a testimony of the major inflection of the *bios philosophikos* that occurs between these two referential poles (Foucault 2011).
8   The whole of Stirner's book (whose original title is *Der Einzige und sein Eigentum*) is based on the relationship between the individual Ego and what constitutes it in its own right, what is most proper to it. It is of this "proper (*Eigenheit*)" that the Ego is most often dispossessed (because it alienates itself in transcendent idols—God, Man, or Society—in which it believes it finds itself). He must learn to reappropriate it, to make it his "property (*Eigentum*)." Before seeking to appropriate things outside ourselves, we must therefore appropriate what we are in our own right and what makes each of us "unique."

Bibliography

Baudelaire, C. (1972), *Les Fleurs du Mal* [1861], Paris: Librairie Générale Française.

Camus, A. (1965), "*L'Homme révolté*" [1952], in *Complete Works. Essays*, eds. L. Faucon and R. Quilliot, 407–709, Paris: Gallimard.

Delruelle, É. (2006), "Faire de sa vie une oeuvre d'art?" Available online: https://aaar.fr/revue/article/faire-de-sa-vie-une-oeuvre-dart-edouard-delruelle/.

Foucault, M. (1994), "À propos de la généalogie de l'éthique: un aperçu du travail en cours" [1984], in *Dits et écrits. Vol. IV*, eds. D. Defert, F. Ewald, and A. Fontana, 609–31, Paris: Gallimard.

Foucault, M. (1997a), "Friendship as a Way of Life" [1981], in *The Essential Works 1954-1984. Vol. I: Ethics. Subjectivity and Truth*, ed. P. Rabinow, 135–40, New York: New Press.

Foucault, M. (1997b), "On the Genealogy of Ethics: An Overview of Work in Progress" [1983], in *The Essential Works 1954-1984. Vol. I: Ethics. Subjectivity and Truth*, ed. P. Rabinow, 253–80, New York: New Press.

Foucault, M. (1997c), "What Is Enlightenment?" [1984], in *The Essential Works 1954-1984. Vol. I: Ethics. Subjectivity and Truth*, ed. P. Rabinow, 303–19, New York: New Press.

Foucault, M. (1999), "Lives of Infamous Men" [1977], in *The Essential Works 1954-1984. Vol. III: Power*, ed. J. D. Faubion, 157–75, New York: New Press.

Foucault, M. (2005), *The Hermeneutics of the Subject. Lectures at the Collège de France 1981-1982* [2001], ed. F. Gros, trans. G. Burchell, New York: Palgrave MacMillan.

Foucault, M. (2011), *The Courage of Truth: The Government of Self and Others II. Lectures at the Collège de France 1983-1984* [2009], ed. F. Gros, trans. G. Burchell, New York: Palgrave MacMillan.

Foucault, M. (2015), "La culture de soi" [1983], in *Qu'est-ce que la critique? Suivi de La culture de soi*, eds. H.-P. Fruchaud and D. Lorenzini, 81–109, Paris: Vrin.

Hadot, P. (1989), "Réflexions sur la notion de 'culture de soi,'" in *Michel Foucault philosophe. Rencontre internationale, Paris 9–11 January 1988*, 261–8, Paris: Le Seuil.

Hadot, P. (2001), *Philosophy as a Way of Life. Interviews with Jeannie Carlier and Arnold I. Davidson*, Paris: Albin Michel.

Lorenzini, D. (2015), *Éthique et politique de soi. Foucault, Hadot, Cavell et les techniques de l'ordinaire*, Paris: Vrin.

Macherey, P. (1988), "Foucault: éthique et subjectivité," in *À quoi pensent les philosophes? Interrogations contemporaines*, eds. J. Message, J. Roman, and E. Tassin, 92–103, Paris: Autrement.

Mees, M. (2021), "La vie comme œuvre d'art? Actualité de l'esthétique de l'existence chez Foucault," *Nouvelle revue d'esthétique*, 28: 61–8.

Nègre, F. (1996), "L'esthétique de l'existence dans le dernier Foucault," *Raison présente*, 120: 47–71.

Rochlitz, R. (1989), "Esthétique de l'existence. Morale postconventionnelle et théorie du pouvoir chez Michel Foucault," in *Michel Foucault philosophe. Rencontre internationale, Paris 9–11 janvier 1988*, 288–300, Paris: Le Seuil.

Sabot, P. (2008), "Lectures de Baudelaire: Benjamin, Sartre, Foucault," *L'École des philosophes*, 10: 37–59.

Sabot, P. (2022), "Identités perdues?," in *Michel Foucault. Discours et politiques de l'identité*, ed. P. Sabot, 223–36, Villeneuve d'Ascq: Presses Universitaires du Septentrion.

Sartre, J.-P. (1950), *Baudelaire* [1947], trans. M. Turnell, New York: New Directions Paperbooks.

Sartre, J.-P. (1956), *Being and Nothingness: An Essay on Phenomenological Ontology* [1943], trans. H. E. Barnes, New York: Philosophical Library.

Shusterman, R. (1997), *Practicing Philosophy: Pragmatism and the Philosophical Life*, New York: Routledge.

Stirner, M. (1995), *The Ego and Its Own* [1844], ed. D. Leopold, Cambridge: Cambridge University Press.

2

The Body at the Limits of Subjectivity. For a Philosophy-Performance as Political Aesthetics through the Thought of Michel Foucault

Arianna Sforzini

Introduction

Throughout his works, from *The Birth of the Clinic* to *The Care of the Self* (1976 and 1990), Foucault writes a history of bodies: medicalized bodies, disciplined bodies, punished bodies, sexualized bodies, governed bodies—governed by others and by oneself—and subjectivized bodies. These histories never form a systematic "theory of the body," because Foucault refuses to univocally define the very notion of the body. In this sense, we do not find in his philosophy the exposition of a distinctive concept, a unique and true nature of the body, but rather a plurality of genealogies that reveal the existence of multiple and heterogeneous bodies, as well as the description of the historical emergence of bodies that did not exist before. What may seem to be the most constant fact of our history, the ultimate, irreducible material core of our "nature"—our body—actually has a history that is not merely the history of knowledge or practices about bodies, but the history of the modifications of the bodies that are the objects and the subjects of these knowledge and practices. Foucauldian discourse on the body teaches to be wary of any assertion of naturalness concerning the dimension or experience of the body. Wherever a "nature" is asserted, in discourses and practices, it is always necessary to critically question the set of relations that have given shape to these discourses and practices, not so much to deny the existence of one or more dimensions of naturality of existence, but to reveal the layers, implications, and centers of social, political, and cultural struggles that the very label of an unchangeable nature masks and neutralizes. The originality of Foucauldian discourse on the body, its critical core, lies in this capacity of questioning and criticizing, through history, the made-up obviousness of eternal ideas about human nature.

In order to delve more deeply into Foucault's histories of the body, this chapter will be constructed along three axes, which traverse Foucauldian thought in a horizontal, vertical, and transversal manner, so to speak.[1] First, I would like to examine what it means for Foucault to write a "history of bodies." I will then show why and how this movement of historicization touches the theoretical and practical heart of Foucault's approach: what essential issues are put to the test in his political and philosophical use of the history of bodies. To this end, I will briefly review the posthumous dialogue between Foucault and Butler on the question of the body. From there, as a third and final moment of the chapter, I will propose to bring together Foucault's analyses of the histories of bodies and subjectivities with an important notion of the contemporary philosophical panorama—that of "*agency*." I will show how a certain conception of performative and political agency, in a "theatrical" approach of bodily existence, can be an interesting and fruitful way to rethink in the present the critical power of bodies.

Bodies in History: Genealogies of Embodied Resistance

What does it mean for Foucault to write a history of bodies? Foucault's 1971 essay on Nietzsche (*Nietzsche, Genealogy, History*) remains an indisputable reference point. This does not imply that Foucault discovered the body and its historicity at the beginning of the 1970s. *The Birth of the Clinic*, for example, first published in French in 1963, is a key text in which Foucault constructs a double line of historicity for medical discourse: historicity of the field of visibility and the visible/invisible division in medicine on the one hand; historicity of the body itself, the object of these visibility, and gaze apparati. *The Birth of the Clinic* makes a history of the medicalized body, starting from the reversal of a modern evidence: that of the superposition of the body of the disease and the body of the patient. The modern clinic immediately assumes an "exact superposition of the 'body' of the disease and the body of the sick man" (Foucault 1976: 3), the correspondence between morbid dynamics and localizations in the volumes and thickness of the body. Yet this coincidence, far from constituting the eternal presupposition of medicine, is of recent invention, "no more than a historical, temporary datum ... This order of the solid, visible body is only one way—in all likelihood neither the first, nor the most fundamental—in which one spatializes disease" (Foucault 1976). It is therefore possible to highlight different bodies convened by as many plural paradigms of medical knowledge. The body emerges already in 1963 as having a history, being inserted into medical practice. The medicalized body is all charged with history. *The Birth of the Clinic* immediately places Foucault in opposition to the two major discourses on the body of which he was contemporary: reductionist scientific positivism (the body-object) and the phenomenology of the lived body (the body-subject). The body is neither the absolute object of positivist science, which medicine could have identified earlier if it had known how to get rid of the metaphysical, religious, and social prejudices of its time, nor the proper body that phenomenology would restore to its native signifying power. Phenomenology is certainly right to maintain that the body is something other than an objective datum, a positivity offered to a scientific gaze, and that it deploys different conditions of existence. These conditions, however, do not speak of an original presence in the world, but of a belonging to history.

And yet, how is it possible to write a history of the body? Is it only a history of scientific discourse on the body? Or does the archaeology of medicine presuppose a historicization of the body itself? To answer these questions, Foucault's genealogical redefinition of the principles of his research in the early 1970s is extremely important and allows him to situate, with the help of Nietzsche, the body at the center of a critical history of knowledge and power. For Foucault, Nietzschean genealogy returns to the concrete history of practices and bodies to deconstruct the metaphysics of history itself. In *Nietzsche, Genealogy, History*, Foucault argues that history must rid itself of all theological and teleological pretensions and renounce the search for a unique and forgotten origin (*Ursprung*). No stable and eternal essence exists beforehand. The very principle of a unique and always identical human nature screens the heterogeneity and fruitfulness of historical processes. Historicized, the "body is molded by a great many distinct regimes; it is broken down by the rhythms of work, rest, and holidays; it is poisoned by food or values, through eating habits or moral laws; it constructs resistances" (Foucault 1977a: 153). Nothing escapes history, not even the physiology of bodies. The project of writing a history of bodies is thus legitimized by an analytical method that avoids both transcendent and abstract universals (immutable concepts) and eternal and fixed immanence (predetermined reality).

According to Foucault, the body corresponds to one of the two notions that Nietzsche opposes to the search for the metaphysical *Ursprung*: *Herkunft*, the descent (the other is *Entstehung*, the emergence). In bodies are rooted the origins of the values, truths, powers, and relations that shape individuals; in other words, bodies are the scenes of the complex web of accidents and events that give shape to what exists and is worthwhile. "Descent attaches itself to the body. It inscribes itself in the nervous system, in temperament, in the digestive apparatus; it appears in faulty respiration, in improper diets, in the debilitated and prostrate bodies of those whose ancestors committed errors" (Foucault 1977a: 147). Historical facts as well as assertions of value or impulses of ideality come from the concrete life of bodies, from its physio-pathological mechanisms, energies, and fragilities. The dynamics of history inscribe their reality and deploy their intelligibility through the skin, the flesh, and the organic folds. The body is therefore not only a privileged object of history, it constitutes its theoretical and practical backbone. Not only does the body have a history, but history is made up of all the relationships and battles of bodies. History is the life of bodies. "Its task is to expose a body totally imprinted by history and the process of history's destruction of the body" (Foucault 1977a: 148).

There is another dimension that complicates the relationship between bodies and history: genealogical history also constitutes a critical instrument, an exercise in dissolving the great philosophical myths of knowledge, such as that of a pure origin, of an immobile identity, of the existence of rational ends, of a substantial nature, and of an absolute truth. And history can play this role of rupture precisely by relying on the explosive power of multiple, heterogeneous, and disparate bodies. The genealogist uses the narrative of bodies to ward off the chimeras of universality and necessity, just as the materialist philosopher invokes medicine, science, and physiology to ward off the utopia of the soul. We must therefore learn to recognize the petty realities beneath the great ideals, the stubborn chance beneath the great teleologies, and the bodies beneath the life of concepts. "Effective" history, says Foucault, "introduces discontinuity into our very being—as it divides our emotions, dramatizes our instincts, multiplies our body and sets it against itself. [It] deprives the self of the reassuring stability of life and nature" (Foucault 1977a: 154). It is able to disturb the paradigms of truth that shape our culture. Foucault the genealogist becomes thus the "surgeon" of the present. He reactivates the Nietzschean figure of the philosopher-physician through a historical-political practice that uses history to make critical "diagnoses" of the present. The historian-genealogist incises the archives of discourse, locates lines of rupture in our knowledge, and brings out problematic knots in our lives. He shatters the obvious in order to bring out new perspectives and new forms of existence.

Genealogies, in short—genealogies through bodies and genealogies of bodies—are never "neutral." They always aim to understand some theoretically and politically important aspects of the actuality of thought and existence. Now, this "non-neutrality" of the genealogical gaze can be seen not only in the result of Foucauldian analyses but also in their starting point. If Foucault is increasingly concerned since the beginning of 1970s with bodies and their intertwining with power relations, it is because this entanglement of power and bodies was suggested to him by his present and his struggles, as Foucault reminds several times in his texts and in his interviews. The emergence of the body in the political field is, for example, in his eyes, one of the key dimensions of the events of May 1968. Far removed from the positions of Marcuse and the heralds of sexual liberation, Foucault clearly perceived that the real breakthrough of 1968 came through the emergence of new fields of problematization in political action: the discovery of "new political objects, of a whole series of domains of existence, of corners of society, of nooks and crannies of life that had been completely forgotten or disqualified by political thought up to that point" (Foucault 1980: 919–20; my translation). In the second half of the twentieth century, the focus of analyses of power shifted from the great institutional battles to the everyday, marginal dimensions that had been virtually ignored by political thought until then: madness, death, disease, crime, sexuality, the right to move freely in space, and to choose where and how to live. Foucault's research, from the *History of Madness* onward, is a clear example of this theoretical and practical shift. It is not surprising then that bodies have become, in an increasingly direct and explicit way, the center and content of struggles and reflections. Foucault experienced the 1968 riots far from France and Paris, in Tunisia, in a strange "outside" in relation to the French socio-political context, which constituted his first "true political experience" (Foucault 1991: 134). Through the revolt of the Tunisian youth, who really risked its lives and bodies, facing the threat of torture and years in prison, Foucault perceived the strength of a political practice that had nothing of the abstract academicism—the catechism, almost—of the French Communist Party Marxism. Tragically, he saw the violence of real power in its wrenching grip on bodies. "I went through a kind of physical experience of power, of the relationship between body and power" (Foucault 1975: 121; my translation). The true discovery of May 1968 for Foucault is not "sex must be free," but "the body can be imprisoned, broken, subjugated and it remains the stake and the focus of political struggle." A true thought of resistance and freedom must then pass through the "lines of contact between body, life, discourse and political power" (Foucault 1975; my translation). For Foucault's present, the body was the heart of political conflict and it probably remains so today, given the number of struggles (e.g., gender issues, decolonial fights, and bioethical debates) that are currently waged as body politics. If the body is a critical object, if the histories of the body are important for present discourse and political practice, it is because these discourses and practices directly imply a grip on the body to which it must be responded, resisted, and reacted.

Between Constructivism and Naturalism? Critical Philosophy as "Somato-creation"

One could ask a question here that might seem naive: does this historicization of bodies, these political genealogies of bodies themselves and not only of discourses on bodies, imply that this body is a totally historical object? Do we really have to imagine that nothing in the body escapes history—which would mean a radical constructivism of Foucault regarding bodily experience? Are there not invariants and constitutive, natural, differences that belong to biology and not to history? Foucault actually thwarts and displaces this question. Even if biology, anatomy, and physiology present transhistorical invariants that determine, at a certain extent, the individual bodily experience, the challenge is precisely to undermine and reduce as much as possible the role of biological determinants in bodily experiences, by showing that what we believe to belong to the biological natural of human beings depends on multiple and heterogeneous networks of historical causalities and casualties. To illustrate this point, I quote an unpublished passage by Foucault, which can be found in box 55 of the Archives deposited in 2013 at the *Bibliothèque nationale de France*. It is most likely (the manuscript is undated) a series of answers prepared by Foucault for an American audience, perhaps at the University of Berkeley in California, who were questioning him in the early 1980s about the archaeological method, and the *Archaeology of Knowledge* in particular. Foucault says, on the question of the body and its invariants:

> To the question of whether there are transcultural biological invariants in the human organism, I hardly see how one could answer no. Of course, as a matter of method, my problem is how far one can push the analysis of historical forms, rather than trying to extend the domain of biological determinants as far as possible. Historical excavation is not intended to show how much we are bound by [these determinants], but how much what appears to us as invariant is in fact bound to the singularity of a situation and a practice. (Box 55, Archives Foucault, BnF; my translation)

Rather than discovering ourselves to be "without nature," we must always take up and reactivate the question of what makes up our nature, and what this notion of nature hides beneath the veil of its universality and invariance.

For these same reasons, can we then reproach Foucault for not being constructivist enough in his analyses of the body, for not having gone far enough in his task of historicization and deconstruction of the body? Would Foucault be, deep down, a naturalist, a vitalist, presupposing at the bottom of his genealogies a non-historical ontological power of the bodies, which would be like a secret force of resistance to the powers that are exercised on the bodies? It is true that, in several of his works, Foucault brings the body into play as the vector par excellence of resistance. As he states in the conclusion of *The Will to Know*, the first volume of the *History of Sexuality* published in French in 1976: "The rallying point for the counterattack against the deployment of sexuality ought not to be sex-desire, but bodies and pleasures" (Foucault 1978: 157). It is not sex that must emancipate bodies, but bodies that must free us from sex. This way of playing the body and its pleasures against sex and its desires remains, however, problematic. For if the body is only historically determined and invested, where should we look for "a rallying point for the counterattack"?

This is precisely the criticism that Judith Butler addresses to Foucault's thought on the body in several of her works. To summarize it very schematically, the conception of a politicized, historical, and cultural body, constructed by a network of relations of power and knowledge, is in contradiction with the affirmation that bodies constitute the condition of possibility of resistance to power. "At times it appears that for Foucault the body has a materiality that is ontologically distinct from the power relations that take that body as a site of investments" (Butler 1993: 33). If we can appeal to bodies against a discursive paradigm, against a power device, it is because they contain an antagonistic power and are not reducible to a pure product of discourses and power relations. Rather, they represent a limit point. The very mechanism of historical inscription, also mentioned in the 1971 Foucauldian article on Nietzsche—"The body ... the inscribed surface of events (traced by language and dissolved by ideas)" (Foucault 1977a: 148)—refers, according to Butler, to this limiting role of the body: in order to be in-scribed, to be written inside bodies, events must act on the body from the outside. Bodies must therefore be, in a way, prior to history and power. Foucault would remain, in essence, Nietzschean, in the sense of a vitalism that would conceive the body as a set of forces more original and primordial than the historical technologies of power and truth. According to Butler, Foucault would have endeavored to remove the body in its materiality from these same operations of deconstruction of which genealogy would like to be the instrument and the vector. He did not go to the end of what the genealogy of power had nevertheless outlined: a body aroused and shaped by the historical-political dynamics, norms, and discourses that are exercised over it, and a resistance of bodies that is dug into the heart of this interiority to language and power. It is only by recognizing the essential co-participation of domination and struggle in the bodies that it will be possible to think of forms of resistance that do not reinforce the mechanism they claim to combat: "gender troubles" that are certainly fragile, made possible by the plasticity and reversibility of the very norms that they turn upside down, but that are the only real resistances capable of jeopardizing the grips of powers and identity assignments. "The culturally constructed body will then be liberated, neither to its 'natural' past, nor to its original pleasures, but to an open future of cultural possibilities" (Butler 1999a: 119).

Butler's dialogue with Foucault is decisive. It goes to the problematic heart of the question of the body through Foucault, revealing both its difficulties and its critical actuality. It is not wrong to say that Foucault oscillates between a radical constructivism of the body and the supposition of a restive immanence. Foucault's genealogy might seem to appeal and give support to an implicit Spinozist (or Deleuzian) vitalism of bodies. Antonio Negri (2000; 2016) uses precisely Foucauldian texts to describe an immanent and productive ontology that sees in concrete existences; in the power of affects, bodies, and desires; and in the invention of new ways of living, the possibility of creating new subjectivities that simultaneously act as instances of de-subjectivation. Nonetheless, the refusal to radically erase the materiality of bodies does not necessarily imply the acceptance of a metaphysical ontology of human nature. For Foucault, it is always a question of making a history of bodies in non-essentialist terms. His genealogies do not constitute, as said before, a philosophy of the body; they are ways of finding in the history of bodies the critical points, the changes of paradigm, and the strategies of conflict. By finding the virtuality of political resistance in minute and concrete existences, in the dynamics of affirmation and dramatization of bodies, Foucault is undoubtedly more Artaudian than Spinozist or vitalist. The capacity of bodies to resist cannot be extracted from historical and immanent games of power. There is no such thing as a natural resistance, nor even a human nature in the sense of a metaphysical and axiological substratum of bodily life.

It is therefore crucial to rethink the struggles of bodies and the political conflicts played out around bodies, without erasing their materiality but without anchoring them in transhistorical, universal, and natural dimensions. This is where theatre as virtuality of thought appeared to me as a good scheme for interpreting Foucauldian analyses, and their reactivation today. In a previous work (Sforzini 2017), I tried to reread Foucauldian genealogies as philosophical theatres of struggles; as many scenes playing out essential problematic nuclei for modern history, reread in the mirror of present. The "scene" is a dimension that is at once very concrete, physical, and corporeal, but at the same time capable of imposing itself, in its repetition of reality, as a power to create an immanent double of the world it is putting on a stage. Making philosophy a theatre, seeing in philosophical discourse and practice a force of immanent reduplication, like that which takes place on the theatrical stages, is a way of staying in the historical and immanent games of power and truths, but at the same time of underlining and bringing into play their real, burning force. Philosophical theatre can be an instrument of indefinite contestation of our social norms, identities, and truths which passes by their dramatization and repetition. Foucault's genealogies stage multiple scenes of resistant historical bodies: the prisoner bodies, the hysterical and alienated bodies, the possessed bodies, the parrhesiastic bodies, the virginal and continent bodies, cynical bodies, etc. One must follow and understand through these antagonist bodies the complex discursive strategies they incarnate, the plural affective forces they create, and the existential and political experiences they invite to make. The theatricalization of Foucauldian discourse allows to participate in the experiences of subversion it describes. As for an artistic performance, philosophy passes from body to body and becomes a vector of transformation. Foucault's philosophical theatre is a "somato-creation" and a principle of physical insurrection, to paraphrase Artaud (see Artaud 2004).

Bodies' Agency and Subjective Performances

Through these historical scenes of bodies' struggles, the very notion of the subject of action and free will has to be philosophically rethought. The analyses of subjective reappropriations of embodied forms of existence go beyond and thwart, in a Foucauldian approach, any dialectic based on conceptual oppositions alienation *versus* dis-alienation, or normalization *versus* autonomy of the self. They define non-dialectical movements of self-assertion within the devices of power (psychiatrization, medicalization, naturalization of instincts and genders, etc.). The self that emerges from the dramatized histories of body and life-techniques—from the "aesthetics of existence," to say it with the late Foucault—is at once constructed and open, determined and free, subject to and creator of multiple strategies of redefinition of personal identity.

One concept in particular, whose history is quite recent, allows to rethink the histories of resistant bodies through their subjective force: the notion of *agency*. The term "agency" is not a creation of contemporary thought. It appears in the history of the English language in the seventeenth century and in philosophical texts from the eighteenth century. As reconstructed by Balibar and Laugier (2004) and Schneewind (1998), in a still very Aristotelian conception, *agency* initially indicates an indefinite property of action, in opposition to the category of passivity, in a semantic constellation where the limits between actor, activity, and act blur. This property, this power of action, is strictly linked to the notion of causality. Hobbes can therefore make the agency a primary ontological cause, a divine force that also determines the free actions of human beings,[2] while Hume subjects it to the same criticism as causality itself[3]: men are mistaken in thinking that the cause of actions, that is, agency, exists as such in nature, whereas it is only a connection between facts operated by the mind. Agency is thus a typically mental and anthropological property: it is a rational way of understanding what makes actions effective in the world. Contemporary moral and analytical philosophy has taken up and reused this concept in a very general sense as the dimension of everything that concerns human action, evacuating the metaphysical question of the ontological reality of the principle of causality. According to Donald Davidson's classic definition:

> Philosophers often seem to think that there must be some simple grammatical litmus of agency, but none has been discovered. I drugged the sentry, I contracted malaria, I danced, I swooned, Jones was kicked by me, Smith was outlived by me: this is a series of examples designed to show that a person named as subject in sentences in the active or as object in sentences in the passive, may or may not be the agent of the event recorded. (Davidson 1980: 43)

The notion of "intentionality" is introduced to make the difference between a simple event and an event of which a subject perceives itself as the author. Agency would therefore presuppose not only the effectiveness of an action but the existence of a subject who recognizes itself and is recognized as the pole of force from which the action derives. Nothing excludes by the way the possibility that this subject may be collective, unconscious, or non-human, for example. Now the definitions of subjectivity and of the mechanisms of formation and existence of subjects are seldom analyzed in the Anglo-Saxon moral philosophical tradition of the second half of the twentieth century, which is discussed here.[4] Nonetheless, theories of intentionality are often linked to a traditional humanist conception of the subject, conceived as sovereign in its faculties of action and knowledge, the heuristic locus of its own truth. Agency would thus seem to coincide with an unhistorical, transparent, and identical "performative" capacity that applies to all actions of bodies, from the most banal such as getting dressed to the most disruptive such as taking up arms for a revolution. Several committed political uses of the notion of agency (e.g., in certain Marxist or feminist movements of the 1960s and 1970s) are based on the presupposition of the existence of an unhistorical subject-substrate that would become the motor of emancipatory struggles. There is a belief in a powerful agent, a committed individual or class group: on the one hand, there is the dimension of power, conceived as domination and repression; on the other hand, there is a particular form of antagonistic subject, invested with an emancipatory, revolutionary agency. The agent is "a form of subjectivity where … the possibility (indeed, the actuality) of resistance to ideological pressure is allowed for" (Smith 1988: XXXV).

A very important nuance to this "sovereign" view of subjective agency can already be woven from the writings of John Austin, the theorist of the performativity of language (e.g., see Austin 1962). In questioning what "doing something" really means, Austin takes among others the example of the "excuse," or better "'plea', 'defence', 'justification' and so on": "the situation … where someone is accused of having done something, or (if that will keep it any cleaner) where someone is said to have done something which is bad, wrong, inept, unwelcome, or in some other of the numerous possible ways untoward" (1956: 1–2) and wants to get out of it. The very possibility of the excuse implies that the sovereignty of the subject of the action is neither monolithic nor absolute. In fact, the traditional logic of thought must be reversed: not starting from the action as if it were a thing and then reflecting on what or who is the cause and origin of it, but seeing the action as a complex process, a "doing something" in which cause and effect merge. How can we distinguish between a successful action and a failed one, between a deliberate action and one that is not done "on purpose"? The excuse shows that the failure, the involuntary, and the irrational are intrinsic possibilities of action, which therefore has no predetermined and absolute criteria of value but can only be understood by broadening the understanding of modalities of intentionality and responsibility. Action is precisely that for which one can feel not responsible: a gap lies in the action itself which makes it not coincide exactly with its author(s) and the intention that could guide it. The subject of action itself can then be conceived as always "other than itself": an interruption, a displacement, and a fracture. Excuses are the mark of an indefinite and displaced subject, constantly transforming itself and acting through its plural dynamisms. The linguistics of performative discourse is therefore in line with older intuitions formulated by psychoanalysis. "The 'I' … is not even master in its own home" (Freud 1920: 247). The "I" is not a subject in the sense of a single substance to which to refer the truthful meaning and intention of all acts; "I" is subject in the sense of the advent of a "performance" at the same time bodily and psychic, conscious and unconscious, individual and collective—a relational, active, and creative force.

> Excuses are as essentially implicated in Austin's view of human actions as slips and overdetermination are in Freud's. What does it betoken about human actions that the reticulated constellation of predicates of excuse is made for them—that they can be done unintentionally, unwillingly, involuntarily, insincerely, unthinkingly, inadvertently, heedlessly, carelessly, under duress, under the influence, out of contempt, out of pity, by mistake, by accident, and so on? It betokens, we might say, the all but unending vulnerability of human action, its openness to the independence of the world and the preoccupation of the mind. I would like to say that the theme of excuses turns philosophy's attention patiently and thoroughly to something philosophy would love to ignore—the fact that human life is constrained to the life of the human body. (Cavell 1994: 87)

It is not by chance that Judith Butler is the main philosopher of both performativity and agency.[5] Something of a "dramatic," theatrical self and the scenes of its truths are at stake in these questions, which again draws an interesting axis of rapprochement with psychoanalysis and the "other stage" of the unconscious. The subject deploys its ontological possibilities in the movement of its concrete existence, namely an open game between spaces of freedom and historical, social and political determinants. It is the subject of its actions, but something in this "doing actions" is constitutively beyond its control. What is mine—my intentions, my capacities, my performances—is not always mine, overflows me, subtracts itself from me, and comes from elsewhere than me. A fundamental otherness is integrated into subjective being. Agency is then the name for this open and plural game between intention and heteronomy, freedom and domination, difference and identity. And it is a force of action that constitutively deals with the bodily conditions of existence of a subject in all its dimensions. The processes of formation of subjectivity contain and problematize everything that situates the subject somewhere, reducing or reinforcing its capacity to act. In other words, if one cannot choose the fundamental features of the situation in which one finds herself/himself living, one can always choose how to replay, criticize, and perform through body agency the (contingent, unnecessary) identities imposed on her/him. The agency always implies a subject that is both corporeal and social, or better; a subject that, precisely because it is embodied in a living body, irreducible to the Cartesian *res extensa*, is a multiple bundle of intersubjective and social relations, in both material and symbolic sense (see Guilhaumou 2012).

Gender Politics, Bodies' Struggles: Between Foucault and Butler

Not surprisingly, feminist studies had already long since underlined this open bodily dimension of agency. As Simone de Beauvoir, among others, stated in her major work *The Second Sex*, first published in French in 1949, women know before and even more than men, from birth and because of their being part of the "weaker," "second sex," that they cannot escape their bodily determinants. At the same time, "one is not born, but rather becomes, a woman" (Beauvoir 1953: 273), in a complex network of social, symbolic, biological, political, and cultural determinants. Women have to act, to perform their existence against, or better through this constrained and inferiorized body that incarnate "the figure that the human female has in society" (Beauvoir 1953). Following a parallel (and yet very different from the point of view of theoretical presuppositions) thought pattern, Judith Butler also analyzes these notions, fundamental to her philosophy, of agency and performativity through the questions of gender and gendered bodies. Far from being an immutable biological givenness, gender is a discursive construction that is called upon to be performed by the subjects, where the dimension of performativity precisely expresses this possibility of repetition but also of transformation and free appropriation of norms and identities that are immanent to power relations. Moreover, this performance of gender is never individual but intersubjective: "That act that gender is [...] is clearly not one's act alone," but a matter of a "shared experience and 'collective action'" (Butler 1988: 519–31). Gender is both a political performance and a subjective agency. If there is no possibility of getting out of history, of transcending power relations and gender determinations, this does not imply that dynamics of transformation, or rather of subversion of norms, is not possible. But they must be rethought in the margins, interstices, and interruptions of a power thought of as a sum of contingent strategies.[6] The ambivalent scene of agency[7] is then this apparently paradoxical movement between the context that determines subjects and their actions, and the possibility that these same subjects have, in their capacity of action, to mimic, transfigure, and transgress the power that has shaped them. Of course, this game, this theatre of subversion is extremely serious; not only it engages our collective responsibility in imagining other forms of life, but it can be very expensive from the point of view of the subject who dares to defy norms and powers, violent and implacable in their mechanisms of repression. Displacing the unintended effects of norms on bodies and genders (by revealing them as intolerable), inventing and re-signifying the symbols that make our existences legible and representable, shaping lives differently, none of these actions can be carried on naively and lightheartedly. And yet, there is no other way to continue making history an open system.

It is precisely the dimension of the body, as we have said, that conveys the incarnate and militant dimension of agency. In spite of Neoplatonic or Cartesian utopias, no existence is disembodied. Performativity is a bodily experience of collective action, and the agency that this performativity expresses is not a sovereign and self-sufficient power but a force of transcendence immanent to embodied existence. "The body implies mortality, vulnerability, agency" (Butler 2004a: 21). Corporeality, in all its precariousness and dependence, is the theatre of an effective power of doing, but it is always delivered to the risk of experiencing violence, normalization, and domination. In this sense, the body is the site of the fundamental ambiguity of the subject, in tension between subjectivation and de-subjectivation, between the words that are said about it and its own expressions, between the sphere of intimacy and collective symbolization. The body is immediately what makes the personal political: an intrinsically collective dimension with all its languages, productions, weaknesses, and struggles.

> Although we struggle for rights over our own bodies, the very bodies for which we struggle are not quite ever only our own. The body has its invariably public dimension; constituted as a social phenomenon in the public sphere, my body is and is not mine. Given over from the start to the world of others, bearing their imprint, formed within the crucible of social life, the body is only later, and with some uncertainty, that to which I lay claim as my own. (Butler 2004a)

The body is a fundamentally paradoxical site between self and other, affirmation and submission. This is why agency can only be both corporeal and performative, produced from the social determinants that subjugate the body, yet unthinkable without the forces of resistance proper to the bodies themselves.

> If I am someone who cannot *be* without *doing*, then the conditions of my doing are, in part, the conditions of my existence. If my doing is dependent on what is done to me or, rather, the ways in which I am done by norms, then the possibility of my persistence as an "I" depends upon my being able to do something with what is done with me. This does not mean that I can remake the world so that I become its maker. That fantasy of godlike power only refuses the ways we are

constituted, invariably and from the start, by what is before us and outside of us. My agency does not consist in denying this condition of my constitution. If I have any agency, it is opened up by the fact that I am constituted by a social world I never chose. That my agency is riven with paradox does not mean it is impossible. It means only that paradox is the condition of its possibility. (Butler 2004a: 3)

As we have seen, Butler distances herself from Foucault's thought on several points, accusing him, despite the radical novelty of his non-essentialist thinking on power, of not pushing the deconstruction of his presuppositions far enough (e.g., with regard to the body and the critical and resistant freedom of the will).[8] The Foucauldian notion of subjectivation, however, through its progressive elaboration from the mid-1970s onward,[9] can be seen precisely as another way of expressing this juncture between heteronomous constitution and transformative action by the self, which is implied by the dimension of agency. Subjectivation is a way of picturing a subject that invents itself by creating different ways of thinking and living: a force of action that is not a predetermined nature but a movement of stylization of the self in history. Within the framework of a conception of power not as a substance that can be held by someone, but as a bundle of relations in action, freedom is not an absolute dimension, but it cannot be denied either, constituting precisely what makes power relations an open game.[10] The paradox between freedom and domination is only apparent, and subjectivation is precisely the capacity for subjective work on external assimilations—what Butler rightly calls agency. The use of the suffix "-tion" (not subject but subjectivation) indicates precisely this character of development and dynamism, something that "happens" (acts and is acted upon)—the shift from an interrogation of essences to a study of processes. To speak of subjectivation is then to posit that the subject is not only caught up in a becoming, but that this becoming defines its own being. The subject is no longer a pre-given essentiality that must be found, but it is constructed according to historically given dynamics. It is transformed in and through experience; it creates itself by performing its own given conditions of existence. It is no longer a question of demonstrating the existence of structures irreducible to experience (while finding in experience a space for projection), in order to establish the subject in its purity. And experience also changes in meaning; it is no longer exteriority and contingency, but a constitutively political milieu of encounters, struggles, and formation. To make oneself—one's body, one's life—a subject in the Foucauldian sense of the term, one would have to learn to make the practice of thought a moment of experimentation, and the existence a gesture of trouble and disruption: a *creative performance*, a performative "somato-creation." The body itself in its agency becomes the performative stage of a critical approach to immanent freedom that is always to react and take up again.

Notes

1   I will reframe and enrich in this chapter some theses already presented in French in my book on Foucault's practices of the body (Sforzini 2014).
2   "The sense from the operation of the external objects, and the agency of external objects is only from God; therefore all actions, even of free and voluntary agents, are necessary" (Hobbes 1841: 331).
3   "These philosophers, instead of drawing a just inference from this observation, and concluding, that we have no idea of power or agency, separate from the mind, and belonging to causes; … they frequently search for the qualities in which this agency consists, and are displeased with every system, which their reason suggests them, in order to explain it" (Hume 1888: 223).
4   See, for example, the works of Gertrude E. M. Anscombe, Peter Geach, and Anthony Kenny.
5   The bibliography on Judith Butler is huge, crossing philosophy, linguistics, gender studies, and psychoanalysis. Without claiming to be exhaustive, I use in particular, for the reconstruction of the Butlerian notion of agency, Zaharijević 2021.
6   As Butler states in the introduction to *Gender Trouble*, she tries to understand "what political agency might be, given that it cannot be isolated from the dynamics of power from which it is wrought. The iterability of performativity is a theory of agency, one that cannot disavow power as the condition of its own possibility" (Butler 1999a: XXIV).
7   "Equally important, agency is the assumption of a purpose unintended by power, one that could not have been derived logically or historically, that operates in a relation of contingency and reversal to the power that makes it possible, to which it nevertheless belongs" (Butler 1997: 15).
8   See, for example, Butler 1989, 1999b, and 2004b.
9   Among the various texts (books, essays, articles, lectures, unpublished manuscripts) in which Foucault deals with the question of subjectivity, I refer here in particular to Foucault 1978, 2005, and 2021.
10 "When one defines the exercise of power as a mode of action upon the actions of others, when one characterizes these actions by the government of men by other men—in the broadest sense of the term—one includes an important element: freedom. Power is exercised only over free subjects, and only insofar as they are free. By this we mean individual or collective subjects who are faced with a field

of possibilities in which several ways of behaving, several reactions and diverse comportments may be realized. Where the determining factors saturate the whole there is no relationship of power; slavery is not a power relationship when man is in chains ... The relationship between power and freedom's refusal to submit cannot therefore be separated. The crucial problem of power is not that of voluntary servitude (how could we seek to be slaves?). At the very heart of the power relationship, and constantly provoking it, are the recalcitrance of the will and the intransigence of freedom" (Foucault 1983: 221–2).

Bibliography

Artaud, A. (2004), *Œuvres*, Paris: Gallimard.
Austin, J. (1956), "A Plea for excuses," *Proceedings of the Aristotelian Society*, 57: 1–30.
Austin, J. (1962), *How to Do Things with Words*, The William James Lectures Delivered at Harvard University, Oxford: Clarendon Press.
Balibar, E. and S. Laugier (2004), "Agency," in *Vocabulaire européen des philosophies: dictionnaire des intraduisibles*, ed. B. Cassin, 26–32, Paris: Le Seuil/Le Robert.
Beauvoir, S. de (1953), *The Second Sex*, trans. H. Madison Parshley, London: Jonathan Cape.
Butler, J. (1988), "Performative Acts and Gender Constitution: An Essay in Phenomenology and Feminist Theory," *Theatre Journal*, 40 (4): 519–31.
Butler, J. (1989), "Foucault and the Paradox of Bodily Inscription," *The Journal of Philosophy*, 86 (11): 601–7.
Butler, J. (1993), *Bodies That Matter: On the Discursive Limits of "Sex,"* London/New York: Routledge.
Butler, J. (1997), *The Psychic Life of Power. Theories in Subjection*, Stanford: Stanford University Press.
Butler, J. (1999a), *Gender Trouble: Feminism and the Subversion of Identity*, London/New York: Routledge.
Butler, J. (1999b), "Revisiting 'Bodies and Pleasures,'" *Theory, Culture and Society*, 16 (2): 11–20.
Butler, J. (2004a), *Undoing Gender*, New York/London: Routledge.
Butler, J. (2004b), "Bodies and Power, Revisited," in *Feminism and the Final Foucault*, eds. D. Taylor and K. Vintages, 184–94, Urbana: University of Illinois Press.
Cavell, S. (1994), *A Pitch of Philosophy*, Cambridge (MA): Harvard University Press.
Davidson, D. (1980), *Essays on Actions and Events*, Oxford: Clarendon Press.
Foucault, M. (1975), "'Je suis un artificier.' Interview with Roger-Pol Droit," in *Michel Foucault, entretiens*, ed. R.-P. Droit, 89–136, Paris: Odile Jacob, 2004.
Foucault, M. (1976), *The Birth of the Clinic: An Archaeology of Medical Perception*, trans. A. M. Sheridan, London: Tavistock Publications.

Foucault, M. (1977a), "Nietzsche, Genealogy, History", trans. D. F. Brouchard and S. Simon, in *Language, Counter-Memory, Practice: Selected Essays and Interviews by Michel Foucault*, ed. D. F. Bouchard, 139–64, Ithaca: Cornell University Press.

Foucault, M. (1977b), *Discipline and Punish: The Birth of Prison*, trans. A. M. Sheridan, New York: Pantheon Books.

Foucault, M. (1978), *The History of Sexuality. Vol. I: An Introduction*, trans. R. Hurley. New York: Pantheon Books.

Foucault, M. (1980), "'Le Nouvel Observateur' et l'Union de la gauche. Interview with Jean Daniel," in *Dits et écrits*, 2 vols., eds. D. Defert, F. Ewald, and J. Lagrange, *Vol. 2. 1976-1988*, text n. 283, Paris: Gallimard, 2001 (first published in *Spirali. Giornale internazionale di cultura*, 15, 1980: 53–5).

Foucault, M. (1983), "The Subject and Power," trans. L. Sawyer, in *Michel Foucault: Beyond Structuralism and Hermeneutics*, eds. H. Dreyfus and P. Rabinow, 208–26, Chicago: University of Chicago Press.

Foucault, M. (1990), *The History of Sexuality. Volume 3: The Care of the Self*, trans. R. Hurley, London: Penguin Books.

Foucault, M. (1991), *Remarks on Marx. Conversations with Duccio Trombadori*, trans. R. J. Goldstein and J. Cascaito, New York: Semiotext(e).

Foucault, M. (2005), *The Hermeneutics of the Subject. Lectures at the Collège de France 1981-1982*, ed. F. Gros, trans. G. Burchell, New York: Palgrave MacMillan.

Foucault, M. (2006), *History of Madness*, ed. J. Khalfa, trans. J. Murphy and J. Khalfa, London: Routledge.

Foucault, M. (2021), *The History of Sexuality. Vol. 4: Confessions of the Flesh*, trans. R. Hurley, New York: Penguin Random House LLC.

Foucault, M., "Boîte 55, Archives Foucault," Bibliothèque nationale de France (NAF 28730).

Freud, S. (1920), *A General Introduction to Psychoanalysis*, trans. E. L. Bernays, New York: Boni and Liveright.

Guilhaumou, J. (2012), "Autour du concept d'agentivité," *Rives méditerranéennes*, 41: 25–34.

Hardt, M. and A. Negri (2000), *Empire*, Cambridge (MA)/London: Harvard University Press.

Hobbes, T. (1841), "The Questions Concerning Liberty, Necessity and Chance, Clearly Stated and Debated between Dr. Bramhall, Bishop of Derry, and Thomas Hobbes of Malmesbury," in *The English Works of Thomas Hobbes of Malmesbury*, ed. W. Moleswort, London: John Bohn.

Hume, D. (1888), *A Treatise of Human Nature. Book I*, eds. S. Bigge and L. Amherst, Oxford: Clarendon Press.

Negri, A. (2016), "When and How I Read Foucault," trans. K. Klotz, in *Between Deleuze and Foucault*, 72–86, Edinburgh: Edinburgh University Press.

Schneewind, J. (1998), *The Invention of Autonomy: A History of Modern Moral Philosophy*, Cambridge: Cambridge University Press.

Sforzini, A. (2014), *Michel Foucault. Une pensée du corps*, Paris: PUF.
Sforzini, A. (2017), *Scènes de la vérité. Michel Foucault et le théâtre*, Lormont: Le bord de l'eau.
Smith, P. (1988), *Discerning the Subject*, Minneapolis: University of Minnesota Press.
Zaharijević, A. (2021), "On Butler's Theory of Agency," in *Bodies That Still Matter. Resonances of the Work of Judith Butler*, eds. A. Halsema, K. Kwastek, and R. van den Oever, 21–30, Amsterdam: Amsterdam University Press.

3

Pleasure, Scandal, and the Body: Foucault on Somatic *Askesis*

Daniele Lorenzini

Introduction

It is well known that, starting in 1980 and largely due to the influence exerted on him by Pierre Hadot's work on spiritual exercises (Hadot 1977), Michel Foucault begins to take an interest in the role that *askesis* plays in ancient philosophy, and to study the various kinds of exercises one can practice in order to shape one's own way of behaving and living in accordance with the principles of a given philosophical school. In this context, Foucault repeatedly emphasizes the difference between ancient *askesis* and Christian asceticism: the term *askesis*, in Greek, has a broad meaning, indicating any type of exercise or practical training whose ultimate goal, far from being the renunciation of oneself, is the elaboration of a positive relationship to oneself characterized by a certain degree of control and self-mastery. This relationship, moreover, does not aim to detach the subject from this world and allow her to have access to the *other* world, but rather to prepare and equip the subject with the necessary tools to deal with the challenges she might encounter in *this* world.

As Foucault argues, the exercises that characterize ancient *askesis*, whose main objective is to put the subject "in a situation in which he can verify whether he can confront events and use the discourses with which he is armed," have two fundamental poles: the first, which I will not address in this chapter,[1] is that of *melete*, or the exercises of "meditation"; the second is that of *gymnasia*, the "training" of oneself that does not only consist in exercises of the imagination, of thought, or of perception, but also and above all in the "training in a real situation, even if it has been artificially induced" (Foucault 1997c: 239–40).

In this chapter, I focus on this vast field of bodily exercises, or what could be called the field of "somatic *askesis*" (Shusterman 2011: 157): exercises of abstinence, physical deprivation, purification, and self-testing, whose function is, however, strikingly different depending on whether one considers the Platonic, Epicurean, or Stoic traditions, or the Cynic tradition. In the former case, these exercises were generally supposed to test the degree of independence acquired by the individual with regard to the external world and events of life; in the latter, bodily *askesis* becomes an ethico-political weapon in the context of what Foucault calls a philosophical militancy. It is this important difference within a general framework that remains nonetheless common that I explore and question in what follows.

Ascetic Techniques of the Body

During the March 17, 1982, lecture of his course at the Collège de France, *The Hermeneutics of the Subject*, within the framework of his analysis of the Hellenistic and Roman "culture of the self," Foucault advances a distinction between two major types of exercises of the body, or of bodily techniques of the self: the regimen of abstinence and the practice of tests (*épreuves*) (Foucault 2005: 426).

On the one hand, drawing from Musonius Rufus' *Peri askeseos*, Foucault explains that ancient *askesis* does not only focus on the soul, but on the body as well, because "virtue must go through the body in order to become active" and effective (Foucault 2005: 426). In particular, Musonius *joins together* the exercises of the body and the exercises of the soul, and he attributes to them two main objectives: first, to train and strengthen courage, that is, the ability to resist external events and misfortunes, to bear them without collapsing and letting oneself be carried away by them; second, to train and strengthen *sophrosune*, that is, the ability to limit oneself, to control and master one's own interior movements (impulses, desires, etc.) (Foucault 2005: 426–7). But where Plato thought it was gymnastics, athleticism, physical struggle, along with their regimens of renunciations and abstinences, that guaranteed to the individual the acquisition of these two virtues—courage and self-mastery—in Musonius' text (and in most Stoic texts, as well as in the Cynic tradition) gymnastics disappears and is replaced by a regimen of *endurance* against hunger, thirst, cold, heat, and so on. One has to make oneself capable of enduring such things by practicing a whole series of abstinences, in order to constitute, not an athletic body, but "a body of patience" (Foucault 2005: 428). In other words, one has to practice abstinence in order to give a form to one's life that allows one to assume a sufficiently detached attitude toward external events.

However, this has little to do with the exercises of "real" poverty we can find the Cynic or anachoretic traditions: the Stoic philosopher, as well as the Platonic and Epicurean ones, does not *renounce* eating, drinking, wearing clothes, possessing wealth, having sexual relations, etc., but finds in the simple appeasement of his necessary and natural needs the "measure" of all these activities. She thus forms a way of life that is not regulated by a regimen of specific interdictions and prohibitions, but by a moderate "style" and the search for the right measure which, alone, can guarantee self-mastery and the tranquility of the soul (Foucault 2005: 429–30).

> Hold fast, then, to this sound and wholesome rule of life; that you indulge the body only so far as is needful for good health. The body should be treated more rigorously, that it may not be disobedient to the mind. Eat merely to relieve your hunger; drink merely to quench your thirst; dress merely to keep out the cold; house yourself merely as a protection against bad weather. It matters little whether the house be built of turf, or of variously colored imported marble; understand that a man is sheltered just as well by a thatch as by a roof of gold. (Seneca, *Letters to Lucilius*, VIII)

On the other hand, there is the practice of tests, which always entails, according to Foucault, a questioning of oneself, and thus a form of self-knowledge: one must know what one is capable of and, above all, one must be able to locate and measure one's progress on the path that leads to virtue, wisdom, and self-mastery: Am I capable of not getting angry, or of avoiding being unjust, or of renouncing profit—even licit profit—for one day? And for two days, or a week, or a month? The test, moreover, is constantly accompanied by a certain work of thought on itself, because it is not simply a question of "imposing a rule of action or abstention on yourself, but of developing an internal attitude at the same time": indeed, to succeed in a given test (*épreuve*), it is not enough to master one's body, but it is also necessary to master one's thought at the very moment when one is faced with reality (Foucault 2005: 432). Thus, Epictetus maintains that it is not enough to abstain from the temptation to follow a beautiful young woman whom one meets in the street, but that it is also necessary to reach a stage where one does not feel anything anymore and no longer thinks anything at all. In the same way, when one embraces one's child, one's wife, or one's friend, one must repeat to oneself: "Tomorrow you will die" or "Tomorrow you will go into exile" (Epictetus, *Discourses*, II. 18; III. 24). In other words, we must consider all the events of our daily existence as opportunities to exercise ourselves, to test ourselves, and to see whether we are capable of detaching ourselves from the things that do not depend on us and only risk disrupting our inner tranquility.

Consequently, unlike the regimen of abstinence, which consists of exercises *localized* in time and space, the test "must become a general attitude in life" (Foucault 2005: 437). Thus, in the Hellenistic and Roman "culture of the self," it is one's entire life—life in all its dimensions (including the most minute, banal, and ordinary)—that becomes a test:

> One must live one's life in such a way that one cares for the self at every moment and that at the enigmatic end of life—old age, moment of death, immortality (immortality as diffusion in the rational being or personal immortality, it doesn't matter)—what one finds, what anyway must be obtained through the *tekhne* one installs in one's life, is precisely a certain relationship of self to self which is the crown, realization, and reward of a life lived as test. The *tekhne tou biou*, the way of dealing with the events of life, must be inserted within a care of the self that has now become general and absolute. (Foucault 2005: 448)

Compared to the modern disciplines that Foucault studies in the 1970s, and that shape individual bodies in order to extract labor force from them in the most efficient way possible (Foucault 1977: 135–69), we are therefore dealing here with another domain, with another series of techniques—ascetic rather than disciplinary (Foucault 2021: 81–2). Of course, these ancient techniques also act on the individual body in order to shape it; but in this case, it is the subject herself who chooses to put them into practice with the aim of giving her life a more accomplished form, thus attaining self-sufficiency, wisdom, happiness, etc. Among these ascetic techniques of the body, which according to Foucault define ancient aesthetics of existence, I will focus more specifically, on the one hand, on the more traditional exercises linked to the "use of pleasures" and, on the other, on the exercises that characterize the scandalous (and bellicose) "stripping of existence" practiced by the Cynics.

Stylistics of Pleasures

The term "*aphrodisia*" designates the "works" or "acts" of Aphrodite (Foucault 1985: 38). Foucault uses it to define the category under which the Greeks of the Classical and Hellenistic periods subsume the various gestures or practices that we call "sexual." More precisely, *aphrodisia* are acts, gestures, and contacts "that produce a certain form of pleasure" (Foucault 1985: 40) and that, consequently, generate a moral problematization—one which, of course, is very different from *our* problematization of "sexuality." At the beginning of the January 28, 1981, lecture of his course at the Collège de France, *Subjectivity and Truth*, when introducing the term *aphrodisia*, Foucault specifies that it "characterizes a quite specifically Greek, Greco-Roman, Hellenistic, and Roman experience," radically different both from the Christian experience of the flesh and from the modern experience of sexuality (Foucault 2017: 76). Besides, *aphrodisia*, flesh, and sexuality do not constitute, according to Foucault, three separate domains of objects, but rather "three modalities of the relation of self to self in the relation that we may have with a certain domain of objects related to sex" (Foucault 2017: 76). In the last lecture of that course, Foucault concludes:

> The Greeks knew neither sexuality nor the flesh. They knew a series of acts called *aphrodisia*, which fall within the same category and involve the same type of behavior, the same practices of the body, and so on. But in any case, these are *aphrodisia*, sexual acts, and not something like the flesh, like sexuality. It is impossible to find [the equivalent] of these categories in Greek thought. *Aphrodisia*, in the Greeks, *veneria* in the Latins, is an activity. It is not a property, a feature of nature, it is not a dimension of subjectivity, it is a type, a series of acts characterized by their form, by the violence of the desire that traverses them, by the intensity of the pleasure one experiences, and by the fact that it is an activity that, due to this violence of desire and intensity of pleasure, is in danger of escaping itself and losing control of itself. (Foucault 2017: 282–3)

Foucault argues that *aphrodisia* were problematized according to two major variables: on the one hand, the quantitative variable, that is, "the degree of activity that is shown by the number and frequency of acts" (the dividing line here is thus between moderation and incontinence) (Foucault 1985: 44); on the other hand, the variable of "polarity," that is, the role—of subject or object—that the individual plays in these acts (the dividing line in this case is between activity and passivity) (Foucault 1985: 46–7). Consequently, in antiquity, the "two main forms of immorality in the practice of the *aphrodisia*" are, for a man, excess and passivity (Foucault 1985: 47). Sexual activity is not considered as an evil in itself, on the contrary, it is seen as natural and indispensable; yet, it carries with it a force that risks confusing the subject and making her lose sight of her goals: self-control, self-sufficiency, tranquility of the soul, and knowledge of the truth. This is why the ancient arts of living necessarily raise the problem of sexual activity and the "economy of pleasures" (Foucault 2017: 36), since "faced with a pleasure which has a dangerously unlimited natural tendency characteristic of the woman," the man must manifest "a rule of moderation" (Foucault 2017: 89).

Moral reflection on *aphrodisia* has therefore never been organized around "a systematic code that would determine the canonical form of sexual acts," but has rather contributed to the elaboration of the conditions and modalities of a "style" to make use of pleasures in a correct way, and to take care of one's body (Foucault 1985: 53). The term that defines this particular form of relationship to oneself, this attitude that proves necessary to make good use of pleasures, is *enkrateia*: it designates "an active form of self-mastery, which enables one to resist or struggle, and to achieve domination in the area of desires and pleasures" (Foucault 1985: 64). The relationship of the subject to "sexual" pleasures must indeed be structured, here, as a struggle and a fight aiming at domination; its objective is not to suppress each and every desire and pleasure, but to prevent the subject from being dragged along or carried away by them.

Within this framework, *askesis* clearly becomes crucial: one must exercise, one must train both one's body and one's soul, in the fields of dietetics—an actual "technique of existence" that defines a "regimen of pleasures" (Foucault 1985: 107, 114)—economics, and erotics, in order to forge a "technique of existence" that does not "require that [Aphrodite's] acts be divested of their primordial naturalness," nor does it "attempt to augment their pleasurable effects," but seeks "to distribute them in the closest conformity with what nature demand[s]" (Foucault 1985: 138).[2] In other words, what is at stake in this *tekhne* is "the possibility of forming oneself as a subject in control of [her] conduct" (Foucault 1985: 138):

> Because it was the most violent of all the pleasures, because it was more costly than most physical activities, and because it participated in the game of life and death, it constituted a privileged domain for the ethical formation of the subject: a subject who ought to be distinguished by his ability to subdue the tumultuous forces that were loosed within him, to stay in control of his store of energy, and to make his life into an *oeuvre* that would endure beyond his own ephemeral existence. The physical regimen of pleasures and the economy it required were part of a whole art of the self. (Foucault 1985: 139)

This art of the self would perdure in the Hellenistic and Roman periods, while undergoing several modifications, and above all a "more intense problematization of the *aphrodisia*" (Foucault 1985: 39). It would eventually give rise to a "culture of the self" that is more austere but still characterized by a *tekhne tou biou* in which the relationship to one's own body and its pleasures remains a crucial element in the constitution of oneself as a moral subject, as well as in the stylization of one's daily life. Foucault highlights the emergence, between the first century BC and the first century AD, of "a new sexual ethic" based on a "hypervalorization of marriage," defined as the sole place of legitimate sexual relations, and on a "devalorization of pleasure," the "elision of pleasure from the sexual act" (Foucault 2017: 104). Sexual ethics is thus elaborated in the form of a "conjugalization of the regime of *aphrodisia*" (Foucault 2017: 177) that would subsequently be transferred to Christianity, giving birth—with the development of monasticism in the fourth and fifth centuries AD—to the experience of the flesh. Foucault can therefore conclude that conjugal sexual morality does not belong to "the very essence of Christianity" (Foucault 2017: 177; on this point, see Lorenzini 2022).

Self-Stripping and Philosophical Militantism

In *The Hermeneutics of the Subject*, Foucault refers to the Stoic exercise consisting, by a "physical" or "realistic" look, in stripping the objects and situations of life of the false values that our judgment attributes to them, thus making them appear "naked," such as they *really* are (Foucault 2005: 294–6). But whereas this exercise consists in the stripping of thought, it is worth noticing that the Cynic philosophers elaborate and practice an exercise of *bodily* stripping that Foucault analyzes in great detail in his 1984 course at the Collège de France, *The Courage of Truth*. There, he focuses on the Cynic's active stripping (*dépouillement*) of his own body and his own existence in the direction of an animality that he claims as a positive value and of a "militant" poverty that he experiences as a permanent test of himself and of others.

Although his most developed analysis of ancient cynicism is to be found in *The Courage of Truth*, Foucault already offers some significant, if very brief, remarks on this topic in 1982 and 1983. Thus, in the February 2, 1982, lecture of *The Hermeneutics of the Subject*, speaking of Demetrius the Cynic, Foucault addresses one of the fundamental features of Cynic philosophy, namely "the comparison of life, and of the person who wishes to achieve wisdom in life, with the athlete" who is constantly exercising himself—and who does so precisely in order to live a "natural" and autarkic life, one stripped of all the (false) dependencies introduced by culture, society, opinion, and so on (Foucault 2005: 321). We are not very far from Stoicism here, and yet, whereas the Stoic, to achieve this objective, acts first and foremost on thought and inner speech, by constantly applying the fundamental distinction between what depends on us and what does not depend on us, the Cynic acts instead on his body and his way of living to make himself concretely, *physically* independent of everything that does not depend on him. It is a true exercise of stripping, of reduction of oneself and one's own existence to their "naked" state.

In the March 9, 1983, lecture of his course at the Collège de France, *The Government of Self and Others*, Foucault offers an analysis of the famous portrait of the Cynic that Epictetus draws in the third book of the *Discourses*. Foucault argues that Cynic philosophy is presented there as a "flagrant way of life" and a "perpetual manifestation of truth" because the Cynic "is someone who detaches himself from all artifice and ornament," and who hides nothing of himself: he "presents himself naked, in his destitution," he lives under the eyes of everyone because "he is a free man, without anything to fear from the outside" (Foucault 2010: 346–7). The Cynic in his life is thus "the manifest truth," the *incarnation* of the philosophical *logos* in a way of living and being (Foucault 2010: 347).

Foucault develops these ideas in his course at the Collège de France the following year, beginning with the February 29, 1984, lecture, where he argues that the Cynic way of life is characterized by extremely precise and coded forms of behavior, as well as by a certain number of extremely recognizable features:

> The Cynic is the man with the staff, the beggar's pouch, the cloak, the man in sandals or bare feet, the man with the long beard, the dirty man. He is also the man who roams, who is not integrated into society, has no household, family, hearth, or country ... and he is also a beggar. We have many accounts which testify that this kind of life is absolutely at one with Cynic philosophy and not merely an embellishment. (Foucault 2011: 170)

This specific way of life does not simply have as its objective, according to Foucault, to "correspond harmoniously, as it were, to the Cynics' discourse and veridiction"; it is not an instance of the "homophonic function" that characterizes Socratic *parrhesia*—the fact that Socrates' words correspond both to his beliefs and to his actions (Foucault 2010: 170). The Cynic's way of life, his everyday existence, possesses on the contrary, with respect to his practice of truth-telling, a threefold function: an instrumental function, a reductive function, and a role of test (*épreuve*). First, the life of the Cynic is the condition of possibility of his truth-telling, because if his mission is that of a scout or a spy who is supposed to tell the truth to humanity as a whole, it is necessary that the Cynic be free of all attachments—family, house, and homeland (Foucault 2010: 170). Second, the Cynic way of life aims at "reducing" all unnecessary obligations and conventions, all opinions "which everyone usually acknowledges and accepts and which have no basis in nature or reason": it is "a sort of general stripping of existence and opinions in order to reveal the truth" (Foucault 2010: 171). Third, the Cynic way of life "brings to light, in their irreducible nakedness, those things which alone are indispensable to human life or which constitute its most elementary, rudimentary essence" (Foucault 2010: 171). The Cynic in Epictetus' portrait can thus conclude—in a clearly paradoxical way—that, having no wife, no children, no servants, no vast house, no riches, and no homeland, but only the earth, the sky, and an old cloak, in fact *he lacks nothing*, for he is without sadness and without fear, absolutely free (Epictetus, *Discourses*, III. 22).

Consequently, the Cynic radicalizes and upsets the traditional philosophical regimen of abstinence: whereas in the Platonic, Epicurean, and Stoic traditions the simple appeasement of necessary and natural needs constitutes the rule of moderation that allows the philosopher to achieve self-mastery and tranquility of the soul, the Cynic rejects all principles of moderation and applies to in his body and the very form of his existence a practice of indefinite deprivation—to the point of the most scandalous begging and animality. Through his body and his life thus "reduced" to the essential, the Cynic bears witness to the truth that other philosophers express in words but do not have the courage to *actually* put into practice. Thus, the Cynic's poverty is, according to Foucault, "real, active, and indefinite" (Foucault 2011: 257). It is "real" because it does not consist in the simple detachment of the soul from material goods and wealth, but in the "stripping of existence which is deprived of the material elements to which it is traditionally linked and on which it is usually thought to depend": clothes, food, housing, possessions, and so on (Foucault 2011: 257). It is "active" because it is not satisfied with indifference to fate and fortune, but engages in "an operation one carries out on oneself in order to obtain positive results of courage, resistance, and endurance"; it is "an elaboration of oneself in the form of visible poverty" (Foucault 2011: 258). Finally, it is "indefinite" or "unlimited" because it does not stop at any given point that one could consider satisfactory, but "is always looking for possible further destitution" in order to reach "the ground of the absolutely indispensable" (Foucault 2011: 258). This is only possible thanks to the modeling of Cynic life on nature, and nature only, and to the valorization of animality as an active principle of criticism of all socially accepted conventions (Foucault 2011: 264–5).

This "reduction" of the Cynic *bios* to nature and the elemental, this transfiguration of the Cynic's life into an athletic combat "manifesting in an immediate and dazzling way the truth of the human being in the stripping of his animality," can only be obtained through *askesis*—a "shortcut to virtue," a short but arduous path that short-circuits traditional education (*paideia*) to climb directly to the summit (at the price, of course, of many difficulties) (Goulet-Cazé 1986: 22–8, 53–71; 2013). This short but arduous path is the path of exercise, that of "practices of destitution and endurance" (Foucault 2011: 207) forging a life without decency and without shame, a life that does in public and under everyone's eyes what only animals dare to do, an "indifferent" life detached from everything and having no needs other "than those it can satisfy immediately" (Foucault 2011: 243). As Frédéric Gros aptly remarks, it is "by dint of scraping existence to the bone, of stripping his life of all artificial conventions or cumbersome riches" that the Cynic reaches "an elemental that absolutely resists," one that is like "the first, solid, and hard layer of immanence," and that "he draws from it an energy without limits," an "immense force that enables him to continue indefinitely his fight and his struggles" (Gros 2012: 295). In Epictetus' words, the Cynic must be, in his own body, "like the visible figure of a truth which attracts": it is through his somatic qualities and his radiant health that he gives proof of the "truth" of his life, thus presenting himself as "the picture of the truth," "the very being of the true, rendered visible through the body" (Foucault 2011: 310).

It should, however, be noticed that this "elementary naturalness" of the body and life of the Cynic philosopher has nothing to do with the Agambenian "bare life" (Agamben 1998), or with a life obtained via the progressive subtraction of attributes from one's *bios*—the culturally, socially, and politically qualified life—in the direction of a pure and simple biological existence (*zoe*). Indeed, if the "animal" life of the Cynic scandalizes, it is because it is fully acknowledged as a human life, and because it explicitly inscribes itself at the hearth of the political community as an *other* (but still entirely recognizable) life. The Cynic principle of destitution and nakedness is, according to Foucault, an ascetic technique aimed at the *positive constitution* of a set of attributes (endurance, resistance, courage, self-sufficiency, self-control, and freedom) through the active shaping of a *bios* that takes the form of perpetual scandal. Rather than a "reduction" of life to its supposed "original" naturalness, what is at stake in the Cynic's somatic *askesis* is therefore the "reduction" of *other people's lives* to their absurdity—which appears in plain sight once they are faced with the Cynic's "true life." In short, scandal is a strategic, ethico-political effect that the Cynic philosopher seeks and tries to obtain, thanks to a long and difficult work on himself:

> In order not to be inferior to the animal, one must be capable of taking on that animality as reduced but prescriptive form of life. Animality is not a given; it is a duty. Or rather, it is a given, offered to us directly by nature, but at the same

time it is a challenge to be continually taken up. This animality, which is the material model of existence, which is also its moral model, constitutes a sort of permanent challenge in the Cynic life. Animality is a way of being with regard to oneself, a way of being which must take the form of a constant test. Animality is an exercise. It is a task for oneself and at the same time a scandal for others. (Foucault 2011: 265)

Thus, by "sculpting" his own statue through the shaping of his body and existence *per via di levare*,[3] the Cynic affirms, or rather *shows*, the non-necessity of all social conventions and rules. According to Diogenes, it is precisely through "bodily *aksesis*," by exercising oneself to endure cold, heat, thirst, hunger, illness, etc., that the human being can achieve virtue, autarky, and happiness: "Only a body shaped by a life of frugality and suffering can enable the soul to become apathetic, and thus man to be free because indifferent to all the blows that Fortune and Fate throw at him" (Goulet-Cazé 1986: 70, 212–3). And it is precisely because he has sculped his own body as a surface that offers no support to the grasp of power, needs, sufferings, and fears, that Diogenes can stand up to Alexander and proclaim himself the only true king (Foucault 2011: 275–8): his self-mastery, his autarky, his independence, and his freedom are based on his ascetic work of constitution of a *bios* that is a crucial tool of ethico-political resistance and a weapon of fight "against and for oneself, against an for others" (Foucault 2011: 283; trans. mod.).

Conclusion

In this essay, I have explored two specific forms of Foucault's "aesthetics of existence," or rather, two types of somatic *askesis* which, while sharing several features, are strikingly different in their function and ethico-political significance. If the genealogical analysis of Greco-Roman *aphrodisia* undoubtedly aims to highlight the non-necessity of the modern apparatus of sexuality, thus inviting us to conceive of sex not as a fatality but as "a possibility for creative life" (Foucault 1997b: 163), it is obvious that the Cynic's philosophical militancy possesses, in Foucault's work, a much more explicit ethico-political value. Indeed, through his bodily *askesis*, the Cynic philosopher transforms his ordinary way of living into a militant practice of resistance—the real core of his radical critique of all social hypocrisy. By increasingly pushing the limits of what he can endure, he implements a singular "devotion," because his concern and care of the others takes a polemical, bellicose form: the form of a fight aggressively addressed at his fellow citizens' vices rooted in their customs, habits, conventions, and sociopolitical institutions.

As an explicit and constant struggle against humanity as a whole, the Cynic's fight does not aim to reject it, but to transform it, thereby contributing to the creation of an *other* society and an *other* world. The Cynic, unlike other ancient philosophers, makes the aesthetic and ethical shaping of his body and life a stake that is immediately *political*, because he inscribes his scandalous existence at the heart of the public space, thus using it as a tool to show his fellow citizens the part of what is "singular, contingent, and the product of arbitrary constraints" in what is given to us "as universal, necessary, [and] obligatory" (Foucault 1997a: 315). Much more effectively than Baudelaire's attitude of modernity, the Cynic's somatic *askesis* therefore epitomizes Foucault's conception of critique as the historical ontology of ourselves.[4]

Notes

1 More details on this topic can be found in Lorenzini 2015: 125–45.
2 The framework here is therefore different from what Foucault, in 1976, had called "*ars erotica*" (Foucault 1978: 57–8), and which eight years later he associates to the ancient Chinese "bedroom" treatises rather than to Greco-Roman *aphrodisia* (Foucault 1985: 137).
3 See Hadot, 1977: 102: "For the ancients, sculpture was an art which 'took away,' as opposed to painting, an art which 'added on.' The statue pre-existed in the marble block, and it was enough to take away what was superfluous in order to cause it to appear." The contrast between sculpture operating "*per via di levare*" and painting operating "*per via di porre*" is attributed to Leonardo da Vinci.
4 This chapter is the English translation of a slightly revised version of my paper "Statues visibles de la vérité: L'*askêsis* corporelle entre éthique et politique," first published in the second issue of *Dorsal: Revista de Estudios Foucaultianos* (2017: 33–47).

Bibliography

Agamben, G. (1998), *Homo Sacer: Sovereign Power and Bare Life*, trans. D. Heller-Roazen, Stanford (CA): Stanford University Press.

Foucault, M. (1977), *Discipline and Punish: The Birth of the Prison*, trans. A. Sheridan, New York: Vintage Books.

Foucault, M. (1978), *The History of Sexuality. Vol. 1: An Introduction*, trans. R. Hurley, New York: Pantheon Books.

Foucault, M. (1985), *The History of Sexuality. Vol. 2: The Use of Pleasure* [1984], trans. R. Hurley, New York: Vintage Books.

Foucault, M. (1997a), "What Is Enlightenment?" [1984], in *The Essential Works 1954-1984. Vol. I: Ethics. Subjectivity and Truth*, ed. P. Rabinow, 303-19, New York: New Press.

Foucault, M. (1997b), "Sex, Power, and the Politics of Identity," in *The Essential Works 1954-1984. Vol. 1. Ethics: Subjectivity and Truth*, ed. P. Rabinow, trans. R. Hurley et al., 163-73, New York: New Press.

Foucault, M. (1997c), "Technologies of the Self," in *The Essential Works 1954-1984. Vol. 1. Ethics: Subjectivity and Truth*, ed. P. Rabinow, trans. R. Hurley et al., 223-51, New York: New Press.

Foucault, M. (2005), *The Hermeneutics of the Subject. Lectures at the Collège de France 1981-1982* [2001], ed. F. Gros, trans. G. Burchell, New York: Palgrave MacMillan.

Foucault, M. (2010), *The Government of Self and Others: Lectures at the Collège de France, 1982-1983*, ed. F. Gros, trans. G. Burchell, Basingstoke: Palgrave Macmillan.

Foucault, M. (2011), *The Courage of Truth: The Government of Self and Others II. Lectures at the Collège de France 1983-1984* [2009], ed. F. Gros, trans. G. Burchell, New York: Palgrave MacMillan.

Foucault, M. (2017), *Subjectivity and Truth: Lectures at the Collège de France, 1980-1981*, ed. F. Gros, trans. G. Burchell, Basingstoke: Palgrave Macmillan.

Foucault, M. (2021), *Speaking the Truth about Oneself: Lectures at Victoria University, Toronto, 1982*, eds. H.-P. Fruchaud and D. Lorenzini, English edition by D. L. Wyche, Chicago: University of Chicago Press.

Goulet-Cazé, M.-O. (1986), *L'ascèse cynique: Un commentaire de Diogène Laërce VI, 70-1*, Paris: Vrin.

Goulet-Cazé, M.-O. (2013), "Michel Foucault et sa vision du cynisme dans *Le courage de la vérité*," in *Michel Foucault: Éthique et vérité (1980-1984)*, eds. D. Lorenzini et al., 105-24, Paris: Vrin.

Gros, F. (2012), "Foucault e la verità cinica," *Iride. Filosofia e discussione pubblica*, 25 (66): 289-98.

Hadot, P. (1977), "Spiritual Exercises," in *Philosophy as a Way of Life*, ed. A. I. Davidson, trans. M. Chase, 81-125, Oxford: Blackwell.

Lorenzini, D. (2015), *Éthique et politique de soi: Foucault, Hadot, Cavell et les techniques de l'ordinaire*, Paris: Vrin.

Lorenzini, D. (2022), "Desire as the 'Historical Transcendental' of the History of Sexuality," in *Foucault, Sexuality, Antiquity*, eds. S. Boehringer and D. Lorenzini, trans. M. Altman and K. Ellerby, 103-11, New York: Routledge.

Shusterman, R. (2011), "Somatic Style," *The Journal of Aesthetics and Art Criticism*, 69 (2): 147-59.

4

Leib, Körper, and the Body Politic

Martin Jay

There can be few more persistent biases than our holistic preference for unity over disunity, integration over disintegration, harmony over discord, and consensus over dissensus. Even when we value fragments or shards of what was once whole, we imbue them with the pathos of nostalgia and mourn their lost integrity. Whether understood in organic or mechanical terms, the complex entities we construe as immanently functional are normatively honored and their opposite stigmatized as pathological. When separation or differentiation occurs, we often label it alienation or estrangement and pine for its overcoming. When stark dualisms are posited—subject/object, mind/body, self/other, culture/nature, soul/flesh, form/content, to name only a few—we hasten to sublate or deconstruct them or search for a *tertium datur* that mediates the opposition. Aesthetic models of coherence, balance, organic unity, and completion normally trump those that favor dissonance, disproportionality, and open-endedness. Decadence is defined precisely by the lack of a triumphant cadence rounding off the end of a story or composition. In short, integration and totalization are identified with life well lived, and their loss with death, decay, and entropy.

An obvious arena for the playing out of these fears and the strategies we employ to meet them is in our corporeal imaginaries. Here the contrast is between bodies understood, on the one hand, as functionally organized, generative, securely boundaried, and inviolable, and on the other as decaying, grotesque, and vulnerable to external invasion.[1] Although often expressed in the vocabulary of biology, with healthy and generative bodies counterposed to their sick, degenerative, or moribund opposites, aesthetic models of wholeness and proportionality are no less prevalent.[2]

The political implications of this bias for corporeal wholeness have been widely appreciated. It was perhaps expressed most explicitly in the familiar metaphor of the body politic, whose long history begins with the ancient

Greeks and reached its apogee in the Middle Ages with works like Al-Farabi's *The Perfect* State and John of Salisbury's *Policraticus*. Its metaphoric efficacy was based on the identification of political functionality with the image of corporeal health, robustness, and beauty. But it could also be used to stigmatize allegedly pathogenic toxins in the body, which were identified with marginalized or abjected internal enemies or foreign intruders (see the discussion in Harris 1998). We all know the sinister outcomes of this kind of rhetorical transfer from the organic body to the political arena.

Rather than examining this familiar analogy, I want instead to interrogate the political implications of another way of conceptualizing the human body, which avoids the simple alternative of healthy holistic integration or dysfunctional decay. I am speaking of a dichotomy that has come down to us from the philosophical anthropological and phenomenological traditions in early twentieth-century Germany and France, which differentiates between the body as *Leib* and the body as *Körper*. Broadly speaking, *Leib* signifies the body as subjectively, if often pre-reflexively experienced, infused with operative intentionality and active purpose, whereas *Körper* suggests the body experienced as an extended object in the world, inert and passive, open to the intentions of others as well as one's own. Significantly, the two different nouns for body are always accompanied by distinct verbs: *Leibsein* and *Körperhaben*, which translate as "to be a body" and "to have a body." These suggest the active quality of the human experience of corporeality, which distinguishes our bodies from the inert objects of inorganic nature. Defying easy reconciliation in some higher dialectical third, the opposition avoids the often sentimental pathos of holistic totalization. And it offers us more conceptual clarity and less normative bias than the opposite extremes of corporeal organization and entropic decay. Instead, it suggests we understand the body neither as a functional organized totality nor a degenerative version thereof, but rather as an active participant in an ongoing process that always involves two experiential modalities. As such, it opens up new vistas on the relationship between bodies and what we call politics, which I want to explore in this chapter.

It is sometimes said that the distinction between *Leib* and *Körper* was introduced by the philosophical anthropologist Helmuth Plessner in 1923.[3] Others have noted its earlier appearance in a 1916 book by Max Scheler titled *Formalism in Ethics and Non-Formal Ethics of Value* (Scheler 1973: 399). Whatever its precise origin, it was further developed by Edmund Husserl, Maurice Merleau-Ponty, and others in the phenomenological tradition and ultimately found its way into the discourse of somaesthetics. There is, in fact, a special issue of the *Journal of Speculative Philosophy* in 2010, introduced by Richard Shusterman's "Soma and Psyche," which explores its costs and benefits in a lucid and thorough way (see Shusterman 2010). In a more recent essay on the distinction, Shusterman tells us that the term "soma" was introduced to overcome whatever dualistic implications might flow from contrasting *Leib* with *Körper* and notes that Husserl himself often spoke of a united *Leibkörper*. Drawing in particular on Plessner's analysis of the imbrication of the two modes of experiencing our bodies, he concludes that "both spontaneous and reflective somatic consciousness (*Leibsein* and *Körperhaben*) are essential for a person's flourishing, for successful functioning, improved performance and developmental growth. Somaesthetics celebrates the value of both" (Shusterman 2018: 19).

While acknowledging the value of balancing the two for the personal goals Shusterman wants to promote, we should, however, hesitate before collapsing them too quickly into an integrated whole if we hope to use the distinction to help us think about politics. Let me quickly sketch what I take to be the main implications of the distinction before passing on to its relevance for political theory. Calling into question the religious dichotomy of soul and flesh and the Cartesian dualism of mind and matter, it alerts us to the entanglement of our experiences of subjectivity and objectivity, the body as perceiver and as the perceived. This oscillation is perhaps most famously exemplified by what Husserl called the "double sensation" experienced when one hand touches the other, whose importance Merleau-Ponty also often stressed. You can either focus on the sensations that represent the "objective" characteristics of the hand you are touching, like the texture of its skin or shape, or on the subjective "sensings" of the hand that is doing the touching (Husserl 1989: 152–3; for a useful summary, see Welton 1999). These two sensations never fuse into one, but can wobble back and forth, as we alternatively attend to one or the other.

Rather than undialectically opposed or ontologically distinct, both are always relationally intertwined, embodying the logic of both/and rather than either/or. *Leib* connotes what Plessner called the "centralized positionality" of the body, its being spontaneously at one with the subject intending its movements and experiencing its feelings. *Körper*, in contrast, is identified with the "ex-centric positionality" of the body in which there is a mediated awareness of it also being a thing in the world. Or more precisely, as Husserl emphasized, it is manifest as an "imperfectly constituted thing" because it is only experienced perspectivally, in part and even misshapen by its limited availability to our senses (Husserl 1989: 167). Such a mediated awareness implies that prior to the experience of "having a body" is the reflexivity enabled by "being a body." But at the same time, the latter is made possible only by the "lived body" always already being situated in the larger world of extended material objects. In other words, the two corporeal modes are recursively and equiprimordially entailed, each latent in or presupposed by the other. If we translate these alternatives into grammatical terms, *Leib* is first-person and *Körper* third-person and the verbs it takes are respectively intransitive and transitive. If we associate them with a specific sensual experience, the former is more haptic, the latter more visual, although only imperfectly because not all of my body is visible within my visual field. In a temporal register, *Leib* is immersed in the qualitatively heterogeneous felt time of what Bergson would have called *durée* or duration, while *Körper* is located in the quantitatively homogeneous spatialized time of the external world (see Wehrle 2020). The central positionality of the former thus also includes the temporal dimension of living in the present moment, whereas the latter is more attuned to the eccentricities of past and future.

A great deal more can be said about the distinction, which produces what has been called "the body-body problem" as opposed to the "mind-body problem" that has vexed philosophy from its beginnings (see Welton 1999: 48). Addressing it would require putting a lot more pressure on such terms as "subjectivity," "intentionality," "perception," "spontaneity," and "temporality." We would have to explore as well the complicated dialectic of internal and external, involving introjection, projection, and the various modalities of intersubjectivity, which would call into question the self-sufficiency of either version of body as an independent entity radically set apart from its environment. We would have to probe the ways in which the body as the generator of desire and the body as the locus of suffering imperfectly map on to the distinction. We would have to ponder the ways that technological mediations of bodily experience, extending from the earliest mirror to the most recent developments in photographic selfies or microcameras that allow us to gaze at the hidden recesses of our bodies, influence the historical mix between *Leib* and *Körper*, which is never a fixed proportion.

These would all be fruitful avenues to pursue in any consideration of the distinction's meaning for politics, but I want to examine something else: the implication of identifying *Leib*, as it often is, with the "lived body." Related to the verbs *leben* (to live) and *erleben* (to experience), and to the adjectives *lebendig* (animated or lively) and *leibhaft* (in the flesh), it foregrounds the body's organic vitality. As such, it inevitably links *Körper*, at least as latent potentiality, with the dead body, in other words with human mortality and our inevitable premonition of it. It is this awareness that is often seen as one of the most salient traits that distinguishes humans from other animals. Here, in English if not in German, we cannot avoid hearing the echo of "corpse" in *Körper*, both rooted, as they are, in *corpus* the Latin word for body.[4] Significantly, in Descartes' *Second Meditation*, where the body is located in space as extended matter without the power of self-movement, it has been described as having all the characteristics of a corpse (see Welton 1999: 54). No matter how much we associate *Leib* with the subjectivity, purposiveness, and spontaneity of life, it is always dependent on the objective materiality making it possible, a dependency perhaps best emblematized by our boney infrastructure, which survives our deaths as a skeleton. As one observer puts it, "a world of organic, autonomous powers circulate within my visceral depths. Their otherness haunts the 'I,' surfacing at times of illness or approaching death" (Leder 1990: 214). There is, in other words, despite the present-mindedness of "I am my body," the anticipatory presentiment of "I will no longer have a body."

In *The Birth of the Clinic*, Michel Foucault argued that only with the gaze of modern medicine was death displaced from the spiritual world and

> *embodied* in the *living bodies* of individuals ... Western man could constitute himself in his own eyes as an object of science, he grasped himself within his language, and gave himself, in himself and by himself, a discursive existence, only in the opening created by his own elimination ... generally speaking, the experience of individuality in modern culture is bound up with death. (Foucault 1973: 196-7)

Whether or not the new attitude of modern medicine toward death was the initial source of our perception of the body as an individual object or merely an institutional and discursive articulation of prior experiences, Foucault's linkage of the objectification of the body with the mortality of the individual is very instructive. It tells us that thinking of the *Leib/Körper* distinction's meaning for politics will inevitably raise an especially vexing issue: How does the realm of human practices and institutions we have come to identify with the political confront the most basic of human concerns, which are literally matters of life and death?

Before venturing a few, inevitably inadequate thoughts on these most daunting of issues, I want to clear some preliminary ground by considering three of the more traditional ways in which vitality and mortality have been considered in relation to politics, both literally and metaphorically. The first is the tradition derived from what the celebrated medieval historian Ernst Kantorowicz famously called "the king's two bodies" (Kantorowicz 1957); the second, the Hegelian identification of death and negation, itself a variant of a longer tradition of what might be called sacrificial sublimation; and the third, what has been known as "biopolitics" and its apparent opposites, "necropolitics" or "thanatopolitics." After we have introduced these alternatives, we can focus on what I hope to show are the different political implications of the distinction between *Leib* and *Körper*.

Drawing on the religious distinction between the *corpus mysticum* of Christ and his creaturely body, the medieval theory of monarchy explored by Kantorowicz differentiated between the eternal life of the institution of kingship and the finite lives of the mortals who temporarily occupy the role of king. One descended from grace, the other from nature, but they mingled in Christ, the Eucharist, and, most importantly from a political point of view, a sacred notion of royalty. The dual nature of monarchy, at once symbolic and literal, allowed continuity of the body politic beyond the deaths of individual rulers through what we might call a political theological transcendentalization of vitality, which was now only fleetingly identified with actual, finite human bodies. Although the religious roots of the distinction grew less explicit and the authority of monarchy itself was diminished after the rise of republican politics, the logic of the king's two bodies remained, as argued by observers such as Claude Lefort (1988) and Eric Santner (2011),[5] in modern political notions of the people and the nation. That is, there is a comparable distinction between a transcendental popular sovereign, the symbolic community of citizens whose authority legitimates a political order, and the empirical people who metonymically claim to represent it, as well as between an allegedly eternal nation and those who assert the right to speak on its behalf.[6]

Life, we might say, is transcendentalized and projected onto an essentialized ideal, kingship or the people, which somehow survives the inevitable deaths of those who are its empirical instantiations. It may, in fact, become so identified with what transcends creaturely finitude that it is located entirely with the hereafter, which begins only with the shuffling off of our mortal coils. Whether or not it reaches that extreme, which renders mundane politics nugatory, it posits, to borrow Foucault's well-known characterization of Kant's distinction between the noumenal and phenomenal subject, a "transcendental-empirical doublet," in which a clear hierarchy of value is assumed. Only the individual soul may, to be sure, enjoy eternal life, but the supra-individual avatars of the *corpus mysticum* on earth are imbued with the same value.

As Derrida notes in an essay titled "Faith and Knowledge," for religions "life has absolute value only if it is worth more than life … respect for life in the discourses of religion as such concerns 'human life' only in so far as it bears witness, in some manner, to the infinite transcendence of that which is worth more than it (divinity, the sacrosanctness of law)." The alleged dignity of life, he continues, "can only subsist beyond the present living being" (Derrida 1998: 51). As is sometimes argued in the case of the Apostle Paul, the elevation of spirit or *pneuma* over flesh or *soma*, the former supposedly universal, the latter merely particular, might have been the source of catholic—with a small "c"—inclusivity. But it could also have very fateful mundane consequences for those groups that were identified solely with somatic particularity, especially the Jews.[7] As we hope to show shortly, the political implications of the phenomenological distinction between *Leib* and *Körper*, which is inherently non-hierarchical, are very different for those outside the charmed circle of the spiritually vital.

If the King's two bodies tradition led to a hierarchically arranged transcendental/empirical doublet in which eternal life was identified with universal or at least collective spirit and death with the mortal individual's creaturely flesh, what might be called the Hegelian tradition of speculative idealism understood the relationship of vitality and mortality in a more dialectical manner. For Hegel, to condense a complicated argument, death was understood as a necessary negation in a process that ultimately led to the reconciliation of apparent opposites, what in the theological terms going back to Gnosticism is called a *pleroma*.[8] As many interpreters of Hegel, including Alexander Kojève and Georges Bataille, have noted, the logic of salutary negation was also that of sacrifice in which the death of the individual was functional in the service of the life of the whole. Death, in other words, is happily recuperated for Hegel in what Bataille called a closed or "restricted economy" rather than bursting its bounds and becoming part of a "general economy" based on excess, waste, expenditure (*dépense*), and the undermining of exchange (Bataille 1993).

In simpler terms, the dialectical heroization of the individual who risks death in order to serve the collective good, whether it be the progress of history, the survival of the community, or the fulfillment of God's will, has been a potent political ploy for a very long time. From Horace's famous exhortation in his ode to valor, "*Dulce et decorum est pro patria mori*" ("It is sweet and proper to die for one's country"), through Patrick Henry's "Give me liberty or give me death" up until Che Guevara's "*Patria o muerte*" ("Fatherland or death"), what is conventionally called "the ultimate" or "supreme" sacrifice has turned death into a justifiable means to realize a higher goal. Not surprisingly, Horace's line is inscribed over the rear entrance to the Memorial Amphitheater at Arlington National Cemetery. Shrouded in the same aura of sanctity that surrounds religious martyrs since at least the days of the early Christians and is still invoked by some to justify suicide bombers in our own day, it draws on a kind of theodicy in which the apparent evil of a violent death—sometimes not only that of the martyr, but also his or her innocent victims—is justified by an alleged higher good.

There has, of course, often been push-back against the dubious consolation to the actual victims offered by this logic. The powerful anti-war poem "Dulce et decorum est," written by Wilfred Owen shortly before his own death in the final week of the First World War, damns Horace's motto as "an old Lie" told to "children ardent for some desperate glory." The recent Cuban demonstrators against the current regime have adopted "*Patria y vida*" ("Fatherland and life"), the title of a popular hip-hop song, as their defiant slogan. Rather than sublimating individual deaths in a narrative of collective redemption, they protest against the logic of sacrificial martyrdom that provides a dubious solace for the premature termination of a particular life.

An even more radical repudiation of the functionalization of individual death in the service of a collective project grew out of a revision of Michel Foucault's analysis of modern biopolitics by an array of international theorists, most notably Giorgio Agamben, Roberto Esposito, and Achille Mbembe. For Foucault, contemporary biopolitics, which was derived from an earlier development of "biopower," involved the exercise of political rationality or what he called "governmentality" by both state and non-state actors to foster the collective health and lives of the populations they control. Unlike the repressive and negative use of power directed at individuals by the traditional juridical and discursive mechanisms employed by sovereign states, it expresses itself in positive terms and focuses on the flourishing of the species body understood demographically.[9] Propagation, births, life expectancy, disease prevention, and sometimes genetic purity are all subjected to regulatory intervention and control, as well as the soft power of hegemonic manipulation based on evermore refined biometrical technologies. Whether in the service of Nazi "racial hygiene," the regulation of carcinogens like nicotine,[10] or, to adopt a more current example, of limiting pandemic infection by mandating vaccinations, the avowed goal of biopolitics is to foster the welfare of populations, not merely affirm the power of the sovereign. It is understood by Foucault, in conformity with his general attitude toward power, as productive and enabling rather than restrictive or constraining.

Foucault had distinguished between a classical version of sovereign biopower whose rationale was "to take life or let live" and a modern biopolitics based on "regularization," which consists in "making live and letting die"

(Foucault 2003: 247). Although drawing on Foucault's distinctions, Agamben, Esposito, and Mbeme have been more interested in the active and darker agenda of what they called thanatopolitics or necropolitics, which deliberately sought death rather than merely passively let it happen.[11] Bracketing the nuances of their arguments, we can discern a common pattern in their explorations of the more sinister effects of the biopolitical agenda and the differentiated populations it targets. They contend that the mechanisms regulating and managing populations identified by Foucault were not as disentangled from the traditional constraining power of sovereignty as he had assumed. Agamben in particular identifies it with a kind of permanent "state of exception," which Carl Schmitt had located only in those moments when the legitimacy of a legal order was undermined. Such a state, he contends, was realized in its most naked form in Nazi concentration camps, where humans were often reduced to the living dead, zombie-like *Musselmänner*, as they were called, before they were literally exterminated. Esposito resisted Agamben's overly broad conclusion that the camps represented a distillation of modernity as a whole in which "bare life" was robbed of any meaningful dignity. But in his analysis of the role of political "auto-immunity," he also acknowledged the function to which certain segments of the population were condemned as toxic pathogens that had to be destroyed or expelled to maintain the health of the community as a whole.

In this analysis, death becomes more than a regrettable by-product of defending the nation or the state against its enemies, which can then be heroically recuperated. Wars, genocides, forced migrations, artificially induced famines, and the like are deliberate strategies for either actively eliminating populations or callously exposing them to likely death. Eugenics could often justify the ruthless "weeding out" of alleged inferior exemplars of the species. Even when efforts have been made to limit civilian casualties in war and make its violence more "humane," the euphemistic defense of their deaths as "collateral damage" speaks to the necessary role they play in thanatopolitics.[12] These are deaths that are not seen, to borrow the terminology of Judith Butler, as "grievable," unlike those of martyrs in the service of allegedly noble causes[13] (Butler 2004: 32). Agamben's "*homo sacer*"—translatable as "accursed man" as well as "sacred man"—was, according to Roman law, someone who can be killed by anyone, but who cannot be the subject of a human sacrifice during a religious ceremony.[14] His life—mere animal *zoe* in Aristotle's terminology, rather than full human *bios*—was so bare of social worth that only the intervention of a god could save him. Mbembe argues that well before the invention of concentration camps, enslavement and colonization subjugated stigmatized populations who were forced to hover precariously between life and death. They were excluded from the national or popular community whose symbolically transcendental life could be invoked to compensate for the mortality of the individuals who comprised it, condemned instead to live in a permanent state of exception. The logic of necropolitical abjection can be seen as well in the way other stigmatized groups—for example, gays during the AIDS panic—could be callously excluded from those whose deaths were worthy of being grieved by the community as a whole (see Haritaworn, Kunstmann and Posocco 2014).

Much more can be said about the implications of these three modes of political engagement with the complexities of human corporeality. Whereas the first two attempt to provide consolations for individual deaths through symbolic transcendence or a dialectical negation of the negation, the third bitterly condemns the ways biopower has served as an excuse for abjecting, indeed even literally eliminating, whole groups deemed pathological or toxic. It is easy to be wary of the first two and sympathize with the victims of the injustices denounced by the third. And yet even in the case of thanatopolitics or necropolitics, there are, I want to argue, certain reasons to be cautious. One was recently revealed in the highly problematic way Giorgio Agamben reacted to efforts to deal with the threat of Covid-19. Arguing in February 2020 that the pandemic was nothing but a hoax artificially created to generate panic and justify an increase in the malevolent power of the state, he magnified the suspicion that thanatopolitics is the hidden agenda of biopolitics into a paranoid rejection of emergency measures to mitigate the spread of the virus (Agamben 2020; for a critique, see Bratton 2021: Chapter 16). Epidemiology, indeed modern medicine as a whole, Agamben charged, is in the service of strengthening the militarization of society, accelerating its transformation into a concentration camp, and degrading humans to the status of animals.

Agamben's dubious response to the pandemic and conspiratorial attack on those who have sought to contain it should not, of course, be turned into an excuse for rejecting *tout court* the analysis of the dark side of biopolitics powerfully developed by Esposito, Mbembe, and others. They have indeed made us all aware of how concern for the health of collective bodies can degenerate into a politics of stigmatization, abjection, and sometimes outright elimination of certain classes of people deemed subhuman. Their lives have indeed been rendered "bare," bereft of meaning, dignity, and recognition. It is only through their anonymous deaths, which allegedly enable the flourishing of those whose lives are considered valuable, do they gain any worth. We should feel justifiable solidarity with these victims of the darker side of biopolitics, past and present, and resolve to overcome the conditions and attitudes that threaten to create their counterparts in the future.

But it should also be acknowledged that the emphasis on thanato- or necropolitics may perhaps distort the ways in which questions of life and death can have political relevance. That is, because its exponents focus entirely on the injuries inflicted on those who are victimized by the dark side of biopolitics, those subjected to violence, suffering, and the premature end of life, as well as the callous disregard of society for their misery, they rarely ponder the implications of universal human mortality. Stressing the consequences of the logic of a Schmittian state of exception, in which rules are suspended and death can be dispensed with impunity by authorities outside the law, they turn away from the existential truth that there is no alternative rule to which mortality is an exception, no escape from our shared finitude. And accordingly, they have little to tell us about how politics might respond to the profound challenges presented by this unforgiving reality.

The distinction between *Leib* and *Körper* may, however, allow us to address this issue in a more sober and straightforward way than these other approaches. Foregrounding, as it does, two dimensions of corporeality, it avoids the hierarchical distinction between idealized spirit and base materiality that allows the king's two body tradition, and its republican inheritors, to elevate the eternal life of the *corpus mysticum* over the finite mortality of those who temporarily occupy its symbolic position. Resisting the dialectical sublation of death as a negation ultimately negated in a redemptive totalization that turns individual loss into a noble sacrifice in the service of the whole, it acknowledges the unresolvable oscillation between two modes of corporeality, which reciprocally entail each other, but can never fully be integrated. And by refusing to situate the threat of mortal danger exclusively in a state of exception in which the lives of some are assured by the deaths of others, it acknowledges that to be human, no matter the luck of your circumstances, is to experience both being a lived body and having one that is, as it were, on loan from the objectifying natural forces that will inevitably reclaim it.

How does this help us think about the realm of human endeavor we call politics? First, it makes us wary of those ideologies that justify current suffering, even unto death, through the service it allegedly provides for the survival of the nation, the people, or whatever idealized cause it identifies with eternal life. Here it joins with the critics of thanato- or necropolitics in warning us against the abjection of allegedly toxic pathogens in a healthy body politics. But it goes beyond them in also casting suspicion on the heroization of sacrifices made by members of the hegemonic group, whose immunization against death is being sought. We may, of course, choose to work on behalf of a cause larger than our own self-preservation, but we should avoid imbuing it with the dubious symbolic charge of biological vitality. Honoring the *Leib/Körper* distinction, in which neither is identified with a transcendent version of eternal life, prevents the illegitimate transfer of the necessary function of individual death in the continuing evolution of the biological species to its putative political or ideological surrogates. It makes us wary of the ways in which images of supposedly healthy or beautiful bodies have been allegorized into national or popular symbols of vitality, and often with implicit gender or racial biases to boot.

If acknowledging the equiprimordiality of the distinction helps us avoid the problematic identification of life with a symbolic eternal body, it also may help us confront the various ways in which modern societies grapple with the rule of universal death, rather than the grim exceptions on which thanato- and necropolitics focus. There is, of course, a vast literature addressing this issue, which has culminated in the magisterial "cultural history of mortal remains" called *The Work of the Dead*, which my Berkeley colleague Thomas Laqueur published in 2015. Among this remarkable book's many services is alerting us to the myriad ways humans have resisted attempts, traceable as far back as the Greek philosopher Diogenes, to treat dead bodies as mere carrion, with no claim on our respect or devotion. Although there have been exceptions in which "bare death" is the mirror image of "bare life"—most explicitly, the concentration camps Agamben too hastily turns into a model of modernity in general—even modern secular cultures with diminished faith in a spiritual afterlife continue reverentially to bury the bodies or treat the ashes of the cremated with enormous symbolic respect. Or at least they do for those lucky enough to escape anonymous mass graves and pauper funerals.

I have nothing to add to Laqueur's exhaustively researched, imaginatively interpreted account of the cultural work the dead continue to do after they have crossed the threshold. Nor do I want to address the various ways in which modern cultures treat mortal remains and their commemoration, or cope with our fears of human finitude.[15] I want instead to offer a few speculations about the way acknowledging our still sentient bodies as *Körper*, vulnerable physical objects which are proleptically haunted by their destinies as corpses, may have political ramifications. Let me begin with a focused, albeit indirect example, the right of "habeas corpus," which goes back in the Anglo-American legal tradition before the Magna Carta, was codified in an act of Parliament in 1679 and then enshrined in Article 1, Section 9 of the American Constitution. The term is from medieval Latin and literally means "let you have the body." It guarantees a court's ability to command the physical appearance of a person accused of a crime to determine whether or not his or her detention is lawful. Although the American Constitution does allow it to be suspended in emergencies caused by rebellion or invasion, an extraordinary power only exercised by President Lincoln during the Civil War, it has long remained a cornerstone of any human rights regime.

As the verb "habeas" suggests, this is a "corpus" understood in the objective sense of *Körperhaben* rather than the subjective sense of *Leibsein*, a passive, vulnerable body that needs to be safeguarded against unlawful detention, or even worse, the sufferings of deprivation and torture.[16] Although strictly speaking a legal rather than political right, it acknowledges the importance of protecting individual physical bodies as such, rather than as mere containers of the immortal souls or moral persons, who inhabit them. Or at least, it understands that the latter cannot exist without the former. As a result, it refuses to turn bodies into empty sites for the exercise of discursive and disciplinary power, inscribed through cultural constructions which are cultural all the way down, as was sometimes suggested by Foucault in his discussion of biopower (for a critique of this position, see Butler 1999). By understanding bodies in their guise of *Körper*, proleptically haunted by their inevitable death, we acknowledge a natural limit to cultural constitution. Politics, for all its efforts to mobilize the human capacity to imbue actions with purpose and turn it into collective will-formation—what Hannah Arendt famously called "acting in concert"—should also honor that limit. Only by doing so can a case be made for the legitimacy of human rights, such as habeas corpus, that resists the absolute power of an idealized popular sovereign without constraints.

A comparable lesson follows from the way in which the concept of the people has been contrasted with that of the population, a distinction whose implications I have tried to spell out elsewhere (Jay 2021). Whereas the "population" implies the total number of persons inhabiting a specific location, the "people" can either signify what the Greeks called an *ethnos*, an ethnically, nationally, or even racially defined community or tribe, or a *demos*, the citizens of a polity, who rule it in a democracy. Although rarely acknowledged, the distinction roughly maps on to that between *Leib* and *Körper*. That is, the active, purposeful notion of a "people" involved in the determination of its own political destiny tacitly draws on the idea of the body as lived; in fact, it elevates it to the level of a collective actor, an organic body politic, with the goal of, at a minimum, survival and, at a maximum, self-flourishing. The "population," on the other hand, is an enlarged notion of the body as *Körper*, experienced as an extended object in the world, inert and passive, vulnerable to the control of others. It is the body that can be managed for benevolent ends by the administrators of biopolitics and for malevolent ones by rulers who practice thanato- or necropolitics.

Understanding a population as an analog of the body as *Körper* can also lead us to consider the individual bodies of which it is composed in the same way. Doing so will perhaps sensitize us to the precarity of their existence, which is often dependent on the benign use of the power granted to active citizens of a people as a *demos*, those who can exercise the privileges of bodies in the guise of *Leib*. That is, it can expand the sense of "I have a body" beyond the self to include the bodies of others, bodies whose fate we may well hold, as it were, in our hands. Active members of a national community or democratic citizenry have the power, and some would argue the obligation, to protect those who find themselves under their jurisdiction, to care for them rather than exploit them. The relevant alternative may not be between animal *zoe* and human *bios*, one infused with spiritual dignity and the other abjectly reduced to mere life, but rather between two equally valuable modes of human corporeality.[17] *Pace* Agamben, the bleak telos of the concentration camp need not turn every well-intentioned exercise of biopolitics into a sinister thanatopolitics. Get yourself vaccinated, dammit!

Second, because the *Leib/Körper* is not an either/or opposition, but a both/and dialectical imbrication, it reminds those of us who may be active citizens, privileged to call ourselves "the people," that we too share an inevitable fate as finite beings, with inert, physically vulnerable bodies, always in some sense objects in the hands of others. The reciprocal entanglement of the two modes of corporeality means that we are never exclusively one or the other, and that any metaphor of a body politic must contain an acknowledgment of both. That is, the image of a healthy, organic, hierarchically organized vital body as the model for a political community like a state should be replaced with one that also includes the mortal body, the body that less actively lives than passively suffers, the body that inevitably anticipates its future as a corpse. Rather than seeking to avoid confronting this sober truth through all the mechanisms of denial and consolation so imaginatively invented by virtually all cultures since time immemorial, it might be wiser to face it head on and create a politics commensurate with our untotalized, unharmonized, and negatively dialectical *Leibkörper*.

Lest this all seem too fuzzy or abstract, I want to finish with a brief glance at one attempt to think historically about the implications of the distinction for politics, which was made by Walter Benjamin in the scattered remarks about the body that can be found throughout his work. As with everything Benjamin wrote, it takes a great deal of hermeneutic acuity and persistence to wrest a coherent argument from his elusive *oeuvre*, but luckily several cogent efforts have focused on this precise issue. Rebecca Comay, Gerhard Richter, and, perhaps most explicitly, Leá Barbisan have painstakingly unpacked his ruminations on the *Leib/Körper* distinction and its implications for politics (see Comay 1994; Richter 2000; Barbisan 2017). What has come to be called Benjamin's "anthropological materialism," a label that can be traced back to a letter Adorno wrote to him on September 6, 1936 (in Adorno and Benjamin 1999: 146), drew on his early encounter with phenomenological theory and continued to inform his later engagement with Marxism. The body in various guises, literal and well as metaphorical, individual as well as collective, his own as well as that of others, is a central concern of *One-Way Street*, *Origin of German Tragic Drama*, *Moscow Diary*, and a number of other works in which he attempts to compose a physiognomy of modern life. It runs like a red thread through his intricate thoughts on language, images, mimesis, allegory, and memory, as well as politics.

Rejecting the vitalist organicism of *Lebensphilosophie* and the totalizing aesthetics of German Idealism, Benjamin was alarmed by the ways in which fascism had mobilized the rhetoric of corporeal wholeness and health for sinister purposes. Instead, he sought to valorize the body in ruins—the fragmented, dismembered body; the body available for allegorization in new combinations. Rather than the site of fully present lived experience, the site of subjective integration, the body he preferred was temporally out of joint, retaining memories of the past and proleptically haunted by—or better put, imbued with faint hopes for—the future. He shared Husserl's sense of the *Körper* as a partial, perspectivally perceived object, writing in a 1918 fragment called "Perception and Body," that "it is highly significant that our own body is in many ways inaccessible to us. We can see neither our face, nor our back, nor our entire head, the primary part of our body" (Benjamin 1991; cited both in Richter 2000: 61, and in Barbisan 2017: 3). Contrary to Husserl, Scheler, and the phenomenological tradition, Benjamin, according to Leá Barbisan, "stretches the relation between *Körper* and *Leib* until it breaks: the body becomes the place where alienness (the object, the world, the outside) penetrates the sphere of the self and deeply disturbs its structure" (Barbisan 2017: 3–4).

But rather than a wholly negative condition to be overcome, it needs to be accepted, even, odd as it may sound, nurtured. As Benjamin put it with his characteristic elusiveness in an unpublished fragment from 1922 or 1923 called "Outline of the Psychophysical Problem":

the content of a life depends on the extent to which the living person is able to define his nature corporeally. In the utter decay of corporeality, such as we are witnessing in the West at the present time, the last instrument of its renewal is the anguish of nature which can no longer be contained in life and flows out in wild torrents over the body. Nature itself is a totality, and the movement into the inscrutable depths of total vitality is fate. (Benjamin 1996: 396)

But the surrender to fate has its costs: "the representation of total vitality in life causes fate to end in madness. For all living reactivity is bound to differentiation, whose preeminent instrument is the body" (Benjamin 1996). Significantly, the *Leib* connects man to humanity at large and its mundane history, into which it is absorbed without remainder, while the *Körper* connects man to God, because it is only through the resurrection of individual bodies that the unique worth of each of us, our differentiation from the rest of humankind, might be ultimately realized. For Benjamin—and here he is providing a surprisingly different reading from Kantorowicz and the king's (or people's) two bodies tradition—it is the mortal body, the corruptible body that must die, rather than the allegedly eternal mystical body, that is the real locus of a possible transcendence.

Benjamin's attentiveness to the relationship between the body as *Körper* and mortality is brought to the fore in his ruminations on the central role of death and the corpse in the German *Trauerspiel*, which refuses the consoling catharsis of traditional Greek tragedy and celebrates mortification instead. Rebecca Comay insightfully situates it in his rejection of the Hegelian model of remembrance as *Erinnerung*, in which alienation is overcome through reconciling sublation, in favor of an alternative he calls *Eindenken*. The former involves a *re*-membering, in which "recollection would be precisely the resurrection of the idealized, transfigured body, a body restored to its organic unity and spiritual integrity as a whole." The latter is instead a "re-*membering*" or "the incoherent, multiply situated reawakenings of shattered body parts re-encountering themselves in time and space"[18] (Comay 1994: 255). This repetitive re-encountering is neither an idealized interiorization of death based on the rhetoric of sacrificial martyrdom nor its foreclosure as utterly outside of the closed circle of life, but rather a riposte to both:

> What is ultimately subverted or exceeded is the very opposition (but therefore also the essential reconciliation) of life and death as the final horizon of every narrative. Death neither terminates nor is redeemed by the life which it not only ends or "finishes" but in fact marks as radically "finite" and, as such, unfinished. Neither resurrection nor proper burial, neither a spiritualization of death nor its securing as life's antithesis, can now be thought. (Comay 1994: 267)

Comay may be too hasty here in denying Benjamin's attraction to the idea of resurrection, which we have seen him ponder in his "Outline of the Psychophysical Problem" and to which he will frequently return in extolling the theological belief in "apokatastasis," the ultimate redemption of everyone and everything in the Last Judgment.[19] But she is right to note that until that end time comes, the body as *Körper* and as corpse serves for Benjamin to resist the consoling fiction of spiritual totalization and unalienated reconciliation. Benjamin's theological terminology here might seem very far away from politics, but it implies a politics that has several intriguing possible implications. First, it undermines the fantasy of a subject-centered politics in which the search for a collective agent able to fashion history intentionally is laid to rest, a fantasy that also has motivated Marxism in many of its more humanist guises. Second, it calls into question the identification of the individual subject with an autonomous ego, fully sovereign in its self-mastery. As Barbisan puts it,

> Benjamin stresses the fundamental "eccentricity" of the human being's body, which undermines every attempt to conceive of the body as a closed entity centered on the "self." The body, split between the "lived body" (*Leib*) and the "thing-body" (*Körper*), torn between the *ego* and the world, disrupts the boundaries of the supposedly autonomous individual. Benjamin conceives of the revolutionary collective according to this unpresentable model: not as a collective subject but as a collective body—as a plastic entity whose political agency relies on its ability to virtually incorporate everyone and everything. (Barbisan 2017: 10)

Finally, by reminding us of the continuity of our bodies as *Körper* with the world of inanimate matter to which we will inevitably return, it diminishes our anthropocentric self-image as the most valuable embodiment of vitality, the crowning species of creation able to lord it over all others. Instead, it restores our link not only with the biosphere as a whole, but with the larger geosphere and hydrosphere that make it possible. Instead of framing the issue of life and death in terms of the opposition between biopolitics and thanato- or necropolitics, it situates it in a more profound context in which the lament of suffering nature also finds a voice.

Lest all this still seem impossibly vague and abstract, let me finish by evoking two recent movements, which have had an international impact beyond the boundaries of the America from which they emerged: "Occupy" and "Black Lives Matter." Without venturing an analysis of their complexities or predicting how effective they will ultimately prove, let me point to three aspects of their practice that comport with our larger argument. Unlike many progressive movements in the past, they have never assumed the posture of organic totalization with a hierarchically defined structure and a vanguard leadership. Remaining stubbornly decentralized, locally focused, and resolutely undisciplined, they have resisted the search for a historical agent capable of "making" history or relying on its putative representative to act in the name of the whole. In addition, they have adopted the tactic of masses of vulnerable bodies occupying or marching through spaces, rather than *soi-disant* meta-subjects actively attempting to seize power. As such, they tacitly make common cause with the legions of migrants and asylum seekers who also march and occupy spaces, asserting their rights as precarious members of a passive population rather than the active citizens of a people, understood either as a *demos* or *ethnos*.

These are all bodies, we might say, as much in the guise of *Körper* as *Leib*. There is, in fact, a robust literature that claims the slogan "Black Lives Matter" should be more precisely rendered as "Black Bodies Matter" (e.g., see Berry 2017).[20] While justifiably protesting against the thanato- or necropolitical reduction of those bodies to mere vessels for what Agamben would call "bare life," they also defiantly assert the value of even the suffering, vulnerable, and disposable bodies that are so reduced. Resisting the consolation that might follow the apotheosis of George Floyd into sacrificial martyr in a just cause, they ask us to face the blunt truth of his meaningless death. Refusing the premature closure provided by the healing process of mourning, they fight to keep the wound open, insisting, as did Walter Benjamin, that apparently interminable melancholy may in the long run prove more redemptive than a shallowly optimistic and hasty suturing of the wound (see Jay 2003). Without embracing the hopelessness that paralyzes Afro-pessimists at their bleakest, they relocate what W. E. B. Dubois famously called the double consciousness of American Blacks, not in their two souls, but in their two bodies. And in so doing, they help us all understand that through our shared mortality and its anticipation in our experience as *Körper,* all bodies not only matter, but in the end *are* in a profound sense only the matter out of which they are made.

Notes

1 There are, of course, occasional celebrants of what Deleuze and Guattari, adopting a phrase from Antonin Artaud, called "bodies without organs," whose undifferentiated, ephemeral structures and permeable borders allow a de-territorialized, discontinuous flow of energetic forces. See Deleuze and Guattari (2004a; 2004b).

2   Obvious examples are Leonardo da Vinci's famous drawing of the "Vitruvian Man" and Winkelmann's Hellenic ideal of noble simplicity and restraint, which could even transfigure Laocoon's body in obvious pain into a symbol of eternal, ideal beauty. Although there are, of course, other aesthetic ideals—think, for example, of the Japanese *wabi-sabi*, combining rustic simplicity with reverence for imperfection and the patina of aging—the bias for organic wholeness remains very powerful in our culture.

3   Helmut Plessner with Frederick Jacob Buytendijk, "Die Deutung des mimischen Ausdrucks. Ein Beitrag zur Lehre vom Bewusstsein des anderen Ichs" (in Plessner 1982: 67–129). For a discussion, see Krüger 2010.

4   In German, *Leiche* or *Leichnam* is used for a dead body, with the latter being a slightly more formal term. Their etymology is the high middle German "*lichname*."

5   Santner argues that the symbolic dimension of the people's body is better understand as a "surplus of immanence," which he calls "the flesh," rather than transcendence.

6   The potential slippage between divine and secular versions of transcendental vitality was already noted by the eight-century Anglo-Latin scholar Alcuin of York, but he warned against it: "Nor should we listen to those who say 'the voice of the people is the voice of God' [*vox populi, vox dei*, which was an old Latin saying] for the turbulence of the mob is always close to insanity." Alexander Hamilton is often quoted as saying something similar: "The voice of the people has been said to be the voice of God; and, however generally this maxim has been quoted and believed, it is not true to fact. The people are turbulent and changing, they seldom judge or determine right."

7   According to David Niremberg (2014), the medieval identification with Christianity with lively spirit and Judaism with base matter or lifeless legalism exemplified this danger, which has echoes in the work of such contemporary Marxists as Alain Badiou.

8   For a discussion from the perspective of Schelling's critique of Hegel, see Das 2013.

9   These concepts were sketchily introduced in work published during Foucault's lifetime only at the end of his first volume of *History of Sexuality*, *The Will to Knowledge* (Foucault 1998), but were developed in his posthumously published lectures at the Collège de France, including *Society Must Be Defended* (Foucault 2003), *Security, Territory, Population*, and *The Birth of Biopolitics*.

10 Ironically, Nazi racial hygiene was expressed not only in the elimination of "inferior" humans, defined racially or in terms of their disabilities, but also by campaigns against smoking (see Proctor 1999).

11 See Agamben 1998; Mbembe 2002 and 2019; Murray 2006 and 2008; Esposito 2008; Trover 2020. There are nuanced differences between the two terms—necropolitics, for example, focuses on the unstable condition between life and death suffered by colonized and enslaved people, rather than literal death—but for our purposes, they are virtually synonymous.

12 See Moyn 2021. Although not explicitly drawing on the theorists we are discussing, his analysis comports with theirs.
13 For a discussion of Butler's contribution to the discourse of thanatopolitics, see Deutscher 2016.
14 The concept has been the focus of considerable controversy. For a recent intervention, which includes consideration of many of the issues and cites the relevant literature, see Antonelli 2019.
15 The flood of literatures on these issues is unabated. For three interesting recent contributions, which examine them from different perspectives, see Khapaeva 2017; Han 2019; Trover 2020.
16 It can, of course, be employed ironically, as Hilary Mantel pointed out in naming the second of her trilogy of novels about Thomas Cromwell *Bring up the Bodies*. Here it referred to the command given to court officials to bring supposed traitors languishing in the Tower, who were regarded as guilty and thus already as good as dead, to face the court in Westminster for a sham trial.
17 The inadequacy of the Aristotelian distinction is also addressed in Jacques Rancière's critique of Hannah Arendt's understanding of genuine politics being denied to those in the "mere life" category. For a discussion, which cites all the relevant literature, see Schaap 2011.
18 Benjamin thus opposes what I have called elsewhere his Frankfurt School colleague Herbert Marcuse's neo-Hegelian faith in "anamnestic totalization" (see Jay 1984: Chapter 7).
19 Benjamin invokes it, for example, in "The Storyteller," in discussing Leskov's debt to Origen (Benjamin 1969: 103), in Convolute N of *The Arcades Project* (in Smith 1989: 46), and in discussing Surrealism, which he credits with "the will to apocatastasis … the resolve to gather again, in revolutionary action and in revolutionary thinking, precisely the elements of the 'too early' and the 'too late' or the first beginning and the final decay" (Benjamin 1999: 698).
20 Googling "Black Bodies Matter" reveals a wealth of other efforts to address this issue.

Bibliography

Adorno, Th. W. and W. Benjamin (1999), *The Complete Correspondence: 1928–1940*, trans. N. Walker, Cambridge (MA): Harvard University Press.

Agamben, G. (1998), *Homo Sacer: Sovereign Power and Bare Life*, trans. D. Heller-Roazen, Stanford (CA): Stanford University Press.

Agamben, G. (2020), "The Invention of an Epidemic." Available online: https://f-origin.hypotheses.org/wp-content/blogs.dir/1827/files/2020/09/agamben_epidemic_invention.pdf (accessed February 22, 2022).

Antonelli, P. (2019), "Sacrificing Homo Sacer: René Girard Reads Giorgio Agamben," *Forum Philosophicum*, 24 (1): 145–82.
Barbisan, L. (2017), "Eccentric Bodies: From Phenomenology to Marxism. Walter Benjamin's Reflections on Embodiment," *Anthropology and Materialism*, 1: 1–14.
Bataille, G. (1993), *The Accursed Share. Vol. 1–3*, trans. R. Hurley, New York: Zone Books.
Benjamin, W. (1969), *Illuminations: Essays and Reflections*, ed. H. Arendt, trans. H. Zohn, New York: Schocken Books.
Benjamin, W. (1991), "Wahrnehmung und Leib," in *Gesammelte Schriften. Vol. VI*, eds. R. Tiedemann and H. Schweppenhäuser, 67, Frankfurt am Main: Suhrkamp.
Benjamin, W. (1996), "Outline of the Psychophysical Problem," in *Selected Writings. Vol. I: 1913–1926*, eds. M. Bullock and M. W. Jennings, 393, Cambridge (MA): The MIT Press.
Benjamin, W. (1999), *The Arcades Project*, trans. H. Eiland and K. McLaughlin, Cambridge (MA): The MIT Press.
Berry, D. R. (2017), *The Price for the Their Pound of Flesh: The Value of the Enslaved, from Womb to Grave, in the Building of the Nation*, Boston: Beacon Press.
Bratton, B. (2021), *The Revenge of the Real: Politics for a Post-pandemic World*, London: Verso Books.
Butler, J. (1999), "Foucault and the Paradox of Bodily Inscriptions," in *The Body. Classic and Contemporary Readings*, ed. D. Welton, 307–13, Malden (MA): Blackwell.
Butler, J. (2004), *Precarious Life: The Powers of Mourning and Violence*, London: Verso Books.
Comay, R. (1994), "Benjamin's Endgame," in *Walter Benjamin's Philosophy: Destruction and Experience*, eds. A. Benjamin and P. Osborne, 251–91, London: Routledge.
Das, Saitya Brata (2013), "The Tragic Dissonance," *Analytica Hermeneutica*, 5: 1–33.
Deleuze, G. and F. Guattari (2004a), *Anti-Oedipus: Capitalism and Schizophrenia*, trans. M. Seem and R. Hurley, London: Penguin Publishing Group.
Deleuze, G. and F. Guattari (2004b), *A Thousand Plateaus: Capitalism and Schizophrenia*, trans. B. Massumi, London: Penguin Publishing Group.
Derrida, J. (1998), "Faith and Knowledge: The Two Sources of 'Religion' at the Limits of Reason Alone," in *Religion*, eds. J. Derrida and G. Vattimo, 1–78, Stanford (CA): Stanford University Press.
Deutscher, P. (2016), "The Precarious, the Immune, and the Thanatopolitical: Butler, Esposito and Agamben on Reproductive Biopolitics," in *Against Life*, eds. A. Hunt and S. Youngblood, 119–41, Evanston: Northwestern University Press.
Esposito, R. (2008), *Bios: Biopolitics and Philosophy*, trans. T. Campbell, Minneapolis: University of Minnesota Press.
Foucault, M. (1973), *The Birth of the Clinic: An Archaeology of Medical Perception*, trans. A. M. Sheridan, London: Tavistock Publications.
Foucault, M. (1998), *The History of Sexuality. Vol. 1: The Will to Knowledge*, trans. R. Hurley, New York: Penguin Books.

Foucault, M. (2003), "*Society Must Be Defended*": *Lectures at the Collège de France, 1975–1976*, eds. M. Bertani and A. Fontana, trans. D. Macey, London: Penguin Books.

Han, S. (2019), *(Inter)facing Death: Life in Global Uncertainty*, London: Routledge.

Haritaworn, J., A. Kuntsmann, and S. Posocco, eds. (2014), *Queer Necropolitics*, London: Routledge.

Harris, J. G. (1998), *Foreign Bodies and the Body Politic: Discourses of Social Pathology in Early Modern England*, Cambridge: Cambridge University Press.

Husserl, E. (1989), "Ideas Pertaining to a Pure Phenomenology and to a Phenomenological Philosophy. Book Two: Studies in the Phenomenology of Constitution," in *The Collected Works of Edmund Husserl. Vol. 3*, trans. R. Rojcewicz and A. Schuwer, Dordrecht: Kluwer.

Jay, M. (1984), *Marxism and Totality: The Adventures of a Concept from Lukács to Habermas*, Berkeley: University of California Press.

Jay, M. (2003), "Against Consolation: Walter Benjamin and the Refusal to Mourn," in *Refractions of Violence*, 11–24, New York: Routledge.

Jay, M. (2021), "We, the People, and Us, the Population," *Salmagundi*, Spring–Summer: 37–45.

Kantorowicz, E. (1957), *The King's Two Bodies: A Study in Medieval Political Theology*, Princeton: Princeton University Press.

Khapaeva, D. (2017), *The Celebration of Death in Contemporary Culture*, Ann Arbor: University of Michigan Press.

Krüger, H.-P. (2010), "Persons and Their Bodies: The Körper/Leib Distinction and Helmuth Plessner's Theories of Ex-centric Positionality and Homo Absconditus," *The Journal of Speculative Philosophy*, 24 (3): 256–74.

Laqueur, T. (2015), *The Work of the Dead: A Cultural History of Mortal Remains*, Princeton: Princeton University Press.

Leder, D. (1990), "Flesh and Blood: A Supplement to Merleau-Ponty," *Human Studies*, 13 (3): 209–19.

Lefort, C. (1988), *Democracy and Political Theory*, trans. D. Macey, Cambridge/Oxford: Polity Press in association with Basil Blackwell.

Mbembe, A. (2002), "Necropolitics," *Public Culture*, 15 (1): 11–40.

Mbembe, A. (2019), *Necropolitics*, trans. S. Corcoran, Durham: Duke University Press.

Moyn, S. (2021), *Humane: How the United States Abandoned Peace and Reinvented War*, New York: Farrar, Strauss and Giroux.

Murray, S. J. (2006), "Thanatopolitics: On the Use of Death for Mobilizing Political Life," *Polygraph*, 18: 191–215.

Murray, S. J. (2008), "Thanatopolitics: Reading in Agamben a Rejoinder to Biopolitical Life," *Communication and Critical/Cultural Studies*, 5 (2): 203–7.

Niremberg, D. (2014), "'Judaism' as Political Concept: Toward a Critique of Political Theology," *Representations*, 128 (1): 1–29.

Plessner, H. (1982), *Gesammelte Schriften. Vol. VII: Ausdruck und menschliche Natur*, eds. G. Dux, O. Marquard, and E. Ströker, Frankfurt am Main: Suhrkamp.

Proctor, R. N. (1999), *The Nazi War on Cancer*, Princeton: Princeton University Press.

Richter, G. (2000), *Walter Benjamin and the Corpus of Autobiography*, Detroit: Wayne State University Press.

Santner, E. L. (2011), *The Royal Remains: The People's Two Bodies and the Endgames of Sovereignty*, Chicago: University of Chicago Press.

Schaap, A. (2011), "Enacting the Right to Have Rights: Jacques Rancière's Critique of Hannah Arendt," *European Journal of Political Theory*, 10 (1): 22–45.

Scheler, M. (1973), *Formalism in Ethics and Non-formal Ethics of Value*, trans. M. Frings and R. Funk, Evanston: Northwestern University Press.

Shusterman, R. (2010), "Soma and Psyche," *Journal of Speculative Philosophy*, 24 (3): 205–23.

Shusterman, R. (2018), "Body Consciousness and the Excentric Self: Between Plessner and Somaesthetics," *Pragmatism Today*, 9 (1): 10–20.

Smith, G., ed. (1989), *Benjamin: Philosophy, Aesthetics, History*, Chicago: University of Chicago Press.

Troyer, J. (2020), *Technologies of the Human Corpse*, Cambridge (MA): MIT Press.

Wehrle, M. (2020), "Being a Body and Having a Body: The Twofold Temporality of Embodied Intentionality," *Phenomenology and the Cognitive Sciences*, 19: 299–51.

Welton, D. (1999), "Soft, Smooth Hands: Husserl's Phenomenology of the Lived Body," in *The Body. Classic and Contemporary Readings*, ed. D. Welton, 38–56, Malden (MA): Blackwell.

5

Care of the Social Self as Embodied

Vincent M. Colapietro

Every man is tasked to make his life, even in its details, worthy of the contemplation of his most elevated and critical hours.

(H. D. Thoreau, Walden)

Introduction

"Philosophy began," Richard Shusterman asserts, "not with a paradigm text, but with an exemplary life—a dramatic model of living—and dying" (Shusterman 1997: 17). He is of course referring to the life of Socrates, as portrayed in the dialogues of Plato.[1] As with all things philosophical, however, the exemplary life of the Platonic Socrates has proven from his time to ours an irresistible invitation to engage in interpretation and critique. Insofar as interpreters and critics identify with this exemplar, this makes their interpretations self-reflections and their critiques self-assessments. In any event, this paradigmatic life is an essentially contested one (Gallie), an invincibly problematic affair. The self who is engaged in questioning itself in the very act of self-interrogation is, for some, an admirable and, for others, a ridiculous figure and for still others an individual worthy of both commendation and mistrust. The figure itself and attitudes toward this figure are marked by irony, so much so that Socratic irony is an integral part of this paradigmatic life.

Given the cultural ideals of ancient Athens, Socrates inexplicably proved to be seductive. He drew youths to himself, though his avowed desire was to draw them to care for themselves, through his insistent and disconcerting questioning. As such, his life was that of a mediator devoted to facilitating transitions, not least of all from an unreflective to an examined life, from a life preoccupied with ultimately unimportant concerns to one focused on a deliberately transformed care for oneself (Plato's *Phaedrus*, 230A ff.: 24; Foucault 1986: 45). Socrates proved to be seductive because the challenge of "turning and returning to oneself" (Foucault 1986) proved to be irresistible. Philosophy as an enticing way of life, more specifically, as a distinctively Socratic fashioning of life, is insistently interrogative.

For anyone committed to such a life, questioning cannot limit itself to inherited conventions and contemporary fashions. It is destined to become reflective, to turn on itself and interrogate its own motives, consequences, and strategies. For example, Friedrich Nietzsche was most deeply allied to Socrates when he was most rhetorically scornful of his predecessor.[2] The question of whether one conceives mortal life itself as an unredeemable sickness (Nietzsche 1990: 39), also, the question of whether the life of dialogical reason is antithetical to the admiration of spontaneous passions and of unapologetic vitality (Nietzsche 1990: 41–2; 52–6), are ones taking shape in the project to know oneself. Those knowers who do not know themselves, who do not have the courage to confront their actual motives and less than subtle subterfuges, especially their strategies of self-deception, are accordingly the object of Nietzsche's scorn.[3] Indeed, the effort of trying to ascertain the relationship itself between self-care and self-knowledge is, at once, an instance of a cognitive (or noetic) drive and a radical doubt regarding the scope of this drive. Perhaps care is more inclusive and basic than knowledge (cf. Whitehead 1961: 176; see also Heidegger on *Sorge*). Perhaps a commitment to caring for oneself breaks at critical points with efforts to *know* oneself. Perhaps living a certain way is requisite for seeing or knowing or even feeling certain things (cf. Wittgenstein; James[4]). Perhaps care for the embodied, social, and improvisational self is, despite Socrates, the paradigmatic form of *philosophical* self-care.

At least as far as the Platonic Socrates goes, however, his exemplary life, his dramatic model, appears to have turned on a radical distinction between somatic and personal well-being.[5] Care for the psyche all but entailed neglect of the body; moreover, care for the individual self all but demanded indifference to the perceptions and judgments of others. The focal object of Socratic concerns seems to be stripped of its embodied and social dimensions. If Socrates is truly taken as our paradigm, then caring for oneself meant for him largely ignoring one's somatic and social self. The illness of one's *psyche* might accompany bodily health; a deformity of one's character might have no bearing on one's social status. Might, however, neglect of the body signal a lack of care for the self, might indifference to the recognition or judgments of certain individuals betray cowardice, an unwillingness to be held to the highest standards of human excellence in some specific regard? From all accounts, Socrates seems to have cared not at all for how he dressed or more generally appeared. Legend has it he was not only snub-nosed but also pot-bellied.[6] Though endowed with a rugged constitution, he went to the gymnasium not to exercise his body but to engage the minds of others. He seems to have been able to take his physical well-being as a given, but not the health of his—or anyone else's—*psyche*. Enchanting utterances might in Socratic exchanges assume a deceptively simple form: they might be nothing more than a plainspoken yet arresting question, upon which far more than a conversation turns (*The Phaedrus*). The paradigm of the life of the philosopher is accordingly one in which disconcerting questions and aporetic challenges are met with a degree of honesty and seriousness rarely seen in any arena of our existence.

The Socratic Soul and the Decentered Subject

In opposition to Heinrich Maier and others, John Burnet and, following him, A. E. Taylor argued that Socrates invented nothing less than the concept of the *psyche* in a sense quite different from anything found in the discourses of that ancient Athenian's contemporaries and certainly in either his philosophical or poetic predecessors. Questions regarding the ontological status of the *psyche* were secondary (if that) to moral ones regarding the integrity of the *psyche*, insofar as this integrity was tied to the actions, passions, and devotions of individuals. "The Socratic doctrine of the soul is," A. E. Taylor insists, "neither psychology, in our sense of the word, nor psycho-physics. It tells us nothing on the question what the soul *is*," except in one critical respect. The soul is "that in us, whatever it is, in virtue of which we are denominated wise and foolish, good and evil" (Taylor 1956: 139). The immortality of the soul is, for Socrates, not the focal concern, though it is hardly a negligible concern; his principal focus is however the shape of one's life, not the immortality of the soul. What the Socratic conception of the human *psyche* opens and encourages are questions regarding the inherently admirable forms of a human life.

Ironically, the ancient concept of the soul was akin to the postmodern decentering of the subject. It was a site in which certain questions might be posed and addressed. The soul itself was akin to the concept of it.[7] The process of decentering subjectivity was no less akin to the conceptualization of this process. The process and its conceptualization are first and foremost sites of interrogation, *topoi* of questioning. What the concept endeavors to grasp is a site, but no less how the concept is used to fulfill this function. Concepts are defined by their functions, especially when their concern is with grasping functions beyond the purely conceptual domain.

The decentering of the subject has not so much left a void as it has opened a space in which important questions about human beings might be framed with fewer inherited distortions or disfigurations. While it might drive toward exposing a chimera, it has not entailed the annihilation or rejection of subjectivity as such. In truth, the decentering of the subject has facilitated the much needed disambiguation of a Protean figure. Michel Foucault's misgivings about phenomenology derive in part from his suspicion that this tradition, tracing its roots to the monumental achievement of Edmund Husserl, cannot help but continue a discourse in which the figure of subjectivity is foundational. As often happens in intellectual history, however, Foucault transposes *explancans* and the *explacandum*. At least at the outset, subjectivity cannot function as a principle of explanation; in a word, it does not serve as an *explacans*. It is rather an *explacadum*, in truth, a phenomenon or a range of phenomena calling for an explanation. What historically has forced us to posit a transcendental consciousness, in principle extricable from historical entanglements, inherently endowed with the capacity to give meaning to what otherwise would be meaningless and possibly even insignificant or negligible in the sense of being unimportant? What has, in other words, so compelled us to posit a sovereign subject who, if only methodologically equipped and conscientious, can at least approximate self-transparency? Can we make sense of this sense-making agency or the seemingly inexorable need for insisting that there be such a reflexive agent? In yet other words, can we make sense of the subject itself without positing it as always already anterior to its own strivings and struggles, its endeavors and accomplishments, as well as indeed failures and frustrations?

"There are some concepts," Maurice Merleau-Ponty observed in "Everywhere and Nowhere," "which make it impossible for us to return to a time prior to their existence [or appearance], even and especially when we have moved beyond them, and subjectivity is one of them" (Merleau-Ponty 1964: 155). The decentering of the subject marks one of those moments in which we have decisively and, in some instances, dramatically (if not melodramatically) moved beyond the concept of subjectivity. In having done so, it is, however, not possible to return to the naïveté when that distinctively modern figure had not yet burst upon the scene. Any post-Cartesian moment is one in which the figure of the subject casts its shadow, even and especially when that figure itself is deemed to be nothing more than a shadow or an illusion.

"Personality, selfhood, subjectivity are," John Dewey quietly announced in the chapter in *Experience and Nature* (1925), devoted to "Nature, Mind, and the Subject," "eventual functions that emerge with highly organized interactions [or transactions], organic and social" (LW 1: 162). *Individual* subjectivity is to some extent a precarious achievement. The ease with which considerations of subjectivity become those of individuality is noteworthy and, in due course, we will have an opportunity to consider these considerations themselves. For the moment, however, the point calling for emphasis is that human subjectivity is on Dewey's account an *emergent function*. While it has "its basis and conditions in simpler events," observable in the lives of other animals and even plants, this function only emerges in very complex circumstances, involving organisms of a very complex constitution. One of the marks of subjectivity is reflexivity. "Plants and non-human animals act *as if* they were concerned that their activity, their characteristic receptivity and response, should maintain itself." In contrast, human subjects are actually concerned with their own activity, in an undeniably reflexive manner. This reflexivity is nowhere more evident than in the deliberate efforts of human agents to make of their very lives works of art. It dramatically displays itself in "an aesthetic of existence."

Two contemporary theorists, Michel Foucault and Richard Shusterman, have proposed such an aesthetic in an especially memorable and indeed illuminating manner. Moreover, they have been criticized, at times severely, for being champions, if only unwitting ones, of a self-indulgent regime neglectful of those far less fortunate, specifically, those unable to devote themselves to the unentangled lives of somatic aesthetes. In my judgment, these criticisms miss their mark. The social, somatic, improvisational self or subject at the center of Foucault's exploration of sexuality and, to a greater extent, Shusterman's somaesthetics is inexorably an entangled and, to some extent, encumbered self. To see their visions of subjectivity as nothing but unwitting celebrations of the neoliberal self constitutes nothing less than an injustice. The individual self is, for both theorists, a socially situated and practically implicated agent who can, in favorable circumstances, deliberately engage in practices of self-fashioning. This engagement is intrinsically tied to the ancient Greek ideal of knowing oneself. In turn, the task of knowing oneself is, for Foucault no less than Shusterman, one of knowing oneself in relation to others and, as it turns out, this task implies knowing or, more accurately, acknowledging others in their irreducible otherness (i.e., as beings who exist apart from oneself and, in addition, as beings who are never fully intelligible to oneself).

As much as I am interested in the work of Foucault and Shusterman, I am ultimately even more interested in human subjectivity as an emergent function and human individuality as a relational capacity. I find their work immensely helpful for understanding both our subjectivity as such a function and our individuality as such a capacity. I want to do justice to their work; but, at least as much, I want to do justice to a range of phenomena, practices, and protocols. Regarding Foucault, I will stress the Nietzschean dimension of his orientation and, regarding Shusterman, I will stress the Deweyan dimension of *his*. But the unabashed embrace of our embodied existence, of the natural world as the only scene of human significance,[8] constitutes one of the places where Nietzsche and Dewey are in deep accord.

Human Subjectivity as an Emergent Function

The "I" proved no less troublesome for Dewey than for Nietzsche. It is one thing to explode the myths of traditional philosophy, quite another to provide a minimally adequate account of human subjectivity. It is one thing to stress the unity of the human creature,[9] another to offer an accurate portrait of the *functional* integrity of the human animal, conjoined to an unblinking acknowledgment of just how precarious and partial the attainment of such integrity is.

In response to a criticism leveled at him by the psychologist Gordon W. Allport, John Dewey conceded much. After expressing appreciation for Allport's "painstaking study and faithful exposition" of Dewey's contributions to psychology (his "scattered and, of late, unprofessional writings"), he admits, "His criticisms are also just." Specifically, he acknowledges "the truth of his remark" that Dewey "failed to develop in a systematic way his underlying psychological principles" (Dewey 1939: 554 [slightly modified]). From his perspective, that is, "from the standpoint of a biological-cultural psychology the term 'subject' (and related adjectival forms) has only the signification of a certain kind of actual existence; namely, a living creature under the influence of language and other cultural agencies has become a person interacting with other persons (concrete human beings)" (Dewey 1939: 555). Earlier in his reply to his critics, he had taken pains to point out "the word 'subject', if it is to be used at all, has the organism as its proper *designatum*. Hence it refers to an *agency of doing*, not to a knower, mind, consciousness or whatever" (Dewey 1939: 542). While the organism is always more than an agent, being ineluctably "an agent-patient" (a being inevitably subjected to the consequences of its own exertions and evasions) (MW: 10), it is never less than "an *agency of doing*." The *organism-and-its-environment*, however, identifies distinct correlates of any conceivable situation in which a living being is implicated, in its irrepressible activity.[10]

But Dewey's indefatigable insistence on the invincible integrity of organism-and-environment tended to deflect his attention from the real, if precarious, integrity of the organic or embodied self. "In a desire to cut loose from the influence of older 'spiritualistic' theories about the nature of the unity and stability of the personal self, (regarded as a peculiar kind of substantial-stuff), I failed," he admitted, "to show how natural conditions (including of course social and cultural conditions) provide support for integrated and potentially equilibrated personality-patterns" (Dewey 1939: 555–6). Without question, "this potentiality often fails of realization": "psychiatric evidence" provides sufficient proof for this all-too-commonplace failure. Even so, this same source of evidence makes no less evident "that conditions which produce integrated [and stable] personality-patterns are as natural as those which produce pathological human beings" (Dewey 1939: 556). In other words, no appeal to spiritual or supernatural factors is needed to explain the integration or stabilization of the myriad impulses, tendencies, and proclivities of the human organism; natural factors and forces suffice. Madness is as natural as sanity. The identification, description, and explanation of the one can be completely framed in naturalistic terms as the other. For Dewey no less than Foucault, this means in historical or historicist terms.

Consider for the moment Foucault's account of authorship. The decentering of the subject and the death of the author were historically bound together and for good reason (see Barthes 1977: 142–8). "It is not enough," Foucault insists, "to keep repeating (after Nietzsche) that God and man have died a common death." Something more positive and potentially illuminating is demanded of us. That is, "we must locate the space left empty by the author's disappearance, follow the distribution of gaps and breaches, and watch for the openings that this disappearance uncovers" (Foucault 1984: 105). In other words, the death of the author does not signal a loss, any more than does the death of the subject more generally; rather it marks a terrain for interrogating historical processes and practices in their complex interplay. Though he says very little (in fact, almost nothing) about them in this context, there is no necessity for Foucault to deny that flesh-and-blood human agents fulfill such functions. The identity and interiority of these agents are, however, shaped by their presumptive functions. It is telling that the essay entitled "What Is an Author?" (the title being itself a question) ends with a series of questions:

We would no longer hear the questions that have been rehearsed for so long: Who really spoke? Is it really he and not someone else? With what authenticity or originality? And what part of his deepest self did he express in his discourse? Instead, there would be other questions, like these: What are the modes of existence of this discourse? Where has it been used, how can it circulate, and who can appropriate it for himself? What are the places in it where there is room for possible subjects? Who can assume these various subject functions? And behind all these questions, we would hear hardly anything but a stirring of indifference: What difference does it make who is speaking? (Foucault 1984: 119–20)

Foucault's considered opinion, however, is more nuanced than this final sentence suggests. It is indeed more pragmatist and thus contextualist than even his most sympathetic readers might imagine. For in his *History of Sexuality* and other late texts, he came to appreciate that, *in certain contexts*, it makes a difference *who* is speaking, moreover, *who* is assuming this or that possible function. Though there are countless contexts in which it makes no difference who is speaking, there are some in which it makes all the difference in the world. This difference itself is one which can make a difference and its demarcation is of course almost always the arduous work of situated subjects making room for themselves in contested terrain.

Exit the Sovereign Subject/Enter Reflexive Agents in Their Historical Specificity

In 1984 Michel Foucault near the end of his life granted an interview to Alessandro Fontana. Allow me to contextualize Allport's remarks about subjectivity as they are encountered in this text. In general, Foucault took the writing of a book to be an *experience* in a sense close to the pragmatist understanding of this Protean term. Part of this sense is that the outcome is somewhat unknown to the author: the experience of exploration was for Foucault, at least, integral to the task of writing a book. When he approached the volumes on the history of sexuality, however, he was in too much control of his material: he knew too well what he wanted to say and how he wanted to structure his text. At first, he had great difficulty executing this project. He readily confessed to Fontano: "By programming my work over several volumes in a plan laid down in advance, I was telling myself that the time had come when I could write them *without difficulty*" (Foucault 1988: 47; emphasis added). Ay, there's the rub. Writing without difficulty did not feel like writing in the only sense worthy of expending such time, energy, and indeed self on a task. "I very nearly died of boredom," Foucault revealed, "writing those books; they were too much like the earlier ones." "For some people [and it is clear Foucault counted himself among them], a book is always a risk. ... When you know in advance where you are going to end up, there's a whole dimension of experience lacking" (Foucault 1988: 47–8). Rather than boring himself to death, rather than eliminating the dimension of risk and, with it, that of experience, he "changed the general plan: instead of studying sexuality on the borders of knowledge and power," he "tried to go further back, to find out how, *for the subject himself*, the experience of his sexuality as desire had been constituted" (again, emphasis added). This prompted him "to examine certain ancient Latin and Greek texts" and his engagement with these texts left him "right up to the end with a lot of uncertainties and hesitancies." But the element of risk and thus that of experience was restored. The sense of not necessarily being able to pull off what he undertook ensured the task of composition would be an experience in which his authorial self was subjected to a severe trial.

The very point of undertaking the task of composition in this manner is tied to an "aesthetics of existence." From his study of those texts, Foucault came to appreciate that "the will to be a moral subject and the search for an ethics of existence were, in Antiquity, mainly an attempt to affirm one's liberty and to give one's own life a certain form in which one could recognize oneself, be recognized by others, and which even posterity might take as an example" (Foucault 1988: 49) or exemplar. The will to be a moral subject so envisioned is, however, inseparable from an ethos of aesthetic existence. "This elaboration of one's own life as a personal work of art, even if it obeyed certain collective canons, was at the centre, it seems to me, of moral experience, of the will to morality in Antiquity" (Foucault 1988). Foucault judges the will to morality described here to stand in sharp contrast to the Christian transformation of moral life.

Changing the subject is, in this context, appropriately ambiguous and, in Foucault's case, both senses are applicable to his endeavors and aspirations. In order to avoid boring himself to death, he broke off in a new direction; that is, he changed the subject. We have already noted this. Instead of "studying sexuality on the borders of knowledge, and power," he tried to discover how, for subjects themselves, the experience of their sexuality as desired had been constituted and often, in no small measure, constituted by these subjects in and through their deliberate engagement in certain recognizable practices. On his account, deliberate attention to the self does not entail ignoring the shared practices in and through which the desiring self constitutes itself as such. Foucault admits, "you want very much to change what you think entirely and to find yourself at the end quite different from what you were at the beginning" (Foucault 1988: 48). But he no less readily acknowledges, "you come to see you've changed relatively little." The degree of change is less important than one's commitment to change, however slight this might come to be. While stressing the continuity between his earlier and later works, he does highlight an emergent focus of his later efforts: "I have tried to analyze how areas such as madness, sexuality, and delinquency, may enter into a certain play of the truth, and also, how, through this insertion of human practice, of behavior, in the play of truth, *the subject himself is affected*" (1988, 48; emphasis added). In retrospective, the earlier works on madness and delinquency along with the later ones on sexuality are concerned with how "the subject himself is affected" (Foucault 1988).

Questions regarding how subjects, as *objects* of certain discourses, were constituted as such are not jettisoned in favor of questions regarding self-constitution. They help to illuminate the context in which the deliberate undertaking of self-constitution is taken up and carried on. The extent to which the earlier projects are truly continuous with the later ones might be exaggerated, a retrospective perspective might slight or blur ruptures and alterations, but Foucault's perception of continuity ought not to be lightly regarded or quickly dismissed. In changing the subject to sexuality, his desire was to change the subject from merely an object of discourse to a self-fashioned work of art. Doing so involved changing both the self of the author (and not only his authorial self) and that of his readers.

His shift of attention to the task of self-fashioning surprised and even disconcerted some of his readers and disciples. This was intensified by the attention to which he devoted in at least one of his seminars to Friedrich von Hayek and Richard von Mises. As Fontana presses this point in the interview from which I have been extensively quoting (Foucault 1988: 50), Michel Foucault is not rejecting the concept of the subject in every sense. He is quite explicit about this: "A distinction must be drawn here. In the first place, I do indeed believe there is no sovereign subject, [no] founding subject, a universal form of subject to be found everywhere. I am very skeptical of this view of the subject and very hostile to it" (Foucault 1988). This is, however, not the only meaning to be attached to this word. While rejecting the sovereign (or transcendental) subject, Foucault acknowledges the situated (or implicated) subject. He implies the necessity to insist upon "the subject [who] is constituted through practices of subjection or, in a more autonomous way, through practices of freedom, liberty, as in Antiquity." Even in this more autonomous manner, self-constitution draws heavily on "a number of rules, styles, and inventions to be found in the cultural environment" (Foucault 1988: 50–1). The culturally situated and practically implicated subject is, I am disposed to suggest, an ingenious and improvisational agent for whom "an aesthetics of existence" is, in favorable circumstances, a live option. Even though any recognizable human being has been constituted a subject "through practices of subjection," such subjugation does not utterly negate the possibility of exerting control over the form, direction, or character of one's own life. As with the pragmatists and even more radically with Nietzsche, there is, for Foucault, no anterior self. The self comes into being in the course of an individual's life and, to some extent, that self is a fiction, an imaginative projection of more or less grounded possibilities (see Short 1997: 305–7).

As a pragmatist, Richard Shusterman is arguably in a better position than Foucault to account for human subjectivity. He can *start* with the human organism without fear of making it into a sovereign subject. He operates in a tradition in which the natural and even the somatic are hardly as freighted as they are in the dominant traditions of European thought. Naturalism and biologism carry within these traditions the implication of a reductionism. This is not the case in either American pragmatism or, more broadly, what might with equal justice be called American naturalism or, even better, pragmatic naturalism (Bernstein 2020).

The most "native" or spontaneous impulses of the human organism from its earliest hours are immediately caught up in a cultural environment. Dewey and Shusterman are philosophers of natality. "Every person is born an infant, and every infant is subject from the first breath he draws and the first cry he utters to the attentions and demands of others" (MW 14: 43). This fact issues into a paradox: "the *meaning* of native activities is not native. It depends upon interaction with the matured social environment" (MW: 14). For the infant, any exertion or expression, "apart from a direction given by the presence of others, apart from the responses they make to it," would be "a physical spasm, a blind dispersive burst of wasteful energy." An exertion or utterance "gets quality, significance, when it becomes a smouldering sullenness, an annoying interruption, a peevish irritation, a murderous revenge, a blazing indignation" (MW 14: 65–6). No less than Foucault, Dewey and Shusterman appreciate how the human organism is an enculterated agent.

"Should Foucault's [later] political praxis be dismissed," Shusterman pointedly asked, "as too narrowly self-centered and self-serving to be truly democratic? Should we regard it not as real politics but as 'radical chic' aimed at an elitist self-distinction?" Then he rightly answered his own questions: "This would be a mistake" (Shusterman 1997: 56). Neither Foucault nor Shusterman retreats from the rough-and-tumble of "real politics" but are concerned to display and, in some instances, dramatize how care for the self is inextricably woven together with care for the context in which care for the self is taken up, carried on, and (especially for Foucault) made different than it has yet been. Care for the somatic self is inescapably care for a *social* self in the making. In turn, the care for the social self in the making is or can be a strategy directed at the unmaking (or undoing), to some extent, of the repressive regimes into which human beings are always initiated, initiated so early and intimately as to be among the very means by which such regimes are sustained. As Shusterman stresses, precisely in his defense of Foucault, "the 'private' self" must be seen "as intrinsically the site and political battleground of the political" (Shusterman 1997: 56). There is nothing redundant in this formulation: the "private" self is a socially constituted self (the sphere of privacy is itself, in great measure, a publicly established arena) and, as such, it is the *political* as well as personal ground of distinctively political conflicts, impasses, and confusions. This "'private' self" is "both the effect and enduring, reinforcing presence of the socio-political forces that constitute and shape us as individual subjects" (Shusterman 1997: 56–7). Such a self is, however, not merely an epiphenomenon; it necessarily exerts a conserving influence and possibly transformative pressure. "Just as socio-political institutions mold us into disciplined, docile selves, so these 'normalized' selves serve in turn to reconstitute and sustain those very institutions" (Shusterman 1997: 57). Repressive institutions, which are always more than simply repressive or inhibitive, being also enabling and in some circumstances self-transformative, institutions, "cannot exist [or endure] without their animating by acting subjects" (Shusterman 1997). In attacking the "normalized self through limit experiences aimed at its radical transformation," the self is also attacking nothing less than "the essential underpinnings of repressive disciplinary institutions" (Shusterman 1997). The private self is, in some instances, not only a public figure but also potentially a publicly disruptive figure.

This implies that human subjectivity is more than either an effect or an agency by which forms of repression prolong themselves. The subject is or can be also just what Dewey claimed for it as a function.[11] While conceding that the "subject is that which suffers, [that which] is subjected [to external forces and disciplinary practices] and which endures resistance and frustration," the subject is "also that which attempts subjection of hostile conditions; that which takes the immediate initiation in remaking the situation as it stands" (LW 1: 184). The repressed subject is always to some extent an impulsive agent, the disciplined self always a rebellious actor thwarting all efforts at complete domestication.

Impulsivity is ineradicable, the beginnings of habituation virtually ubiquitous. Nature, in the inchoate form of spontaneous impulses, and culture, in that of the inevitably constraining form of inherited dispositions, do not constitute a dualism, only a functional, contextual, and fluid distinction which, on occasion, can be profitable for situated subjects, social individuals, to draw, especially for purposes of self-fashioning.

Our attention to the self as a figure of subjection and repression ought not eclipse our appreciation of the self as one of the sites of reconstruction, one of the means by which selves and their situations are transformed, sometimes radically. If Shusterman appreciates in a more robust and less qualified manner than does Foucault the subject as the source of reconstruction, he also appreciates how Foucault, especially in his later writings, at least implicitly endorses such a view of the subject.

Care for the self is at once a personal project and a political act, an always more than merely private undertaking and always less than an adequate response to the political situation in which subjugated subjects are implicated. But it can be an effective and noteworthy response, as the work and indeed the lives of Michel Foucault and Richard Shusterman show in their philosophical practice, a practice going far beyond the textual or discursive. Their most characteristic texts, however, bear eloquent witness to a nuanced understanding of human subjectivity. Beyond this, they illuminate phenomena and practices of utmost importance for anyone conscientiously devoted to the *bios philosophicus*, when that individual attends imaginatively, critically, and personally to the somatic, social, and improvisational facets of one's own emergent subjectivity.

Subjectivity is inherently social. But, then, sociality is itself intrinsically personal and can be memorably individual. Such individuality is, as Dewey insisted, shaped and revealed by its response to what is other than itself. Reflexivity and sociality are themselves tied together. The relationship of the self to itself cannot be torn apart from the relationship of the self to others. Reflexivity is complexly mediated by internalized others, just as sociality is no less complexly structured by the virtually ubiquitous presence of external others. The ongoing, complex interplay of these and other factors call for critical attention, imaginative reframing, and personal assessment. For they are critical factors in the emergence, stability, and alteration of subjectivity.

No theorists have been more attuned to the complexity and subtlety of this interplay than those to whom this volume is dedicated. As a result, no theorists have been more instructive in discerning not only the mechanisms at work in maintaining repressive institutions but also selves at play in the hope of undermining, to some extent, inherited forms of repression and debilitating regimes of discipline. "Bodies and [their] pleasures" can be more than a slogan. It can be, as Foucault and Shusterman demonstrate, a signpost in the direction of practices in and through which selves make of their inherited circumstances "a more congenial medium" for spontaneous human impulses of a generous, affirmative, and truly vital character (Dewey MW 14: 230). Finding or creating opportunities for life to say "Yes" to life is neither a small nor a self-indulgent task (James 1979).

Those who would desecrate the body cannot help but desecrate the embodied self (see Nietzsche 1966: 13; also, 33). Those who would ignore the sociality of the self, in the name of a private, invulnerable sphere in which an invincibly private self presumes absolute sovereignty (LW 1: 57, 77), cannot but erase the social self. The social, somatic, and improvisatory self of everyday life ought not to be sacrificed for an immaterial, immortal soul or simply the Socratic *psyche* in its alleged autonomy from our embodied condition (see Lovibond 1983). It might be voluntarily sacrificed for the sake of a life in which its own somatic impulses and inescapable sociality are allowed freer and even wilder expression. That is, the somatic, social, and imaginative self might expose itself to limit-experiences and other severe challenges as an expression of self-care, encompassing a bid for self-knowledge. In doing so, human life deliberately exposes itself to radical risks, for the sake of possible transfiguration.

One need not be committed to an *ethos* of absolute rupture or complete novelty (see Shusterman 1997) to be committed to exposing oneself to such risks, to subjecting oneself to such challenges. The hope of realizing, in the concrete here and now, a fuller realization of "an aesthetics of existence" justifies such exposure and subjection. One need not cut a Baudelairean figure to be animated by the hope for personal transfiguration. The extent to which one is at home in one's culture—and this personally means being at home in one's own skin in various cultural arenas—is, however, going to have a profound implication for the *experience* of one's embodied subjectivity or selfhood. This might incline one to more ameliorative projects or to more disruptive endeavors. This does not in either case take identity as a given. It does try to acknowledge how, for example, the forging of a gay life, without necessarily committing to a settled identity, might be more arduous and delicate than the challenges confronting a cis male. In general, the meliorative task of the situated pragmatist is to some extent different from the disruptive endeavors of the genealogical critic. Though it varies from case to case, the task of such a pragmatist and the disruptions of such a critic overlap, often to a very large degree. To the extent they do not, they tend to be complementary.

Conclusion

Richard Shusterman has learned much from Michel Foucault. Arguably, Foucaultians have much to learn from Shusterman, not least of all how a pragmatist approach to human subjectivity allows us to reject the sovereign or transcendental subject without effacing historically specific forms of human selfhood. We encounter in Shusterman's writings a more robust affirmation of subjectivity, allied to an unblinking recognition of the decentered status of the subject, than we do in Foucault's.

It is indeed impossible for us to return to the time before Montaigne, Descartes, Luther, Hume, and other modern thinkers, "even and especially if we have moved beyond" their conceptualizations of subjectivity. The subject as "an *agency of doing*"—and undoing—of self-contestation but also of self-fashioning, is what matters most. At least for a pragmatist such as Richard Shusterman, this term concretely designates the human organism in its irrepressible vitality and activity, but also its immediate and radical enculturation. The spontaneous exertions of the human infant attain their meaning largely through the responses of others (MW: 14). It is impossible for us to measure the degree to which the human organism is subjected to cultural pressures, the extent to which "language and other cultural agencies" shape the very interiority of the *psyche*. The unique response of individual organisms to these cultural influences both displays and contributes to shaping the individuality of the self. They are hardly mechanical; they are often ingeniously improvisational.[12] It is nonetheless possible to affirm the agency of this organism. If there is (in a sense) originally no doer behind the deed (see Nietzsche 1969: 45), there comes to be in time a more or less integrated cluster of habits, including the emergent function of, again, a more or less integrated set of reflexive propensities. That is, there comes to be an agency to which feelings, thoughts, and actions can properly be attributed, including by that agent itself. These propensities include ones concerning the avowal and disavowal of thoughts, feelings, and actions.[13]

One might dissociate oneself from one's own body and relationship to others. Hyperbolic, methodic, and universal doubt allegedly disencumbers the subject of both its embodiment and these relations. The Cartesian subject elevated to a sovereign status is, for theorists such as Nietzsche, Dewey, Foucault, and Shusterman, not a triumph over skepticism; it is an incitement to doubt. In opposition to this and related forms of subjectivity, one might identify oneself as a somatic and social self; and go on to envision care for the self as a project in which care for the embodied self and the social nexus in which that concrete being is implicated, however much they in practice might pull apart, in principle can mutually enhance and deepen each other (i.e., the somatic and the social dimensions of human subjectivity are not inherently antagonistic). Foucault's aesthetics of existence and Shusterman's somaesthetics help us to see just how this is so. And, in the end, the *how* matters most.

Notes

1. See Dewey, "The 'Socratic Dialogues' of Plato" (LW 2: 124–4).
2. See, for example, *Twilight of the Idols*, especially "The Problem of Socrates" (Nietzsche 1990: 39–44).
3. In his *Genealogy of Morals*, Nietzsche writes: "We are unknown to ourselves, we men of knowledge—and with good reason. We have never sought ourselves— how could it happen that we should ever find ourselves?" "So we are," he adds, "necessarily strangers to ourselves, we do not comprehend ourselves, we *have* to misunderstand ourselves" (Nietzsche 1969: 15). The very ways in which we knowers from Socrates forward have made a show of trying to know ourselves are, in Nietzsche's judgment, diversions, and evasions.
4. In "The Gospel of Relaxation" William James contends: "Action seems to follow feeling, but really action and feeling go together; and by regulating action, which is under the most direct control of the will, we can indirectly regulate the feeling, which is not" (James 1983: 118).
5. In "Profiles of the Philosophical Life" Shusterman sharply distinguishes between "two models for enhanced life and self-improvement"—"a quasi-medical one of health and an aesthetic model of art and beauty." The former however allegedly entails a commitment to "the soul's immortality and its troublesome division from the body." "The aesthetic model [in the Platonic dialogues] is," he claims, "less dependent on these problematic doctrines and even more potently portrayed" (Shusterman 1997: 24). At any rate, Shusterman opts for the aesthetic model and rejects the quasi-medical one. But it is far from evident, at least to me, that the latter involves a commitment to the soul's immortality or the dualism of *psyche* and *soma*. Both models might, in different ways, be illuminating.
6. "Socrates belonged, in his origins," Nietzsche asserts, "to the lowest orders: Socrates was rabble. One knows, one sees for oneself, how ugly he was. But ugliness, an objection in itself, is among Greeks almost a refutation. Was Socrates a Greek at all?" (Nietzsche 1990: 40).
7. The *psyche* in its ancient senses is complexly related to subjectivity in the modern sense.

8   Zarathustra, as portrayed by Nietzsche, beseeches his brothers, "*remain faithful to the earth*, and do not believe those who speak to you of otherworldly hopes! Poison-mixers they are, whether they know it or not. Despisers of life are they, decaying and poisoned themselves, of whom the earth is weary: so let them go" (Nietzsche 1966: 13). Remaining faithful to the earth means embracing the somatic character of human life. These "godlike men," these poison-mixers, "want one to have faith in them, and doubt to be sin." But "it is not in afterworlds and redemptive drops of blood, but in the body, that they too have most faith." But their body is "a sick thing … to them." So, "listen rather, my brothers, to the voice of the healthy body: that is a more honest and purer voice. More honestly and purely speaks the healthy body that is perfect and perpendicular: and it speaks of the meaning of the earth" (Nietzsche 1966: 33; cf. LW 1: 40–1). Whatever differences in rhetoric, Dewey substantively agrees with Nietzsche's celebration of the body and *this* world. See especially Dewey's "Antinaturalism *in Extremis*" (1944).

9   Even so, see one of Dewey's later essays, "The Unity of the Human Being" (LW 13: 323–37). This was originally an address to the American College of Physicians (St. Louis, April 21, 1937).

10 One of the crucial points for which Dewey argues in "The Reflex Arc in Psychology" is that what is ordinarily called a stimulus is not a goad, as though the organism is inert apart from stimuli, but a pivot around which a course of behavior turns (EW 5: 96–9). In other words, the human organism, like all other forms of organic life, is irrepressibly active. Stimuli redirect or encourage a course of activity; they do not initiate that course. The organism is always already exerting itself in some manner. Such is its constitution.

11 It is noteworthy, if only in a footnote, to recall a remark made by Jacques Derrida in response to Serge Doubrovsky's challenge. Doubrovsky began by noting, "You always speak of a *non-center*. How can you within your own perspective, explain or at least understand what a perception is," since "a perception is precisely the manner in which the world appears *centered* around me." He goes on to bring language also into the discussion: in any instance of speaking, "I inevitably find the center again. For it is not 'One' who speaks, but 'I'" (Doubrovsky in Discussion in Derrida 1970, 271). To this challenge, Derrida is no less emphatic than clear: "First of all, I didn't say there was no center, that we could get along without the center. I believe that the center is a function, not a being—a reality, but a function. And this function is absolutely indispensable. The subject is absolutely indispensable. I don't destroy the subject; I situate it. That is to say, I believe that at a certain level of philosophical and scientific discourse one cannot get along without the notion of subject. It is [however] a question of knowing where it comes from and how it functions" (Derrida 1970: 271).

12 In *Becoming John Dewey: Dilemmas of a Philosopher and Naturalist*, Thomas C. Dalton documents Dewey's fascination with the experimental data regarding how infants learn to crawl, stand up, and eventually walk. It turns out they do this in quite various ways and exhibit a remarkable degree of somatic ingenuity in mastering these tasks (see Dalton 2002: 230–6).

13 What is true of houses is true of experiences: "Experience when it happens has the same dependence upon objective natural conditions, physical and social, as has the occurrence [or coming-to-be] of a house." Experience "as its own objective and definitive traits; these can be described *without reference to a self*" (emphasis added). Dewey goes on to insist: "for some purposes and with respect to some consequences, it is all important [regarding houses] to note the added qualification of personal ownership of real property, so with 'experience.' In the first instance and intent, it is [however] not exact nor relevant to say 'I experience' or 'I think.' 'It' experiences or is experienced, 'it' thinks or is thought, is a juster phrase" (LW 1: 179; cf. MW 14: 216).

Bibliography

Barthes, R. (1977), *Image Music Text*, New York: Hill & Wang.
Bernstein, R. J. (2020), *Pragmatic Naturalism: John Dewey's Living Legacy*, New York: Graduate Faculty Philosophy Journal.
Burnet, J. (1916), *The Socratic Doctrine of the Soul*, London: British Academy, Oxford University Press.
Colapietro, V. M. (1990), "The Vanishing Subject of Contemporary Discourse: A Pragmatic Response," *The Journal of Philosophy*, 87 (11): 644–55.
Culler, J. (1981), *The Pursuit of Signs*, Ithaca (NY): Cornell University Press.
Dalton, T. C. (2002), *Becoming John Dewey: Dilemmas of a Philosopher and Naturalist*, Bloomington: Indiana University Press.
Derrida, J. (1970), "Structure, Sign, and Play in the Human Sciences," in *The Languages of Criticism and the Sciences of Man*, eds. R. Macksey and E. Donato, 247–72, Baltimore: Johns Hopkins University Press.
Dewey, J. (1896), "The Reflex Arc in Psychology," *Psychological Review*, 3: 357–70; also in *The Early Works of John Dewey. Vol. 5*, 96–109, Carbondale (IL): Southern Illinois University Press (cited as EW 5).
Dewey, J. (1939), "Experience, Knowledge and Value: A Rejoinder," in *The Philosophy of John Dewey*, ed. P. A. Schilpp, 515–601, New York: Tudor Publishing Co.
Dewey, J. (1983), "Human Nature and Conduct," in *The Middle Works of John Dewey. Vol. 14*, ed. JoAnn Boydston, 1–231 and ix–xxiii, Carbondale (IL): Southern Illinois University Press (cited as MW 14).

Dewey, J. (1984), "Individualism, Old and New," in *The Later Works of John Dewey. Vol. 5*, ed. JoAnn Boydston, 39–123, Carbondale (IL): Southern Illinois University Press (cited as LW 5).
Dewey, J. (1988), *Experience and Nature*, in *The Later Works of John Dewey. Vol. 1*, ed. JoAnn Boydston, 3–326 and vii–xxiii, Carbondale (IL): Southern Illinois University Press (cited as LW 1).
Dewey, J. (1991), "Experience, Knowledge, and Value: A Rejoinder," in *The Philosophy of John Dewey*, ed. P. A. Schilpp, 515–608, New York: Tudor Publishing Co.; also in *The Later Works of John Dewey. Vol. 14*, 3–90, Carbondale (IL): Southern Illinois University Press, 1991 (cited as LW 14).
Foucault, M. (1984), *Foucault Reader*, ed. Paul Rabinow, New York: Pantheon Books.
Foucault, M. (1986), *The History of Sexuality. Vol. 3: The Care of the Self* [1984], trans. R. Hurley, New York: Vintage Books.
Foucault, M. (1988), *Politics Philosophy Culture: Interviews and Other Writings 1977–1984*, ed. L. D. Kritzman, New York: Routledge.
Foucault, M. (1990), *The History of Sexuality. Vol. I: An Introduction*, trans. R. Hurley, New York: Vintage Books.
Foucault, M. (1997), *Ethics, Subjectivity and Truth*, ed. P. Rabinow, trans. R. Hurley et al., New York: The New Press.
Gallie, W. B. (1968), *Philosophy and the Historical Understanding*, New York: Schocken Books.
Heidegger, M. (2010), *Being and Time*, trans. J. Stambaugh, Albany (NY): SUNY Press.
James, W. (1979), "The Moral Philosopher and the Moral Life," in *The Will to Believe & Other Essays*, 141–62, Cambridge (MA): Harvard University Press.
James, W. (1983), "The Gospel of Relaxation," in *Talks to Teachers on Psychology*, 117–31, Cambridge (MA): Harvard University Press.
Lovibond, S. (1983), *Realism & Imagination in Ethics*, Minneapolis: University of Minnesota Press.
Merleau-Ponty, M. (1964), *Signs*, Evanston (IL): Northwestern University Press.
Nietzsche, F. W. (1966), *Thus Spoke Zarathustra*, trans. W. Kaufmann, New York: Viking Press.
Nietzsche, F. W. (1969), *The Genealogy of Morals. Ecce Homo*, trans. W. Kaufmann, New York: Vintage Books.
Nietzsche, F. W. (1990), *Twilight of the Idols. The Anti-Christ*, trans. R. J. Hollingdale, New York: Penguin Classics.
Plato (1972), *Phaedrus*, trans. R. Hackforth, Cambridge: Cambridge University Press.
Short, T. L. (1997), "Hypostatic Abstraction in Self-Consciousness," in *The Rule of Reason: The Philosophy of Charles Peirce*, eds. J. Brunning and P. Forster, 289–308, Toronto: Toronto University Press.
Shusterman, R. (1997), *Practicing Philosophy: Pragmatism and the Philosophical Life*, New York: Routledge.

Shusterman, R. (2009), "Somaesthetics and C. S. Peirce," *The Journal of Speculative Philosophy*, 23 (1): 8–27.

Shusterman, R. (2014), "Somaesthetics and Politics: Incorporating Pragmatist Aesthetics for Social Action," in *Beauty, Responsibility, and Power: Ethical and Political Consequences of Pragmatist Aesthetics*, eds. L. Koczanowicz and K. Liszka, 5–18, Amsterdam/New York: Rodopi.

Shusterman, R. (2019), "Bodies in the Street: The Soma, the City, and the Art of Living," in *Bodies in the Streets. The Somaesthetics of City Life*, ed. R. Shusterman, 13–37, Leiden/Boston: Brill.

Smith, J. E. (1966), "Is the Self an Ultimate Category?," in *Philosophy, Religion, and the Coming World Civilization*, ed. L. Rouner, 135–50, The Hague: Martinus Nijhoff.

Taylor, A. E. (1956), *Socrates: The Man and His Thought*, Garden City (NY): Doubleday Anchor Books.

Thoreau, H. D. (1966), *Walden & Resistance to Civil Government*, ed. W. Rossi, New York: W.W. Norton & Co.

Whitehead, A. N. (1961 [1933]), *Adventures of Ideas*, New York: Free Press.

Wittgenstein, L. (1968), *Philosophical Investigations*, New York: Macmillan.

6

Somaesthetics and the Philosophical Life

Richard Shusterman

Origins

Somaesthetics emerged from two closely related projects of my philosophical research: pragmatist aesthetics and the idea of philosophy as an art of living. As pragmatism advocates an aesthetics of active engagement, it also insists that all action (artistic, practical, or political) requires the body, our tool of tools. Building on *Pragmatist Aesthetics'* insistence on the body's central role in artistic creation and appreciation, I conceived of somaesthetics as a field to highlight and explore the soma—the living, sentient, purposive body—as the indispensable medium for all perception, including aesthetic appreciation. Moreover, as I argued in *Practicing Philosophy*, if, like the ancients, we understand philosophy not as a mere theoretical enterprise but as a way of life, then we must recognize the soma as the necessary medium of philosophical life, which in turn implies that the goal of improving our art of living calls for somaesthetic cultivation.

Although *Practicing Philosophy* is where I first discussed somaesthetics by name, the advocacy of somatic care of the self in the art of living was already central in the first edition of *Pragmatist Aesthetics* (1992). Expressing pragmatism's democratic thrust, the book's crowning chapter explored the art of living as a project not limited to professional philosophers, artists, or other elites but instead as open to anyone willing to live in a critical, reflective, attractively ethical manner; and it urged that such living should involve a significant relationship to one's soma, since the soma is our essential medium of life. In this sense, leading a philosophical life does not require a job in philosophy nor even extensive reading of canonic philosophical texts, though it would surely profit from them. Treating philosophy as an open, essentially contested, and gradable range concept rather than a rigidly defined categorical concept of yes/no demarcations, we can say that someone who not only reads and writes philosophy but also seeks to exemplify it as a critical, reflective embodied art of living is more of a philosopher than someone who confines herself only to philosophy's texts. In this sense, we could describe Wittgenstein as more of a philosopher than Quine, which does not mean that he is a better philosopher (though I believe he is). In the same sense, one might describe Tolstoy as more of a philosopher than Frege, while still regarding Frege as a better philosopher.

Advocates of the philosophical life often contrast it to mere theorizing, as in Thoreau's famous critique, which democratically breaks philosophy out of the exclusivity of elite professionals and opens it to anyone who is willing to make the effort of its demanding way of life:

> There are nowadays professors of philosophy, but not philosophers. Yet it is admirable to profess because it was once admirable to live. To be a philosopher is not merely to have subtle thoughts, nor even to found a school, but so to love wisdom as to live according to its dictates, a life of simplicity, independence, magnanimity, and trust. It is to solve some of the problems of life, not only theoretically, but practically. (W: 270)

Ancient advocates of the philosophical life, however, recognized that action and theory were complementary for the philosophical enterprise, whose most compelling examples effectively integrated thoughtful texts and embodied conduct. Already in the Hellenistic age, writing constituted an important tool for artfully working on oneself—as a medium for self-knowledge and for self-transformation. Hence the very exponents of philosophy as an art of living made writing (in such diverse forms as letters, diaries, confessions, essays, treatises, handbooks, and poems) a central part of that art. Somaesthetics emerged to support the revival of the philosophical life and highlight and develop the centrality of the body in its meliorative care of the self.

Despite its roots in philosophy as a way of life, somaesthetics should not be identified as a particular formula or recipe for philosophical living. Nor is it simply a branch of pragmatist aesthetics. Having evolved beyond my initial vision of it, somaesthetics is now an interdisciplinary field of research (albeit a very modest one) that is concerned with the critical study, meliorative cultivation, and use of the soma as the site of sensory appreciation (aesthesis), effective performance, and creative self-fashioning. Involving both discursive theory and embodied practice, somaesthetics engages the social, physical, and technological contexts that shape the soma's experience. It therefore involves a variety of disciplinary orientations, from physiology and politics to human-computer interaction design. Rather than recommending a particular way of life with a specific set of values and a single method (or uniform group of methods) to achieve them, somaesthetics is a pluralistic field of inquiry in which different theorists can propose and argue for their preferred somatic methods and goals. In providing an overarching theoretical structure and set of conceptual tools to promote better integration and understanding of the diverse somatic disciplines and ideologies of contemporary and past cultures, somaesthetics sees its most fundamental goal as improving the quality of our lived experience through enhanced capacities of perception and performance.[1] This concern with how the somatic is integrated into self-knowledge and self-cultivation is evidence of somaesthetics' roots in the idea of philosophical life as a critical, meliorative, aesthetic-cum-ethical project whose commitment to self-knowledge and self-care has more than self-centered, self-serving ends. To clarify my somaesthetic approach to the philosophical life, I will compare it to theories of the two most influential contemporary advocates of philosophy as an art of living: Pierre Hadot and Michel Foucault.

Therapy or Beauty

Socrates, as Plato portrays him, offers two influential models of philosophical life that persist in later antiquity: a quasi-medical one of health and an aesthetic model of art and beauty. In *Crito*, *Gorgias*, and *Republic*, he suggests that the philosopher's role is analogous to the physician's. The doctor cares for the body's health, the philosopher aims at improving the soul's. Philosophy is superior to medicine, because the body's health is ultimately doomed by death, while the immortal soul is not so limited. Here the philosophical life can permanently triumph, though at the cost of commitment to the soul's immortality and its division from the body. This therapeutic model of philosophical life, which Hadot embraces and brilliantly analyzes, is the most prevalent in antiquity (see PWL).

The aesthetic model of philosophical life requires no commitment to the soul's immortality and independence from the body. It finds passionate expression in Plato's *Symposium*, where he praises love's desire for beauty as the source of philosophy, and lovingly describes the philosophical life as a continuous quest for higher kinds of beauty which ennobles the philosopher. This quest is not simply to perceive such beauties but to create or "give birth" to the beautiful: beautiful speeches and thoughts, beautiful pursuits and practices, that exemplify insight and virtue. Such beautiful progeny, like the begetting of children, reflects the life-drive for immortality, and they help us achieve it by remaining after our death as beautiful memorials of our life. With such an aesthetic model of philosophy, it becomes important for Socrates and Plato to sharply distinguish philosophy from art and assert its superiority for the practice of living. Poets and their interpreters are therefore condemned for not really knowing the arts of living of which they speak; they create through Muse-inspired madness, and, like other artists, only imitate appearances. Aristotle's defense of art as *poiesis* (the reasoned making of external things) still sharply distinguished it from *praxis* (the realm of conduct and ethics). The result has been a long tradition of dividing art from philosophy and excluding it from the serious conduct of life, whose governing principles were instead sought in divine will or essential human rationality.

However, modern skepticism about divinely ordained moralities and about deducing a compelling ethics from some putative human essence and universal rationality has revitalized the aesthetic model of philosophical living, the idea that ethical life should be practiced as an art. Baudelaire and Nietzsche were among its nineteenth-century prophets, urging the individual to artfully stylize and recreate oneself, "to become what one is" (adapting the subtitle of Nietzsche's *Ecce Homo*). Foucault is its most prominent contemporary proponent, and I follow him in advocating an aesthetic model of philosophical life, though we diverge in our visions of it. While favoring the aesthetic over the therapeutic model of philosophical life, I should insist that the two are not contradictory. In both somatic and spiritual matters, health and beauty often overlap or interconnect, so that therapies for healing bad health can richly contribute to life's aesthetic quality. Conversely, experiences of beauty often have a therapeutic effect. I prefer the aesthetic to the therapeutic art of living because of its more positive character, its focus on creating beauty rather than healing disease.

Scholars have long recognized the strong affinities between somaesthetics and Foucault's aesthetics of existence, long before I followed his example by studying the history of sexuality through the prism of aesthetic self-stylization. The French philosopher Bernard Andrieu, in introducing my essay in his anthology of key texts in philosophy of body, describes my "somaesthetics as less an aesthetics of pleasure than an aesthetics of existence, in the Foucauldian sense, of the living body," noting how its somaesthetic "reflection invites the transgression of disciplinary norms" (Andrieu 2010: 343–4, 348). Pleasure, however, is a very important value not only for somaesthetics but also for Foucault, who famously advocated "bodies and pleasures" (HS 1: 157), though our visions of body and pleasure diverge in significant ways. Before examining these and other differences between somaesthetics and Foucault's aesthetics of existence, I should clarify the central differences between my somaesthetic vision of the art of living and Hadot's magnificently erudite portrayal of the philosophical life, a crucial influence on Foucault's work and on the continuing study of the topic today, including my own.

Somaesthetics versus Hadot's Philosophical Life

One key difference is the issue of obedience to schools versus personal, individual expression. Hadot emphasizes the necessary role of the formal philosophical schools for practicing philosophy as a way of life. Here each school

> represents a form of life defined by an ideal of wisdom ... [with] its corresponding fundamental inner attitude ... and ... exercises designed to ensure spiritual progress toward the ideal state of wisdom, exercises of reason that will be, for the soul, analogous to the athlete's training or to the application of a medical cure. ... The dogmas and methodological principles of each school are not open to discussion ... [so that] to philosophize is to choose a school, convert to its way of life, and accept its dogmas. This is why the core dogmas and rules of life for Platonism, Aristotelianism, Stoicism, and Epicureanism remained unchanged throughout antiquity. (PWL: 59–60)

In contrast, somaesthetics (as a product of pragmatist pluralism, which itself is a product of modernity's individualism) emphasizes personal freedom and the value of individual expression rather than insisting on allegiance to a particular school and strict obedience to "all the constraints ... of the framework of the school" and its "dogmatic imperatives" (PWL: 62). For the somaesthetic philosophical life, as I understand it, a key goal in one's care of oneself is liberation from docile conformity to imposed constraints of inherited or imposed rules and habits so that one can develop one's own particular character and vision of personal fulfillment: ineluctably drawing on existing ideas, social values, and somatic practices but seeking one's own creative pattern of deploying them.

Somaesthetics is closer here to Foucault's idea of aesthetics of existence. Although he develops this idea from his study of Greco-Roman ethics and thus recognizes the influence of the philosophical schools in defining certain ethical-aesthetic models or rules of conduct, he shies away from seeing them as rigid prescriptions to be strictly obeyed. He moreover acknowledges that such ancient models cannot be properly applied to present-day contexts because the notion and values of the self (along with many other pertinent concepts for ethics) are very different in contemporary society, where individual self-expression is much more central. Somaesthetics shares with Foucault an appreciation of individual freedom and creative self-expression, though we differ somewhat on how to understand these things.

Another key difference, already noted, is Hadot's vision of the philosophical life as essentially therapy rather than aesthetic flourishing in a life of beauty. For him, "philosophy is a therapeutics: 'We must concern ourselves with the healing of our own lives'" (PWL: 87). Since the soul is the essential factor in our lives, "[s]piritual exercises are required for the healing of the soul," and a major part of such exercises is "a training for death" to free the soul from its fears of dying (PWL: 96). Although the ancient philosophical schools viewed death differently, some affirming the soul's immortality while Epicureanism denying this, they all affirmed, claims Hadot, "the concept of philosophy as a means of achieving spiritual death ... and ... the idea of philosophy as the ascent of the soul into the celestial heights" by elevating its vision "from individuality and particularity to universality and objectivity" (PWL: 242). In contrast, somaesthetics, like Foucault, affirms a more aesthetically oriented notion of self-cultivation, and it focuses on cultivation of the whole incarnate person rather than narrowly on the soul. Its spiritual exercises are also somatic ones, because it regards our body and soul as an ontological unity: the soma, a living, sentient, purposive, and culturally informed body.

Hadot's neglect of the body's use, powers, and pleasures in his conception of the philosophical life is a third key point where he differs from somaesthetics, which shares Foucault's emphasis on "the claims of bodies, pleasures and knowledges, in their multiplicity and their possibility of resistance" (HS 1: 157). At the center of Hadot's vision of the philosophical life are "spiritual exercises" (such as attention, reading, meditation, and memorization) which he sees as parallel to but sharply contrasted with "physical exercises" (PWL: 102). He insists we should understand "spiritual exercise ... as an attempt to liberate ourselves from a partial passionate point of view—linked to the senses and the body—so as to rise to the universal, normative viewpoint of thought." It is how "philosophy subjugates the body's will to live to the higher demands of thought," "to die *to one's individuality and passions*, in order to look at things from the perspective of universality and objectivity" (PWL: 94–5). Or again,

> The spiritual exercise of apprenticeship for death, which consists in separating oneself from the body, its passions, and its desires, purifies the soul from all these superfluous additions. It is enough to practice this exercise in order for the

soul to return to its true nature, and devote itself exclusively to the exercise of pure thought. (PWL: 103)

Indeed, for Hadot, "all spiritual exercises are, fundamentally, a return to the self" in its essential form which, for him, is the soul. In this return "the self is liberated from the state of alienation into which it has been plunged by worries, passions, and desires" resulting from our embodied existence, so that the true self or soul is "liberated" toward "universality and objectivity, and participating in universal nature or thought" (PWL: 103). Somaesthetics, like Foucault, rejects the possibility of this God-like point of view in our experience, insisting instead on the situated historicity and partiality of all human thinking. It likewise maintains that our embodied situatedness is positively enabling for life. As life requires interaction with its environment, so situated thought and action are more useful and rewarding; as the soma is a key locus of pleasure, its cultivation can greatly improve the quality of our lives; as embodiment is necessary for both action and feeling, the soma is not a barrier but a necessary foundation for ethical conduct.[2]

A fourth key difference between somaesthetics and Hadot's vision of the philosophical life is his insistence that such life requires a radical rupture with ordinary life and its norms of conduct. For Hadot, "to be a philosopher implies a rupture with what the skeptics called *bios*, that is, daily life, when they criticized other philosophers for not observing the common conduct of life, the usual manner of seeing and acting" (PWL: 56). Connecting this with the notion of spiritual exercises, Hadot elaborates:

> To the same extent that the philosophical life is equivalent to the practice of spiritual exercises, it is also a tearing away from everyday life. It is a conversion, a total transformation of one's vision, life-style, and behavior. Among the Cynics, champions of *askesis*, this engagement amounted to a total break with the profane world, analogous to the monastic calling in Christianity. The rupture took the form of a way of living, and even of dress, completely foreign to that of the rest of mankind ... In fact, however, all philosophical schools engaged their disciples upon a new way of life, albeit in a more moderate way. The practice of spiritual exercises implied a complete reversal of received ideas ... The individual was to be torn away from his habits and social prejudices, his way of life totally changed ... We ought not to underestimate the depth and amplitude of the shock that these changes could cause, changes which might seem fantastic and senseless to healthy, everyday common sense. (PWL: 103–4)

As Hadot notes, "The radical opposition explains the reaction of non-philosophers, which ranged from the mockery we find expressed in the comic poets, to the outright hostility which went so far as to cause the death of Socrates" (PWL: 104).

In contrast, the adoption of a somaesthetic philosophical life, though transformative of the self and its habits, requires no radical rupture with everyday conduct and social norms. Its critical meliorative dimension can find adequate expression in a change of attitude and relation to such conduct and norms rather than in their flagrant transgression. In other words, one can perform the same sort of actions that one performed before and that basically accord with the essential norms shared by society, but the difference is that one performs those actions more mindfully, effectively, and gracefully—with greater critical awareness of their meaning, their benefits, and their shortcomings, along with greater attention to possible improvements of action and of social norms. Although one's critical somaesthetic reflection can bring one to depart from social norms in divergent or transgressive conduct and in radical political protest, it does not necessarily follow from the critical, reflective, meliorist mindfulness that defines the somaesthetic philosophical life.[3] To a superficial observer, such a non-transgressive philosophical life may look like a conventional life, because its distinction is not strikingly visible on the surface but resides in the depth of its critical attitude, mindfully reflective subjectivity, and meliorative, self-stylizing drive, which together can blossom into salient divergence and transgressive conduct when deemed appropriate.

Hadot's advocacy of the philosophical life not only opts for the therapeutic over the aesthetic model but even explicitly critiques the latter, ultimately taking Foucault as his target. In explaining the work of spiritual exercises for transforming the self, he invokes Plotinus's famous sculptural image to advocate purity and simplicity:

> If you do not yet see your own beauty, do as the sculptor does with a statue which must become beautiful: he removes one part, scrapes another, makes one area smooth, and cleans the other, until he causes the beautiful face in the statue to appear. In the same way, you too must remove everything that is superfluous, straighten that which is crooked, and purify all that is dark until you make it brilliant. Never stop sculpting your own statue, until the divine splendor of virtue shines in you. (PWL: 100)

Somaesthetics, in elaborating its aesthetic account of the philosophically life, also appeals to this image of sculpting the self as advocated by the American proto-pragmatist Thoreau, a prophet of simplicity who argued for a life of beauty without the need for wealth, luxury, or social privilege. We can enjoy such beauty simply by more attractively shaping the environments in which we dwell by transforming the soma's powers of perception and performance to create more appealing atmospheres that are fairer ethically and aesthetically. Somaesthetics has repeatedly invoked Thoreau's artistic metaphor of self-cultivation:

> It is something to be able to paint a particular picture, or to carve a statue, and so to make a few objects beautiful; but it is far more glorious to carve and paint the very atmosphere and medium through which we look, which morally we can do. To affect the quality of the day, that is the highest of arts. Every man is tasked to make his life, even in its details, worthy of the contemplation of his most elevated and critical hour. (W: 343)

Unlike Hadot, I follow Thoreau in clearly highlighting the somatic dimension of such ethical-aesthetic sculpting. "Every man is the builder of a temple, called his body, to the god he worships, after a style purely his own, nor can he get off by hammering marble instead. We are all sculptors and painters, and our material is our own flesh and blood and bones. Any nobleness begins at once to refine a man's features, any meanness or sensuality to imbrute them" (W: 468). Hadot denies that "the Plotinian image of sculpting one's own statue" should be understood as suggesting "a kind of moral aestheticism" in which self-cultivation involves a reconstructive addition or development, "to adopt a pose, to select an attitude, or to fabricate a personality for oneself." He rejects the aesthetic connotation of Plotinus's statue image on the grounds that "[f]or the ancients, sculpture was an art which 'took away,' as opposed to painting, an art which 'added on.' The statue pre-existed in the marble block, and it was enough to take away what was superfluous in order to cause it to appear" (PWL: 102). Rather than quibble by claiming that straightening the crooked means more than merely uncovering a form and that clay and bronze sculpture involve construction, we can simply critique Hadot's argument for wrongly ignoring that minimalist purity is also a form of aesthetic value. He also fails to see that the very effort to make something "become beautiful" (even by simply revealing its hidden beauty) clearly entails an aesthetic drive. In speaking of beauty, aesthetic value is already implied, even if the beauty advocated rejects certain aesthetic styles such as those relying on ornamentation and serving ostentatious dandyism.

Perhaps what blinds Hadot is Foucault's account of aesthetics of existence. For it boldly links the ethical-aesthetic *askesis* of ancient philosophy's care of the self (with its various disciplines of meditation and other spiritual exercises) to the cosmetic *askesis* of the Baudelairean dandy who cares for the self by cultivating it as a distinctive, original work of art. That life of aesthetic, singular stylization demands an originality that implies a rupture with ordinary life and social norms, but does so in a way that Hadot regards as excessively superficial and self-regarding. He chides Foucault for "defining his ethical model as an aesthetics of existence—[and thereby] propounding a culture of the self which is too aesthetic. In other words, this may be a new form of dandyism, late twentieth-century style," focused "too exclusively on the culture of the self" (PWL: 211). Rescuing the aesthetic vision of philosophical life from the charge of narcissistic dandyism has been a key aim of somaesthetics and its critique of Foucault's aesthetics of existence. Having shown how somaesthetics' vision of the philosophical life aligns itself with Foucault's in opposition to Hadot's, I now turn to the ways it departs from Foucault.

Foucault and Somaesthetics: Differences of Genealogy and Style

Some of the differences between Foucault's thought and mine reflect different philosophical genealogies. Of course, in having Foucault as a core inspiration, somaesthetics obviously inherited much from the sources that shaped his aesthetics of existence. But those sources were tempered by other traditions that influenced my somaesthetic vision of philosophical life. One key orientation I shared with Foucault was Nietzschean thought. Particularly important were Nietzsche's insistence on embodiment and his advocacy of the art of living as creative, meliorative self-stylization "to become what one is"; his appreciation of Greek culture's love of beauty and valorization of the body; his genealogical, historicist perspectivism that recognizes the social shaping of our values, including our attitudes toward the body.

In Foucault, we also find traces of Nietzsche's radical privileging of heroic, innovative genius, which Nietzsche combined with elitist disdain for the herd mentality of common folk, common pleasures, and conventional ethics. Foucault also displays the influence of Georges Bataille's radical critique of established values and commonsense, and his celebration of transgression through intense limit-experiences that challenge the ordinary realm of conduct, thought, and language. This embracing of the positive value of established negativities (madness, crime, perversion, nonsense, and death) for challenging the oppressive regime of the normal is shared by Maurice Blanchot, another important figure in the Nietzschean tradition of transgression and limit-experience that Foucault avows. "I know very well why I read Nietzsche. I read Nietzsche because of Bataille, and I read Bataille because of Blanchot" (DE 2: 1256).

Such disdain of the common is not present in my thought. The perfectionist aims of somaesthetic meliorism—of ethical, cognitive, and aesthetic elevation—have always been tempered by the abiding influence of pragmatism's deeply democratic spirit and of Wittgenstein's appreciation of the ordinary. My critique of the oppressive evils of neoliberal capitalism and its conformist, consumerist ideology has been rightly described as reformist rather than radically revolutionary (see Małecki and Schleusener 2014: 216–34). Somaesthetics is not averse to transgression, but that is only one of its tools, and not its most favored. Instead, it explores how certain forms of nonconformist body practices can effectively challenge oppressive, socially imposed somatic norms without doing so in ways that are extremely violent or damaging to oneself or to others. Rather than a menu heavy with the shock therapy of transgressive negation to challenge the unfortunate status quo, pragmatist somaesthetics posits not a complacent optimism but a defiantly resolute meliorism, set on exposing the multiple imperfections in our selves and our society so that we can find remedies to go beyond them. Lacking the fascination with madness and death as ways to encounter the reality outside our conventional thought (through an *expérience du dehors* as Blanchot and Foucault describe it [DE 1: 548]), somaesthetics shares Montaigne's focus on enriching life by cultivating more sensitive sanity to expand the range and deepen the appreciation of our welfare and pleasures, both personal and shared. But it departs from Montaigne in advocating the need for significant socio-political change.

Nietzsche is famous for showing us "how to philosophize with a hammer" by ferociously attacking conventional values and established beliefs. Foucault's genealogical critique of established ideologies maintains much of this explosive style, though wrapped in more discreet rhetoric. Somaesthetics, though not devoid of passionate critique, is generally more temperate in style. The Italian philosopher, Salvatore Tedesco, in his Introduction to the translation of *Body Consciousness*, explicitly contrasts my style to Nietzsche's by describing it as "a technique recalling Chinese acupuncture rather than Nietzschean hammering" (Tedesco 2013: 5). The acupuncture metaphor adroitly implies how East Asian philosophies have profoundly inspired my work in somaesthetics with its interest in gentle, mindful somatic therapies such as the Feldenkrais Method. A reviewer of *Body Consciousness* for *Le Monde* therefore described its somaesthetics as *une philosophie douce*, gesturing with that term also to the *medicines douces* of the orient, alternative medicines designated as *douce* (i.e., gentle or sweet) in contrast to the more aggressive Western styles of medical intervention (Zerbib 2007: 12).

Recalling Bataille's and Blanchot's key influence on Foucault, we might also trace the divergence between his account of the philosophical life and that of somaesthetics to a difference in inspiring artistic genres. Literature, particularly in its elite avant-garde form, was obviously crucial for Foucault. He saw literature as a field of creative, transgressive experimentation and limit-experiences, not only because it violates the norms of ordinary language but because of its passion for dealing with limit-experiences of death, love, crime, and impossible desire. In a discussion on poetry, he claims it is precisely in "the domain of language that the play with limit, contestation, and transgression appears with most vivacity" (DE 1: 426).

Although literary theory was central to my early philosophical work, it was dance (and its related somatic movement disciplines) that provided the key inspiration for somaesthetics.[4] Dealing not with fictions, but real bodies (both my own and those I cared for in the context of my work as a somatic educator/ therapist), I learned to appreciate the powers of tender, thoughtful touch and of slow, gentle movement. This complemented my interest in the passionately wild dancing and aggressive gestural styles of hip-hop culture and my later adventures with the spontaneous, sometimes frantic movements of the Man in Gold, bolting to escape unfriendly reactions to his strange appearance (see Shusterman 2016) Somaesthetics, in my philosophical life, embraces a plurality of movement styles, just as pragmatist aesthetics appreciates popular as well as high art. Despite the intense democratic thrust of his work, Foucault showed no taste for popular art.

Somaesthetics follows Foucault in emphasizing the crucial role of embodiment in the art of living, but differently conceives the embodied locus of this art. For Foucault, "subject" and "body" are the key elements, both essentially shaped by culture. Those terms reflect the culturally entrenched occidental dualism of mind and body, or subject and object, despite Foucault's critique of the ahistorical foundationalism and exclusions of that dualist tradition and its regimes of power/ knowledge. If ancient philosophy highlights the thoughtful "moderate subject … [who practices] an aesthetics of existence" by controlling the body, then early modernity "discovered the body as object and target of power," a material "manipulable body" for disciplinary "*dressage*" (DP: 136; HS 2: 89).

Somaesthetics breaks more completely with the dualist tradition by introducing the notion of soma. This locus of experience (of active perceiving and doing but also of passive undergoing) is a sentient, purposive, dynamic, evolving, vulnerable, and imperfect body-mind union that is essentially shaped by culture. This shaping not only involves how recently past and contemporary culture forms our somatic desires, habits, tastes, and values, but also the ways that prehistorical culture, through millennia of our evolutionary past, have shaped even our anatomy and physiology, including the brain. The soma embraces, as a complex, living whole, what German phenomenology dualistically distinguishes as *Körper* and *Leib*. This enables somaesthetics to focus on the body not only as a physical thing to care for to survive and to express our aesthetic values but also as a perceptive, purposive, and affective subjectivity through which we experience the world and its pleasures. Through its ability to take what Helmut Plessner calls an *excentric* position or critical distance from itself, the soma is also a subjectivity that can grasp itself as object and thus care for itself as a materiality although it is always more than that (Shusterman 2018: 10–20). Through disciplines of somaesthetic reflection, the soma, as subjective agency, can take its own experience and feelings as an object of analysis and material for transformation.

From the classical pragmatists William James and John Dewey, somaesthetics embraced a deep philosophical commitment to the concept of experience, including its nondiscursive, qualitative dimension. Here I oppose my neopragmatist mentor Richard Rorty, who advocates the aesthetic life but rejects the concept of experience as philosophically useless, and therefore criticizes somaesthetics as similarly misguided because it relates to the nonlinguistic as well as the discursive (Rorty 2001: 197–210). Foucault provided crucial support for somaesthetics in this respect because, while recognizing the enormous powers and scope of discourse, he also finds an important philosophical role for experience. Besides this focus on experience, his aesthetics of existence and my somaesthetics share the central concepts of pleasure, aesthetics, and art. Exploring our convergences and divergences on these topics will clarify our different approaches to the art of living.

Varieties of Experience

Like classical pragmatism and somaesthetics, Foucault regards experience as essentially embodied and structured by social forces beyond the individual, which shape her habits, beliefs, perceptions, and desires. But we equally emphasize the transformative potential of experience. Although most experience serves to reinforce the established habits of perception, thought, and action that prestructure experience, some experiences are importantly transformational in ways that significantly alter our habits and radically question established norms. As aesthetic experiences can constitute such transformational events, they are significant both for Foucault and somaesthetics. Foucault further claims exploratory writing can constitute such transformational experience, ostensibly because of the new research, thinking, and writing it involves. "An experience is something from which one comes out transformed … [T]he book transforms me and transforms what I think. … I am an experimenter in the sense that I write to change myself and not to think the same as before" (DE 2: 860–1).

Besides aesthetics and writing, other experiences can be transformative through their intensity or their challenging of norms, including violent, transgressive experiences whose traumatic reverberations grievously shake the subject's sense of self and world. Following Bataille and Blanchot, Foucault privileges such "limit-experiences," avowing that his fascination with them is what essentially underlies and inspires his work, even his careful, erudite historical studies:

> I tried, in particular, to understand how man transformed into objects of knowledge some of these limit-experiences: madness, death, crime. This is where we find the theses of Georges Bataille, but taken up again in a collective history which is that of the West and its knowledge … I have already spoken to you about limit-experiences: this is the theme that really fascinated me. Madness, death, sexuality, crime are for me the more intense things. (DE 2: 876, 886)

Somaesthetics has given far less attention to such limit-experiences, though I did devote a long study to sexuality, inspired by but strikingly different from Foucault's (see AE). One reason for this diminished attention to those other limit-experiences is that Foucault has already done an impressive job with them. A deeper reason is somaesthetics' aim of meliorist care. While appreciating the potential value of transgressive limit-experiences, somaesthetics is also wary of their dangers and damage to both the self and others. Not all transformation is improvement; not every alteration is a benefit. Change for mere change's sake may be a good recipe to avoid boredom, but it does not imply progress in self-care, in empowering enrichment of the subject. Indeed, Foucault seems less eager to bolster the self through transformation than to undermine or negate it. We see this in his critique of phenomenology:

> The experience of the phenomenologist is, basically, a certain way of looking reflectively at any object of experienced life, at everyday life in its transitory form in order to grasp its meanings. For Nietzsche, Bataille, Blanchot, on the contrary,

experience is to try to reach a certain point of life which is the closest possible to the unlivable. What is required is the maximum of intensity and, at the same time, of impossibility. Phenomenological work, on the contrary, consists in deploying the whole field of possibilities linked to everyday experience. Moreover, phenomenology tries to recapture the meaning of everyday experience in order to find out in what way the subject that I am is indeed, in its transcendental functions, the founder of this experience and of these meanings. On the other hand, the experience in Nietzsche, Blanchot, Bataille has the function of tearing away the subject from itself, to make so that it is not itself anymore or that it is brought to its annihilation or dissolution. This is an enterprise of de-subjectivation. The idea of a limit-experience, which tears the subject away from itself, this is what was important for me in the reading of Nietzsche, of Bataille, of Blanchot, and which made it such that, as boring, as erudite as my books are, I always conceived them as direct experiences aiming to tear me away from myself, to prevent me from being the same. (DE 2: 862; or RM: 31–2)

Somaesthetics is situated between Foucault and phenomenology. Like Foucault, it aims at transforming the subject through novel experiences and unhabitual, somatically-centered conduct rather than simply studying (and thereby reinforcing) the subject's everyday experience and sense of self. Unlike Foucault, somaesthetics' goal of transformation is not annihilation or dissolution of the subject, but instead its cultivation into something better. Foucault's advocacy of limit-experiences celebrates the explosively violent and aggressively transgressive. His metaphors are typically combative. He writes: "I believe, following Nietzsche, that truth is to be understood in terms of war. The truth of truth, that's the war" (MFE: 135). And he insists on identifying himself not as a philosopher or a historian, but as an expert in battle explosives: "I am an explosives expert (*un artificier*). I make something that ultimately serves for a siege, a war, a destruction. I am not for destruction, but I am for enabling an advance, for tearing down the walls," to demolish the established discursive regime of power-knowledge (MFE: 92).

Somaesthetics acknowledges the value of defiance, belligerence, and even violence in challenging oppression (for instance in its studies of rap), but it insists that there are also other useful methods in our somatic toolbox for resisting domination and for dissolving its repressive effects on the subject by using gentler means. Here the Daoist dimension of somaesthetic philosophy comes into play with its recognition of the gentle power of water, whose compliant fluidity can cut through stone and make it crumble. Like phenomenology, somaesthetics appreciates the ordinary but never to enthrone it as adequate or ultimate.

Instead, somaesthetics sees the ordinary as an essential ground for melioristic transformation, as an enabling context for going beyond the limits of everyday experience. Somaesthetics affirms intense somatic experiences of crossing limits that are transformative without involving transgressive violence or crime, that are not "impossible," "negative experiences" that annihilate the subject; somaesthetics also explores techniques for achieving such positive, livable, limit-experiences through somatic techniques that can be sweetly pleasurable as well as challengingly arduous. In the practice of philosophical life, somaesthetics recognizes the value of intense, transgressive limit-experiences that edify by radically challenging the subject's sense of self. I learned to appreciate that value through the dizzying frenzy of possession in my experiences with the Man in Gold.[5]

Pleasure

Foucault and somaesthetics assign a central role to the pleasures of experience, not only the classically philosophical enjoyments of the intellect, but also full-bodied sensual pleasures. But our paths diverge from this hedonic base, as somaesthetics is more pluralistic in its appreciation of ordinary pleasures. Despite Foucault's sympathetic study of the measured pleasures of "the moderate subject" and its "aesthetics of existence" in ancient Greece, despite his professed aim "to make ourselves infinitely more susceptible to pleasure" (FEW: 137), when it comes to contemporary culture and his own hedonic agenda, Foucault focuses narrowly on the extreme pleasures of limit-experiences. He disdains what he calls "those middle range of pleasures that make up everyday life" (like a "glass of wine"), insisting that "a pleasure must be something incredibly intense" or it is "nothing" (FEW: 129). Real pleasure belongs only to "incredibly intense" and overpowering limit-experiences, including death.[6] The "complete" or "real pleasure," Foucault avowed, "would be so deep, so intense, so overwhelming that I couldn't survive it. I would die … [S]ome drugs are really important for me because they are the mediation to those incredibly intense joys that I am unable to experience, to afford, by myself." Confessing "a real difficulty in experiencing pleasure," Foucault needs to be overwhelmed to enjoy it (FEW: 129).

This narrow taste for intense limit-experiences reflects Foucault's personal problems of anhedonia; but it is also symptomatic of our culture's general insensitivity to the subtle pleasures of somatic sensibility and mindfulness that somaesthetics promotes. Somaesthetic perception and reflection can transfigure the ordinary into experiences that are extraordinary in pleasure and insight. Our culture's numbness to these somatic subtleties (with its corresponding performance fetishism for the fastest, highest, and strongest) promotes the quest for sensationalism, whether it be strong drugs, sadomasochistic sex, drinking binges, or the thrills of transgressive speeding in reckless joy-rides with outsized carbon footprints. As I've elsewhere argued (BC), a one-sided diet of limit-experiences will eventually turn the sensational into the routine, if it does not ruin you first. The neuroscience of sensory fatigue shows that intensification of pleasure cannot simply be achieved by mere intensity of sensation. Sensory appreciation is typically dulled when blasted with extremes. The most intensely enjoyed music is not the loudest. A tender grazing touch can surpass the pleasure of a thunderous thrust.

Aesthetics and Art

We can see from their names alone, that Foucault's aesthetics of existence and somaesthetics take aesthetics and art as foundational concepts for the philosophical art of living. But we diverge on what constitutes such life, because we differently understand these two concepts, which are vague, ambiguous, complex, historically fashioned, and essentially contested. Despite some clear distinctions of usage, they often overlap in theoretical and ordinary discourse. We sometimes distinguish aesthetic value from artistic value: natural beauty exemplifying only the former. But we typically regard works of artistic value as having aesthetic value, even when the works in question lack or eschew aesthetic value in the strict sense of perceptual sensory satisfaction from which our term and concept of aesthetic originate (based on the Greek word for sensory perception, αἴσθησις). Such sensorily unsatisfying works of art gain aesthetic status through their distinctive artistic value in terms of their creative, often striking innovation in the field of art. Foucault's aesthetics of existence commits this common conflation of aesthetic and artistic value, while privileging the latter. Somaesthetics, while recognizing both forms of value, is more careful about distinguishing them, and more appreciative of traditional aesthetic values in its art of living.

Foucault derives his idea of the art of living from his study of the ancient Greeks who practiced "a kind of ethics which was an aesthetics of existence," reflecting "the will to live a beautiful life, and to leave to others memories of a beautiful existence." Lamenting that today "in our society art has become something which is related only to objects and not to individuals, or to life. That art is something which is specialized or which is done by experts who are artists," he challenges: "But couldn't everyone's life become a work of art? Why should the lamp or house be an art object, but not our life?" So, building on the Greek model, Foucault urges "the idea of *bios* as material for an aesthetic piece of art." "From the idea that the self is not given to us, I think that there is only one practical consequence: we have to create ourselves as a work of art" (FR: 341, 343, 348, 350–1).

But what counts as creating oneself as "an aesthetic piece of art"? Because the concepts of aesthetics and art are both ambiguous and contested, they suggest very different genres of aesthetic living. Whereas the classical Greek aesthetic demanded beauty, harmony, measured proportion, and unity, today's dominant artworld aesthetic is far less concerned with realizing these values and often seems bent on challenging them. Shaped by the ideology of romanticism and the avant-garde, our modernist high-art aesthetic makes novelty or singularity the prime desideratum of a work of art, though this demand is not made by the aesthetics of popular art. These different conceptions of aesthetic result in different styles or demands in the art of living. Is it enough to shape one's life into a satisfyingly harmonious, well-integrated, and dynamic form? Or does making one's life a work of art require something more, or completely other—a radical originality, a distinctive singular expression that breaks with previous forms and limits as the avant-garde work of art aims to do?

Failing to clarify these different notions of aesthetic, Foucault's aesthetics of existence problematically slides from one to the other. He insightfully reconstructs the ethical ideal of aesthetic living embodied in ancient Greek practices of self-stylization, where one's conduct (regarding sex, diet, etc.) was not dictated by strict, universal rules whose violation meant sin, but instead aesthetically chosen "to give [one's] existence an honorable and noble form" (HS 3: 185). Although such choices involved a measure of free aesthetic self-expression, they were also guided and constrained by models of what Greek society regarded as noble and admirable. Artistry was exercised in aesthetically deploying established models to give attractive form to the particularities of one's life. Not everyone could succeed in living an aesthetic life, for most had neither the material means nor the taste and character to do so. Yet, even if difficult, the aesthetic life did not demand inventing a whole new style of living; indeed, drastically violating established standards of beautiful (*kalon*) living would constitute unaesthetic vulgarity.

For modern times, however, Foucault advocates an aesthetic life far more extreme in its demands, because it takes as its exemplar the avant-garde artist or Baudelairean dandy who refuses all established models in the aim of creating something radically new. Not content with self-stylization, such an artist "tries to invent himself" (FR: 42), to "create a new way of life" (DE 2: 1128; EWF: 158), to transform himself into "something radically 'other'" (RM: 46, 121; DE 2: 867, 893). For Foucault, "we must produce something that does not yet exist and about which we cannot know how and what it will be … [which means] the destruction of what we are and the creation of something totally other, a total innovation" (RM: 121–2; DE 2: 893). While recognizing that the Greek art of living was based on a limit-respecting aesthetic, including "a 'quadri-thematics' of sexual austerity" (HS 2: 21), Foucault recommends an aesthetic of limit-defying transgressive experimentation to test, explode, and transform the self. Although he adroitly links such venturesome experimentation to Baudelaire's dandy aesthetics and Kant's enlightenment motto of daring to know, Foucault's deep immersion in the radical French currents of contemporary high art (e.g., as friend of Boulez, lover of Barraqué, admirer of Bataille and Blanchot, and collaborator with the Tel Quel group) could suffice in itself to make him identify the aesthetic narrowly with the radical innovation and transgression of art's avant-garde. In any case, he disregards (if not disdains) the traditional aesthetic values and non-transgressive styles that both the moderate subject of ancient Greece and the vast majority of people today affirm as genuine sources of pleasure. Pragmatist-inspired somaesthetics—with its critical appreciation of the popular arts (including disruptive genres like rap) and its pluralistic, democratic disposition—valorizes also transformative experiments that aim at piecemeal improvements rather than transgressive upheaval into a radical other. It recognizes a wide spectrum of creative experiments in individualistic self-stylization that are neither radically transgressive nor conformist, the kind that might appeal to independent, critical, and moderate subjects who do not want their lifestyles and beliefs dictated by a school, as in the philosophical schools of ancient Greece or in monastic orders today.

Recognizing the colossal disparity between today's transgressive high-art aesthetic and the limit-regarding aesthetics of existence of ancient Greece, Foucault proposes a fascinating way to link them through one particular form of the ancient philosophical life that was strikingly distinctive but not much favored. The school of Cynics, he argues, displays a militantly rebellious, strenuously singular, revolutionary style of life that aims to express the truth of their ideas. And this mode of life, after its formative influence on Christian asceticism, continues in its modern incarnations, first in the political revolutionary of the nineteenth century and then in the revolutionary artist of the twentieth. In offering a way to reclaim as artistically aesthetic the transgressive limit-experiences that violate accepted aesthetic tastes and negate the subject, and in offering a way to ground this negative, disruptive aesthetic in the ancient practice of the philosophical life as an aesthetics of existence, cynicism clearly fascinated Foucault. Devoting most of his final lectures to examining this school of philosophy, he showed how brilliantly yet paradoxically it exemplified the philosophical life as a beautifully heroic life of truth-telling—not only in its discourse but in its raw, elemental, unconcealed, and unrefined style of life, in its crude, vivid truth to primal nature.

Foucault, of course, recognized that the rude, beggarly animality of the Cynics was not beautiful but shamefully ugly by Greek standards. However, through his account of Diogenes and other Cynics, Foucault sought a way to equate philosophy's true life with the beautiful life, while identifying that true life with the Cynics' transgressive life of transvaluation of values, captured in Diogenes' motto "change the value of the currency." For Foucault, the Cynic lived more truly because more naturally; he lived more naturally by flouting societal conventions. Moreover, by bravely defying them in speech and in action, the Cynic's life is heroic, hence admirable or beautiful in the moral sense, which the Greek word for beautiful (*kalon*) also denoted. Whether this threefold identification of the true life, the Cynic's life, and the beautiful life is ultimately successful is a question too complex to explore here.[7]

More generally, it is worth asking: In what sense or in what degree must an aesthetic life be a life of truth? Despite some famous idealistic proclamations of their identity, the values of truth and beauty are not always convergent or compatible. Truth-telling is often an ugly affair; and beauty often relies on deceptive artifice. If "beauty is only the promise of happiness" that reality fails to fulfill, if art represents an effort to defy, escape, or transform the ugly truth of the real, then is the art of living essentially a way of defying or hiding from life's ugly, boring, or frightful truths? "Birth, and copulation, and death. That's all the facts when you come to brass tacks," as T. S. Eliot's Sweeney bluntly complained of life's ennui. We should also ask in which way and to what degree must the philosophical life be a heroic life? What constitutes heroism in the aesthetics of existence or somaesthetics? Ancient Greek culture was fixated on bold heroism, and its philosophy shared that passion, whose traces still survive today. Socrates embodied that fearless, combative, heroic ideal, while Confucius did not; yet Confucius founded a rich and politically influential philosophical tradition that pervades East Asian culture. We certainly need admirable exemplars to guide us in the thought and action of our philosophical lives. Foucault has been a crucial exemplar, indeed a hero, for me and for somaesthetics. But sometimes heroes are better to admire than to follow.

Notes

1. For a detailed account of the structure of somaesthetics with its three branches and three dimensions, see BC: 15–29 and TB: 25–46.
2. Hadot, of course, must admit that pleasures are central to Epicureanism's philosophical life, but he regards such pleasures as essentially intellectual, dismissing (erroneously in my view) the value the Epicureans gave to the sensual dimension of simple, natural bodily pleasures. "For the Epicureans, in the last analysis, pleasure is a spiritual exercise. Not … sensual gratification, but the intellectual pleasure derived from contemplating nature, the thought of pleasure past and present, and lastly the pleasure of friendship" (PWL: 88).
3. At one point, with respect to the Skeptics, Hadot seems to concede the possibility of leading a genuine philosophical life in terms of one's inner attitudes without significantly departing from the established norms of conduct. "It is true that even while the Skeptics chose to conform to the common conduct of life, they remained philosophers, since they practiced an exercise demanding something rather strange, the suspending of judgment, and aiming at a goal, uninterrupted tranquility and serenity of the soul, that the common conduct of life hardly knew" (PWL: 56).
4. My two first books were devoted to literary theory: *The Object of Literary Criticism* (1984) and *T.S. Eliot and the Philosophy of Criticism* (1988). For the influence of dance and somatic therapies on my philosophy, see the Prefaces to PA and BC.
5. I describe the value of those experiences for my theorizing and my altered, expanded sense of self in "Aesthetic Experience and the Powers of Possession" (2019) and in the Preface to *The Adventures of the Man in Gold* (2016).
6. In praising the limit-experience of suicide, Foucault describes it as "a fathomless pleasure whose patient preparation, without respite but without fatalism either, will enlighten all your life" (DE 2: 779).
7. I provide more detailed discussion of this issue in Richard Shusterman, "Foucault and Somaesthetics: Variations on the Art of Living," forthcoming in a symposium on "Foucault's Legacy in Contemporary Thinking: Forty Years Later (1984–2024)," in *Foucault Studies*, 2024.

Bibliography

Andrieu, B., ed. (2010), *Textes Clés de Philosophie du Corps: Expérience, Interactions et Écologie Corporelle*, Paris: Vrin.

Droit, R.-P. (2004), *Michel Foucault, Entretiens*, Paris: Odile Jacob (cited as MFE).

Eliot, T. S. (1969), "Sweeney Agonistes," in *The Complete Poems and Plays of T.S. Eliot*, 115–26, London: Faber.

Foucault, M. (1979), *Discipline and Punish*, trans. A. Sheridan, New York: Vintage Books (cited as DP).

Foucault, M. (1980), *The History of Sexuality. Vol. 1: An Introduction*, trans. R. Hurley, New York: Vintage Books (cited as HS 1).

Foucault, M. (1984), *The Foucault Reader*, ed. P. Rabinow, New York: Pantheon Books (cited as FR).

Foucault, M. (1986a), *The History of Sexuality. Vol. 2: The Use of Pleasure* [1984], trans. R. Hurley, New York: Vintage Books (cited as HS 2).

Foucault, M. (1986b), *The History of Sexuality. Vol. 3: The Care of the Self* [1984], trans. R. Hurley, New York: Vintage Books (cited as HS 3).

Foucault, M. (1991), *Remarks on Marx*, trans. R. J. Goldstein and J. Cascaito, New York: Semiotext(e) (cited as RM).

Foucault, M. (1997), *The Essential Works 1954–1984. Vol. I: Ethics. Subjectivity and Truth*, ed. P. Rabinow, New York: New Press (cited as FEW).

Foucault, M. (2001), *Dits et Ecrits. Vol. 1–2*, Paris: Gallimard (cited as DE 1 and DE 2).

Foucault, M. (2011), *The Courage of Truth: The Government of Self and Others II. Lectures at the Collège de France 1983–1984* [2009], ed. F. Gros, trans. G. Burchell, New York: Palgrave MacMillan.

Hadot, P. (1995), *Philosophy as a Way of Life: Spiritual Exercises from Socrates to Foucault*, trans. M. Chase, ed. A. I. Davidson, Oxford: Blackwell (cited as PWL).

Małecki, W. P. and S. Schleusener (2014), "What Affects Are You Capable of? On Deleuze and Somaesthetics," in *Deleuze and Pragmatism*, eds. S. Bowden, S. Bignall, and P. Patton, 216–34, London: Routledge.

Rorty, R. (2001), "Response to Richard Shusterman," in *Richard Rorty: Critical Dialogues*, eds. M. Festenstein and S. Thompson, 153–7, Cambridge: Polity Press.

Shusterman, R. (1984), *The Object of Literary Criticism*, Amsterdam: Rodopi.

Shusterman, R. (1988), *T. S. Eliot and the Philosophy of Criticism*, London/New York: Duckworth and Columbia University Press.

Shusterman, R. (1992), *Pragmatist Aesthetics: Living Beauty, Rethinking Art*, Oxford: Blackwell (cited as PA).

Shusterman, R. (1997), *Practicing Philosophy: Pragmatism and the Philosophical Life*, New York: Routledge (cited as PP).

Shusterman, R. (2008), *Body Consciousness*, Cambridge: Cambridge University Press (cited as BC).

Shusterman, R. (2012), *Thinking through the Body*, Cambridge: Cambridge University Press (cited as TB).

Shusterman, R. (2016), *The Adventures of the Man in Gold: Paths between Art and Life*, Paris: Hermann.

Shusterman, R. (2018), "Body Consciousness and the Excentric Self: Between Plessner and Somaesthetics," *Pragmatism Today*, 9 (1): 10–20.

Shusterman, R. (2019), "Aesthetic Experience and the Powers of Possession," *Journal of Aesthetic Education*, 53 (4): 1–23.

Shusterman, R. (2021), *Ars Erotica: Sex and Somaesthetics in the Classical Arts of Love*, Cambridge: Cambridge University Press (cited as AE).

Shusterman, R. (2022), *Philosophy and the Art of Writing*, London: Routledge (cited as PAW).

Tedesco, S. (2013), "Presentazione. Esercizi spirituali di somaestetica," in *Coscienza del corpo. La filosofia come arte di vivere e la somaestetica*, ed. R. Shusterman, 5–13, Milano: Christian Marinotti Edizioni.

Thoreau, H. D. (1969), "Walden," in *The Portable Thoreau*, ed. Carl Bode, 258–572, New York: Viking Press (cited as W).

Zerbib, D. (2007), "Richard Shusterman: Les Effets Secondaires d'une Philosophie Douce," *Le Monde*, November 30, 2007: 12.

7

Somaesthetics, Foucauldian Aesthetics of Existence, and Living Ethically as White

Chris Voparil

My aim in this chapter is to examine Michel Foucault's and Richard Shusterman's conceptions of an aesthetics of existence as responses to challenges of contemporary race matters. Specifically, I situate their work in relation to recent calls for new ways of living and being in the world as white (e.g., Alcoff 2015; Yancy 2016; Sullivan 2019). As Shannon Sullivan has argued, to make a positive contribution to the quest for racial justice white people "need to develop a racial identity alternative to what a white racist society demands of them"—that is, "a different set of virtues, a different *ethos*" (Sullivan 2014a: 139, 147). Challenging white supremacy demands not only the critique of white power and privilege, but a reconstruction of what it means to live and be in the world as white.

Calls for the transformation and even the elimination of whiteness abound in recent work in Critical Philosophy of Race and Critical Whiteness Studies. However, these well-intentioned efforts face myriad obstacles and lacunae as they attempt to develop concrete practices for change. In ways we are still coming to understand, white privilege and white supremacy "warp" white people (Sullivan 2019: 109), both epistemically and ethically. The prevalence of white ignorance, understood as a form of cognitive-affective dysfunction that thwarts efforts at self-knowledge (Medina 2013), renders white people "incapable of behaving ethically especially with regard to racial matters, *and* they generally cannot see or understand themselves as unethical" (Sullivan 2014b: 596).[1] Little clarity exists about how to remedy these ethical and epistemic deficits and advance the reconstructive project of developing a new ethics and aesthetics of white existence.

In what follows, I argue that Foucault's aesthetics of existence and Shusterman's somaesthetics possess resources that enable us to move beyond these challenges and transform the ethically compromised white subjectivity that is sustained and perpetuated by white privilege and white ignorance. The ethical shortcomings identified by Sullivan require alternative ways of practicing the freedom available to white agents. In Foucault's distinctive sense of ethics, they need to develop a new relationship to themselves—a new *rapport à soi*—as normalized white subjects. Among Foucault's great insights we can count his understanding of bodies as sites where normativity is inscribed and practiced, and his view that subverting disciplinary power which produces and constructs rather than restricts and constrains requires not speaking truth to power or critique of ideology but a "critical ontology of ourselves" (Foucault 1984c: 45–50). Shusterman's somaesthetics advances this work by translating Foucault's transgressive impulses and valorization of limit-experiences into everyday aesthetic experience via a notion of somatic style, understood as vehicle for performing differently the larger norms that our bodies authorize.

Neither Foucault nor Shusterman has written on whiteness in relation to their aesthetics of existence. Others have examined the role of the aesthetic and of embodied habits in both perpetuating white racism and improving issues of equity and justice (e.g., Granger 2010; James 2013; Taylor 2017). My focus here is how Foucault's and Shusterman's insights into ethical-aesthetic self-transformation can be marshaled for a positive program of developing new ethical practices of white subjectivity and, ultimately, reconstructing whiteness.

After surveying in the first section the obstacles that efforts to cultivate white ethical improvement must overcome, I provide in the second an overview of the aesthetics of existence and its ethical resources, and underscore the limitation, in the face of white ignorance, of its reliance upon increased self-knowledge. The third and fourth sections develop the positive resources that Foucault and Shusterman offer in their understandings of somatic normativity and conception of ethics as aesthetic self-stylization. My main claim is that our best hope for developing ethically improved white self-transformation resides in conceiving of whiteness as a style of existence and developing practices and habits of alternative embodied styles of living and being as white people.

The Challenges of Transforming Whiteness

For those who seek to transform whiteness, rather than eliminate it altogether, the goal is "a morally livable white identity" that is "both white and morally defensible" (Alcoff 2015: 171).[2] In recent work, the path to a new ethics of living for white folk that gets beyond or at least establishes a different relation to white power and white privilege typically involves two dimensions: disrupting dominant habits and practices that sustain white normativity and developing new habits and practices to take their place. As José Medina holds, "self-problematization" is the first obligation of privileged subjects (Medina 2013: 22). White privilege protects a type of moral certainty and arrogance that must be pierced (Applebaum 2008: 297). Terrance MacMullan similarly calls whiteness a "lived script" that needs to be disrupted (MacMullan 2009: 141). As George Yancy describes it, the aim is "to *disarticulate* whiteness" from practices, discourses, and institutions that maintain white power (Yancy 2016: 229). The larger context of this disruptive work is challenging the narratives of normalization that undergird and perpetuate whiteness (Jolles 2012). Sullivan sums up the overall aim of the interruptive project: "to find a way of disrupting a habit through environmental change and then hope that the changed environment will help produce an improved habit in its place" (Sullivan 2006: 9).

While necessary, the work of disruption on its own is not sufficient. New habits and practices of white subjectivity must be developed. Existing accounts vary in their attempts to capture the nature of this novel subjectivity. Sullivan advocates white critical self-love (Sullivan 2014a: 162). Linda Alcoff (2015) describes a complex form of white double consciousness, transposing W. E. B. Du Bois's famous account of Black double-consciousness onto the terrain of white experience to capture two conflicting forces governing white experience: the influence of racist histories, on the one hand, and the "everyday amiable connections and affective pulls across racial lines," on the other (Alcoff 2015: 129). This double consciousness can take regressive and progressive forms—the former a "comforting escape hatch" from these histories, and the latter, by contrast, inviting a morally responsible acknowledgment of our racist past and present (Alcoff 2015: 168). Marjorie Jolles calls for "a toggling with normativity: a back-and-forth process of narrative identification and disidentification" (Jolles 2012: 316). Yancy fixes upon the need for practices of "un-suturing" that make possible a whiteness that is "exposed, vulnerable, open to being wounded" (Yancy 2016: 255).

To move forward, Alcoff argues, what is needed is "a new imaginary or narrative that can make sense of the white participation in … multiracial, multiethnic political coalitions" (Alcoff 2015: 128–9). Yet manifold challenges remain. One is knowing which parts of white subjectivity need to be disrupted and which require accepting or facing head on. MacMullan describes how the dynamics generate perplexing paradoxes, including how "to identify as *white* when it comes to taking responsibility for current and past injustices enabled by the idea of whiteness, and to identify as *not white* when describing an alternative to the current categories of race" (MacMullan 2009: 95). Paul Taylor aptly depicts this white liberal double bind as the "situation that well-intentioned white people find themselves in when they sincerely want to deal productively with race-related issues, but seem condemned to screw up no matter what they do" (Taylor 2007: 202). The call in thinkers like Foucault "to invent new and hitherto unimagined conducts expressive of our ideals" (Marchetti 2011: 142) may well become, in the context of whiteness, merely an exercise in the perpetuation of white privilege.

Beyond these practical dilemmas, deeper epistemic and ethical deficits further obstruct efforts to transform whiteness. One is white ignorance, or what Medina describes as the "cognitive-affective functioning" that sustains structures of white supremacy and privilege and that involves both "racial self-ignorance and social ignorance of racialized others" (Medina 2013: 18). Charles Mills called it a "group-based cognitive handicap" that prevents people from seeing and doing the right thing in relation to racial injustices (Mills 2007: 15). This kind of ignorance involves more than the absence of knowledge; white ignorance is an active form of unknowing which Mills characterizes as a "collective amnesia" that manifests in "a white refusal to recognize the long history of structural discrimination that has left whites with the differential resources they have today" (Mills 2007: 28–9). Despite these liabilities, white ignorance as experienced does not hinder white people; rather, it is "incredibly functional" and confers psychic benefits (Sullivan 2014a: 595), as well as material ones, including the ability to encounter the world as "a place called home, a place of privileges and immunities, a space for achievement, success, freedom of movement" (Yancy 2012: 45).

My primary concern here is with the ethical implications of these warping effects of white ignorance and privilege. As Sullivan compellingly argues, part and parcel of this ethically compromised white subjectivity is an inability to see oneself as unethical that forestalls any attempt to alter behavior in an ethically positive fashion with respect to race (Sullivan 2014b: 595; 2019: 109). The various forms of evasion, denial, and self-exculpation practiced wittingly or unwittingly by "good white people" (Sullivan 2014a) when confronted with white racism— what Sullivan also has dubbed "toxic goodness" (Sullivan 2019: 111)—constitute a further array of obstacles to white ethical improvement.

The Ethics of Somaesthetics and the Aesthetics of Existence

In this section, I briefly sketch the conceptions of an aesthetics of existence advanced by Shusterman and Foucault and illuminate their role in ethical and political transformation. For both thinkers, larger disciplinary norms are altered by cultivating different ways of living and being that fail to support those norms. A chief barrier these projects face when transposed to the context of whiteness is their reliance on the kind of self-knowledge and awareness that white subjects, as a result of white ignorance, profoundly lack.

The aim of somaesthetics to provide "a clear pragmatic orientation, something that the individual can directly translate into a discipline of improved somatic practice" (Shusterman 2000b: 535)[3] makes it a useful resource for developing a practical approach to white ethical self-transformation. Understood as "the critical study and meliorative cultivation of the experience and use of one's body as a site of sensory appreciation (*aesthesis*) and creative self-fashioning" (Shusterman 2014: 6), somaesthetics' potential as a vehicle for transforming whiteness is very promising. Across numerous essays and books, Shusterman has developed the critical and transformative potential of the soma, "the bodily, sensory subjectivity through which we perceive things, including the soma itself as a bodily object in the world" (Shusterman 2019: 14). In his view, "somatic self-examination provides a model of immanent critique," as well as "a means of strengthening our somatic capacities (which include our capacities for courage, endurance, empathetic social perception and nurturing care) so that we are better equipped to engage in social and political struggles" (Shusterman 2014: 8, 12).

For his part, Foucault saw the ancient Greek model of "an aesthetics of existence" as "a practice, a style of liberty" that involved norms of behavior conceived on the model of an "elaboration of one's own life as a personal work of art," in contrast to the later Christian morality as "obedience to a system of rules" (Foucault 1989: 451). In lectures, interviews, and the final volumes of *The History of Sexuality*, Foucault used various categories and vocabularies to pursue a preoccupation with the modes and practices of the self-constitution of subjectivity.[4] Understood as "an exercise of self on self," he described these practices as "a sort of close combat of the individual with himself in which the authority, presence, and gaze of someone else is, if not impossible, at least unnecessary" (Foucault 2007: 205). He termed these exercises "technologies of the self," which comprise "the ways in which we relate ourselves to ourselves, contribute to the forms in which our subjectivity is constituted and experienced, as well as to the forms in which we govern our thought and conduct" (Davidson 1994: 119).

More than a conceptual project, for Foucault attending to the constitution of our subjectivity was part of larger transformative work he called a "critical ontology of ourselves," understood as "an attitude, an ethos, a philosophical life in which critique of what we are is at one and the same time the historical analysis of the limits that are imposed on us and an experiment with the possibility of going beyond them" (Foucault 1984c: 50). More bluntly, he held that "At every moment, step by step, one must confront what one is thinking and saying with what one is doing, with what one is" (Foucault 1984b: 374). The critical ontology of ourselves is "a way of practicing freedom that does not vacillate between the two poles of specific liberation and revolutionary transformation," but instead enables ways of being free under particular normalizing conditions (Dumm 1996: 143–4).

For both Foucault and Shusterman, crucially, there is no wall between the aesthetic and the ethical in these conceptions. Among the most attractive elements of a Foucauldian aesthetics of existence and a somaesthetic approach to meliorative self-fashioning is their mutual discernment of the importance for ethics of practices of aesthetic self-transformation. Inspired by the Greeks' lived responses to the ethical question of "how should one live?," the shared aim of this art of living, as Shusterman writes, is "not truth for truth's sake, but rather ameliorative care of the self (*epimeleia heatou*), and, as a consequence, the betterment of the society in which the self is situated" (Shusterman 1997: 17). Indeed, if we accept that there is more to the good life than discerning and fulfilling universally valid, logically derived obligations, as Shusterman explains, then "the project of an ethical life becomes an exercise in living aesthetically" (Shusterman 1992: 245). "Ethical decisions of how to live," on this view, "could not be logically derived from man's essence or from uncontestable principles, but instead require, like aesthetic judgments, creative and critical imagination" (Shusterman 1997: 6).

An aesthetics of existence for Foucault likewise is fundamentally ethical in his distinctive sense of pertaining to one's *rapport à soi*, or the way the individual constitutes herself as a moral subject of her own actions (Foucault 1984a: 352). As Arnold Davidson puts it, "Foucault thought of ethics as that component of morality that concerns the self's relationship to itself" (Davidson 1994: 118). The basic insight here is that ethics not only involves moral norms and traditional moral codes but the relationship to oneself within individuals subject to those norms—"an orientation of modification, experimentation, and transformation of the self by and through the self" (Koopman 2013: 192). Foucault described this "self-formation as an 'ethical subject'" in further detail as:

> [A] process in which the individual delimits that part of himself that will form the object of his moral practice, defines his position relative to the precept he will follow, and decides on a certain mode of being that will serve as his moral goal. And this requires him to act upon himself, to monitor, test, improve, and transform himself. (Foucault 1990: 28)

In various places, Foucault further elaborated the elements of this process in terms of four components: the ethical substance, the mode of subjection, the self-forming activity, and the *telos* (Foucault 1984a: 352-5; 1990: 26–8). Colin Koopman gives a helpful account of how central Foucault's elaboration of "an alternative ethics of the transformation of ourselves" was to his broader reading of modernity (Koopman 2013: 183). The key insight was that "the self, taking itself as a work to be accomplished, could sustain an ethics that is no longer supported by either [ancient Greek or modern] tradition" (Veyne 1993: 7).

Similarly, for Shusterman, the soma "grounds our ethical life in a very basic way" (Shusterman 2019: 16). The body is "the essential medium or tool" through which ethical values and social norms are inscribed and perpetuated—"enforced through our bodily habits, including habits of feeling (which have bodily roots)" (Shusterman 2019: 16n). For Shusterman, ethics "must be involved with a relationship to self because the very task of the ethical agent in dealing ethically and effectively with others inescapably involves matters of self-knowledge, self-discipline, and self-care" (Shusterman 2011a: 4).

Bringing these projects of ethical and aesthetic self-transformation to bear on the distinct challenges of living ethically as white faces a number of obstacles. While Foucault himself didn't discuss whiteness, he was aware of the issue that "[r]ecent liberation movements suffer from the fact that they cannot find any principle on which to base the elaboration of a new ethics" (Foucault 1984a: 343). Foucault's broader critical genealogical project largely mirrors the two dimensions promoted by recent work on transforming whiteness: first, a historical questioning of our existence and the factors that have constructed us as we currently are; and, second, a discernment of "the possibility of no longer being, doing, or thinking what we are, do, or think" (Bernauer and Mahon 1994: 144). James Bernauer and Michael Mahon continue, "If one side of this resistance is to 'refuse what we are,' the other side is to invent, not discover, who we are by promoting 'new forms of subjectivity'" (Bernauer and Mahon 1994: 147). If, as

Sarin Marchetti recounts, Foucault was "interested in tracing a 'genealogy of problems, of *problématiques*,' which prompted the discovery or invention of new ways of conceiving one's conduct as ethically meaningful, so to react to, and escape from, forms of oppressive coercion by either social or religious institutions and powers" (Marchetti 2011: 128), the applicability to the transformation of white conduct in the face of white supremacy and privilege is apparent. Clearly, the practice of freedom, for Foucault, is the struggle against normative authority in "the subtler forms operative in social life and indeed the recesses of our own subjectivity" (Colapietro 2011: 36).

However, the challenge is how to problematize whiteness given that it is experienced as enabling and empowering. One possibility highlighted by Cynthia Gayman is that "the work of the intellect described by Foucault, must first be catalyzed by an experiential disruption, leading to recognition of what pragmatist philosopher John Dewey described as the 'problematic situation'" (Gayman 2011: 63). As noted earlier, the issue is that white privilege and white ignorance are experienced typically not as disruptions but as expansive and unproblematic ways of being in the world. Even if we experience what Medina (2013) calls "epistemic friction" in our interactions with others, change is derailed by the various mechanisms for deflecting and dismissing these transformative impulses, as Sullivan (2014a) catalogs, as well as by the barriers to white perception of oneself as unethical. Whiteness as such is rarely experienced as a "problem."[5]

The ethical import of an aesthetics of existence or an ethics of self-care or self-formation is also curtailed by the existence of white ignorance. In dominantly white societies, white self-knowledge itself is precisely what is lacking. Even increased somatic awareness may be unavailable. Given that the melioristic impulse at the heart of self-improvement nevertheless relies on improved self-knowledge, the inability to perceive oneself and one's habits and actions clearly and accurately poses deep challenges to projects of ethical self-cultivation and its reliance on work of self on self to both identify and remedy our ethical shortcomings.

For Shusterman and Foucault, the first step in self-transformation is self-knowledge: "probing one's present limits so as to grasp the needed dimensions and directions of change" (Shusterman 1997: 40). For his part, Shusterman cites self-knowledge as "sought as part of a larger project of self-cultivation and self-mastery" (Shusterman 2011a: 10). As he explains, "productive efforts of self-cultivation and self-creation require ... a significant amount of self-knowledge to guide one's efforts in building on one's strengths and recognizing one's weaknesses so that they can be overcome, concealed, or deployed to one's advantage" (Shusterman 2011a: 8). Even though he recognizes limits on the pursuit of self-knowledge, he insists that "what seems fundamentally crucial to projects of governing, caring for, and cultivating oneself is to know oneself" (Shusterman 2011a: 4–5).[6] Foucault, likewise, averred that "[t]his transformation of one's self by one's own knowledge is, I think, something rather close to the aesthetic experience" (Foucault 1989: 379). The perniciousness of white ignorance threatens to prevent the essential procurement of self-knowledge and self-awareness on which improving somatic habits and practices depends. A potential remedy, which we will take up in the fourth section, is hinted at by Shusterman when he counsels distinguishing between "the cognitive content of such knowledge and the affect we attach to it" and calls for developing a "resilient affective style" in response (Shusterman 2011a: 11).

Somaesthetics and Living White Normativity Differently

I turn now to the resources in somaesthetics for getting past these obstacles to transforming whiteness, many of which are congenial to Foucault's own conception of "ethics as a self-transformative process" (Koopman 2013: 191). Shusterman's work on pragmatist aesthetics, on philosophy as a way of life, and on somaesthetics has been in productive dialogue with Foucault from an early stage.[7] Shusterman long ago grasped how the aesthetics of the soma includes "how the body moves and experiences itself" (Shusterman 1992: 261) and developed this into a "systematic conception of philosophy as a distinctly embodied practice of transformative self-care" (Shusterman 2000b: 532). He also credits Foucault for including a crucial somatic dimension in his aesthetics of existence (Shusterman 2021: xi), for working in all three dimensions of somaesthetics (analytic, performative, and practical), and for "proposing alternative bodypractices to overcome the repressive ideologies entrenched in our docile bodies" (Shusterman 2000b: 535–9). This meliorative orientation of somaesthetics is crucial. It manifests in "an ascetic yet aesthetic quest for something better than one's current self" (Shusterman 2000b: 546). Shusterman affirms "Foucault's pragmatic somaesthetics" and discerns in it "a clear pragmatic orientation, something that the individual can directly translate into a discipline of improved somatic practice" (Shusterman 2000b: 539, 535).

What I want to argue is that there are resources for overcoming the challenges of altering whiteness in the understanding of normativity as embodied in lived practices that Foucault and Shusterman share. On this view, the path to ethically improved ways of living as white resides not in theoretical discourse or critique of white privilege but a different aesthetics of existence. Individual reflection and social critique are not enough to overcome (embodied) white ignorance.

Shusterman's somaesthetic analyses help us understand how "[o]ur ethical concepts and norms—along with the social and political institutions that both reflect and reinforce them—depend on social forms of life including the ways we experience our bodies and the ways that others treat them" (Shusterman 2014: 9). This stance locates the source of the normativity manifested in disciplinary or normalizing discourses not in large-scale ideologies or worldviews but in our daily lived practices and the bodily comportment that supports them. On this view, the chief locus of change is not rational critique of belief systems but how norms are lived and embodied in our selves and in our quotidian interactions with others. Cressida Heyes makes this point most clearly: "Thinking ourselves differently is important, but even more so is practicing ourselves into something new; I value the asketic effort over the intellectual struggle for self-knowledge" (Heyes 2007: 9).

Among the insights that Shusterman gleans from Foucault are both how power functions through inscribing domination on bodies and how altering our bodily practices and ways of living and being the world is a site of resistance. As Shusterman explains, "entire ideologies of domination can thus be covertly materialized and preserved by encoding them in somatic norms that, as bodily habits, get typically taken for granted and so escape critical consciousness." "But just as oppressive power relations impose repressive identities that are encoded and sustained in our bodies," he continues, "so they can be challenged by alternative somatic practices" (Shusterman 2000b: 534–5).[8]

The key Foucauldian perception here is that responding to disciplinary power, like that manifested in whiteness, given its productive, subject-forming, rather than merely constraining, force, demands self-transformation rather than liberation (Koopman 2013: 209). He zeroed in on where techniques of domination and techniques of the self intersect: "the points where the technologies of domination of individuals over one another have recourse to processes by which the individual acts upon himself ... And ... the points where techniques of the self are integrated into structures of coercion and domination" (1993: 203). As we have seen, the experience of white privilege empowers rather than restrains. In Thomas Dumm's view, Foucault's late turn to ethics is driven by the search for an alternative to the forces of normalization. Drawing on Georges Canguilhem's insights, Dumm suggests that the care of the self, for Foucault, is "an element in a series of resistances to the terms that have operated to define the self in reference to the pregiven identities of normalizing discourse" (Dumm 1996: 137). Although in the context of Black (rather than white) experience, Paul Taylor also has extolled "the liberatory potential of the aesthetic" and called for development of "an aesthetics of resistance" (Taylor 2017: 219, 227).

The importance of these insights for transforming whiteness is that we must go beyond altering cognitive beliefs. It means targeting unconscious and embodied habits, particularly the "somatic social norms that, as bodily habits, are typically taken for granted and so escape critical consciousness" (Shusterman 2008: 22). Oppressive social norms are sustained by somatic scripts, which include racist, sexist, homophobic, and other forms of prejudice and discrimination that have a visceral basis impenetrable by rational argument. The enabling norms of whiteness likewise rely on somatic scripts. Sullivan highlights the centrality of physiological reactions and "affective knowledge," and how "white privilege continues to operate as much, if not more through human biology than through mental beliefs, hidden and 'invisible' because it is a product of gut reactions rather than conscious decision or choice" (Sullivan 2014b: 593). Yancy describes these features as "somatic normativity" (Yancy 2016: 221). Social norms depend on the cooperation of our bodies (Stitzlein 2008: 70).

Somatic exploration, then, is a means to "challenge and dissolve entrenched subjectivities by disturbing their entrenched somatic habits" and the larger norms they support (Shusterman 1997: 35). However, as we have seen, in the case of white experience, the lack of access to reliable knowledge about oneself is a limitation. Nevertheless, the value of a somaesthetic approach is that it is not solely oriented to discursive knowledge. Rather, it includes "the nondiscursive somatic dimension of life" (Shusterman 1997: 31). Even though we cannot escape our language-infused forms of life, "we can still use the body's nonlinguistic experiences to escape or explode some particular discursive yoke that oppresses or constrains" (Shusterman 1997: 34). It is this appeal to bodily comportment that offers a way to challenge and transform white ignorance and privilege.

Counter-Conduct and Whiteness as a Style of Existence

A somaesthetic approach foregrounding habits, practices, and bodily comportment enables us to view whiteness itself not as a free-floating abstraction but as something we *do*. Barbara Applebaum elucidates that whiteness is "a doing: less a property of skin than *an enactment of power reproducing its* dominance in both explicit and implicit ways." On this view, white privilege and white fragility are forms of "*doing* whiteness" (Applebaum 2017: 868–9). As Yancy puts it, "whiteness is a powerful *embodied* form of being-in-the-world" (Yancy 2016: 221). Yet, as noted earlier, for all the richness of existing analyses of white normativity and calls for a novel white subjectivity, they can be frustratingly abstract and lacking in practical guidance. The ethical deficiencies that, thanks to white ignorance, accompany living and being as white, seem to put the prospect of positive ethical self-transformation out of reach.

In this final section, I draw on both Foucauldian and somaesthetic insights to suggest a site and set of practices for transformative white agency—that is, an alternative way of living and being ethically as white. If white normativity is located in the habits of white bodies, then altering white somatic comportment is how to transform the norms of whiteness. What we need, then, is "a radically different aesthetics of dwelling, of being-in-the-world, of being near, a different way or style of somatic comportment, sensing, feeling, emoting, perceiving" (Yancy 2016: 255). To make this case, I argue that we treat whiteness as an aesthetic style of existence and cultivate what Foucault termed "counter-conduct." I suggest that ways of living whiteness differently can be achieved through an alternative aesthetics of existence that manifests counter-conduct and divergent somatic style. A bit of explanation is required here to establish the ethical sense in which both style and counter-conduct are understood, as well as to explain the advantages of thinking of whiteness as a style.

Although he does not discuss whiteness specifically, Shusterman describes style more broadly as "a disposition or habit to perform or appear in a certain manner or set of ways." It entails "an intentionality that animates the various ways the person acts, feels, thinks, and desires—an animating spirit that underlies her looks and other somatic dimensions of sensory appearance and that helps define a person's character or personality" (Shusterman 2011b: 151, 156).[9] Similarly, Ladelle McWhorter holds that "[s]tyle involves all our practices of self-overcoming and self-transformation. It comprises all our *askeses,* our disciplined pleasures … Style is the form that human existence takes, and it is the process of forming that existence. The work of style is the artistry with which we live our lives" (McWhorter 1999: 190).

So what would it mean to consider whiteness a style? This idea is not without precedent. Sullivan has named the racial style that functions to maintain white privilege "whiteliness" (Sullivan 2006: 165). Yancy has called for "a form of white antiracist *Bildung*" to develop "a new way of seeing, a new way of knowing, a new way of being" that can be understood as "a corporeal style, and a dispositional sensibility that troubles the insularity of whiteness." The objective is to encourage alternatives to "acting whitely" (Yancy 2016: 42) beyond dominant—and often inscrutable to white people themselves—modes of performing whiteness. Whatever else it may be, whiteness is a somatic style.[10]

Why a style of living should be regarded as a matter of ethics already has been addressed by Foucault. As Davidson establishes in an illuminating commentary, on the ancient model from which Foucault draws, "[e]thical problems were not resolved by producing a list of required, permitted, and forbidden actions, but were centered around one's attitude to oneself, and so to others and the world—one's style of living" (Davidson 1994: 134).[11] Thinking of style in this way removes ethics from "the quest for universal standards of behavior that legislate conformity and normalization" and instead "seeks to open possibilities for new relations to self and events in the world" (Bernauer and Mahon 1994: 153–4). Andrew Dilts puts it this way: "what it means to become an ethical subject is to engage in practices of the self … that are explicitly self-conscious of their status as forming the self in relation to existing rules of conduct, or styles of existence" (Dilts 2011: 144).

Shusterman likewise has written about Foucault's "ethics of self-stylization" (Shusterman 1997: 56), elucidating how Foucault understands the body as "a medium of aesthetic self-stylization through demanding discipline and critical control" (Shusterman 1997: 35–6), as well as "[t]he essential connection of somatic and ethical style" (Shusterman 2011b: 148).[12] Shusterman defines a somatic style as "a disposition or habit to perform or appear in a certain manner or set of ways" (Shusterman 2011b: 151). A crucial reminder here is that "style" is not to be understood as merely a surface pretension. As Shusterman explains, "style is simply an integral part of one's own being, so that changing one's style means in some way changing one's self" (Shusterman 2011b: 156). Altering one's style indeed is part and parcel of altering somatic normativity: "our moral feelings and dispositions are always already somatic, just as our somatic style is always already shaped by the spirit and ethical norms of the social world" (Shusterman 2011b: 158). Applebaum explains why contextualizing performances of whiteness within a normative frame is so important: "Because norms only exist in our particular performance of them, norms are not stable and can be subverted" (Applebaum 2017: 869).

The full power of somatic style in the context of normalizing forces is revealed when we link it to Foucault's notion of "counter-conduct." Davidson has provided the fullest account of this underappreciated idea in Foucault: "counter-conduct, political and ethical, is an activity that transforms one's relation to oneself and to others; it is the active intervention of individuals and constellations of individuals in the domain of the ethical and political practices and forces that shape us" (Davidson 2011: 32).[13] Counter-conduct enacts unconventional behavior that opens new ethical and political possibilities: "To become other than what we are requires an ethics and politics of counter-conduct" (Davidson 2011: 37). Importantly, Foucault does not neglect the role of social context in supporting counter-conduct—for example, in his discussion of friendship (Davidson 2011: 34)—calling to mind John Dewey's view of "community and political engagement as central to aesthetic self-construction" (Shusterman 1997: 8).[14]

While, again, these ideas have not been applied to whiteness specifically, we have an analog in Foucault's discussion of "[g]ay counter-conduct" as "a new mode of life" (Davidson 2011: 33). Among the features which distinguished gay life for Foucault was its mode of "*askésis*" and "style of life" (Davidson 1994: 131). Shusterman pursues Foucault's potential for "creating a radically new way of life and self-stylized ethical subject" in the context of Foucault's work on transgressive S/M practices. However, Shusterman's turn to style and stylization is a way to overcome what he dubs "Foucault's dilemma"—namely, that

> self-transformation must be different enough to resist the homogenizing pressures of normalizing powers and yet be accessible enough to be understood and adopted by ordinary subjects normalized by those powers. Some way must be found to transcend standardized norms without exceeding the reach of common people. (Shusterman 1997: 58)

One insight applicable to the context of race is how "our selves are not fixed ontological identities but, instead, socially constructed roles that we play with respect to others." As a result, the path to self-transformation of those identities is "deliberately adopting different role-playing performances" (Shusterman 2000b: 541).

What, then, would a novel white aesthetic style look like? A relevant example of an alternative somatic style of whiteness is the "wigger" discussed by Crispin Sartwell: "the white person who acts like a black person," particularly in the context of hip-hop music and culture (Sartwell 2005: 35). "Wiggerism" is "an aesthetic repertoire that pits itself against the aesthetic canons associated with whiteness" in part by making visible aspects of white aesthetics that are otherwise "unmarked and normative" (Sartwell 2005: 36). As Sartwell explains, wiggerism is a form of self-critique: "part of what most wiggers are attacking is themselves; part of what they are violating is the inscription of white culture on their own bodies and expressions" (Sartwell 2005: 43).[15] To put it in Foucault's terms, they are enacting a new ethics or *rapport à soi*. This example affirms how "[p]olitical resistance to oppressive normalizing powers is pursued by transforming the normalized self into something radically different and more attractively powerful" (Shusterman 1997: 57).

Clearly, wiggerism is only one example; more work on developing alternative somatic styles of whiteness no doubt is needed.[16] The point is that under the pressure of the norms of white supremacy and white privilege, the Foucauldian path to resistance is through conducting ourselves differently, both ethically and aesthetically.

Conclusion

The argument advanced in this chapter started with recent insights into the ethical deficiencies that accompany normalized white subjectivity and that curtail its capacity for self-improvement. It held that ignoring the dimensions of the moral life associated with Foucault's thinking around the ethic of an aesthetic approach to existence—knowledge of oneself, care of oneself, and one's style of life—undermines our capacity "to take account of ourselves, of who we have become, of how we might become different" (Davidson 1994: 135). If white bodies are constituted by and perpetuate practices, discourses, and institutions of white supremacy (Yancy 2016: 44), altering the habits and lived experiences of those white bodies is part of transforming those practices, discourses, and institutions themselves. The performative nature of whiteness calls for cultivating alternative somatic styles of living it.

The relevance for ethical and political self-transformation of an aesthetics of existence already has been theorized by both Foucault and Shusterman. I sought here to utilize their insights in a positive program of change capable of overcoming the challenges associated with transforming whiteness. I argued that the critical and meliorative emphases of somaesthetics offer practices and habits of somatic normativity that circumvent reliance on increased self-knowledge, which white ignorance often renders unavailable. By approaching whiteness as something we do—a somatic style—we can foster a Foucauldian ethics oriented to alternative forms of aesthetic self-stylization. Our best hope for promoting ethically improved white self-transformation resides in conceiving of whiteness as a style of existence and developing practices and habits of alternative embodied styles of living and being as white people.

What, then, are the prospects for ethical and aesthetic transformation of whiteness? Shusterman acknowledges that "working on one's self through one's body is not in itself a very serious challenge" to socio-political structures, though "it could perhaps instill attitudes and behavioral patterns that would favor and support social transformation" (Shusterman 1992: 260). If we take to heart Foucault's insights into the nature of disciplinary power and the most effective ways of resisting it, altering the ethics or *rapport à soi* of white people becomes a crucial and neglected site for change. As Heyes observes, "[o]ne of Foucault's key insights was that disciplinary power, at the same time as it manages and constricts our somatic selves, also enhances our capacities and develops new skills" (Heyes 2007: 7). While in short supply, conceiving of "somaesthetic practices the subvert normalization" (Heyes 2007: 127) is the most promising path to promulgating new ways of living ethically as white. That for the Greeks an ethically virtuous life was also one worthy of emulation (Shusterman 2009: 36–8) is cause for hope.

Notes

1 Cressida Heyes similarly holds that "the somatic individual is unethical to the extent that its narratives foreclose the possibility of becoming something new" (Heyes 2007: 112).
2 I discuss the transformativist and eliminativist approaches to whiteness in Voparil (forthcoming).
3 This essay also appears in Shusterman (2000a).
4 For helpful overviews of this work, see Davidson (1986; 1994).
5 The Deweyan account that Gayman develops to challenge "psycho-sexual subordinating patterns [that] are established and become entrenched as unchallenged ways of life" is compelling. The issue in the context of whiteness is that the reliance on experiential disruption may not apply: "Discerning this pattern of subjugation required a shift in student perception and, to recall Dewey's insight, this was not merely a cognitive shift but an experiential jolt" (Gayman 2011: 71). See also Koopman (2011; 2013). Still, contexts intentionally designed to problematize white experience from the outside can be imagined.
6 Shusterman helpfully clarifies that the meaning of the Delphic injunction pre-Plato was that "[k]nowing oneself was thus essentially a lesson in humility" and examines both the value and dangers surrounding the quest for self-knowledge, though not in relation to whiteness specifically (Shusterman 2011a: 6, 18).
7 Shusterman has referred to Foucault as "an exemplary but problematic pioneer" of somaesthetics and affirmed his "seminal vision of the body as a malleable site for

inscribing social power" (Shusterman 2000b: 530, 534), as well as expressed worries about his aesthetics of existence being an instance of "the postmodernist ethics of taste" (Shusterman 1992: 238). Shusterman has advocated, for democratic life, a "popular aesthetic" of self-transformation rather than the "aesthetics of avant-garde genius" sometimes favored by Foucault (Shusterman 1997: 60). See also Shusterman (1997: Chapter 1; 2021).

8   While her analysis does not involve whiteness, I take inspiration from Heyes's probing of somaesthetics for "strategies of resistance to normalization" vis-à-vis gender (Heyes 2007: chap. 5).
9   Style also is a function of what Shusterman calls our "body schema"—the "entrenched habits, dispositional mechanisms, or tendencies of movement, feeling, and attitude that are incorporated in our bodies and enable us to act skillfully and intelligently without having to think about what we are doing with our bodily parts" (Shusterman 2011b: 156).
10 See Yancy and Ryser (2008) on the performative dimension of whiteness.
11 Referencing the four dimensions of Foucauldian ethics, Davidson continues: "I propose we take each particular conceptual combination of ethical substance, mode of subjection, self-forming activity, and telos as representing a style of life." He urges further that "the care of self must itself be placed in the context of a style of life, that in order to make sense of the care of the self we must widen our vision to include the style of life that gives form and direction to the self's relation to itself" (Davidson 1994: 125, 134).
12 Paul Veyne also highlighted the ethical dimension in Foucault as "a work of the self on the self, a self-stylization" (Veyne 1993: 8).
13 See also Marchetti (2011).
14 Heyes also notes the communal potential of Foucauldian resistance via "gather[ing] together people who, in defying normalization, are open to the possibility of becoming something new and unanticipated" (Heyes 2007: 123).
15 The example Sartwell discusses at length is the US rapper Eminem.
16 See Voparil (forthcoming) for a more in-depth account, including the potential of performative and practical somaesthetics.

Bibliography

Alcoff, L. M. (2015), *The Future of Whiteness*, Malden (MA): Polity Press.
Applebaum, B. (2008), "White Privilege/White Complicity: Connecting 'Benefiting from' to 'Contributing to,'" *Philosophy of Education Yearbook*: 292–300.
Applebaum, B. (2017), "Comforting Discomfort as Complicity: White Fragility and the Pursuit of Invulnerability," *Hypatia*, 32 (4): 862–75.

Bernauer, J. and M. Mahon (1994), "The Ethics of Michel Foucault," in *The Cambridge Companion to Foucault*, ed. G. Gutting, 141–58, New York: Cambridge University Press.

Colapietro, V. (2011), "Situation, Meaning, and Improvisation: An Aesthetics of Existence in Dewey and Foucault," *Foucault Studies*, 11: 20–40.

Davidson, A. I. (1986), "Archaeology, Genealogy, Ethics," in *Foucault: A Critical Reader*, ed. D. C. Hoy, 221–33, Cambridge (MA): Basil Blackwell.

Davidson, A. I. (1994), "Ethics as Ascetics: Foucault, the History of Ethics, and Ancient Thought," in *The Cambridge Companion to Foucault*, ed. G. Gutting, 115–40, New York: Cambridge University Press.

Davidson, A. I. (2011), "In Praise of Counter-Conduct," *History of the Human Sciences*, 24 (4): 25–41.

Dilts, A. (2011), "From 'Entrepreneur of the Self' to 'Care of the Self': Neo-Liberal Governmentality and Foucault's Ethics," *Foucault Studies*, 12: 130–46.

Dumm, T. L. (1996), *Michel Foucault and the Politics of Freedom*, Thousand Oaks (CA): Sage Publications.

Foucault, M. (1984a), "On the Genealogy of Ethics: An Overview of Work in Progress" [1983], in *The Foucault Reader*, ed. P. Rabinow, 340–72, New York: Pantheon Books.

Foucault, M. (1984b), "Politics and Ethics: An Interview," in *The Foucault Reader*, ed. P. Rabinow, 373–80, New York: Pantheon Books.

Foucault, M. (1984c), "What Is Enlightenment?," in *The Foucault Reader*, ed. P. Rabinow, 32–50, New York: Pantheon Books.

Foucault, M. (1989), *Foucault Live: Collected Interviews, 1961–1984*, ed. S. Lotringer, New York: Semiotext(e).

Foucault, M. (1990), *The History of Sexuality. Vol. 2: The Use of Pleasure* [1984], trans. R. Hurley, New York: Vintage Books.

Foucault, M. (1993), "About the Beginning of the Hermeneutics of the Self: Two Lectures at Dartmouth," *Political Theory*, 21 (2): 198–227.

Foucault, M. (2007), *Security, Territory, Population: Lectures at the Collège de France, 1977–1978*, ed. M. Senellart, New York: Palgrave MacMillan.

Gayman, C. (2011), "Politicizing the Personal: Thinking about the Feminist Subject with Michel Foucault and John Dewey," *Foucault Studies*, 11: 63–75.

Granger, D. A. (2010), "Somaesthetics and Racism: Toward an Embodied Pedagogy of Difference," *The Journal of Aesthetic Education*, 44 (3): 69–81.

Heyes, C. J. (2007), *Self-Transformations: Foucault, Ethics, and Normalized Bodies*, New York: Oxford University Press.

James, R. (2013), "Oppression, Privilege, & Aesthetics: The Use of the Aesthetic in Theories of Race, Gender, and Sexuality, and the Role of Race, Gender, and Sexuality in Philosophical Aesthetics," *Philosophy Compass*, 8 (2): 101–16.

Jolles, M. (2012), "Between Embodied Subjects and Objects: Narrative Somaesthetics," *Hypatia*, 27 (2): 301–18.

Koopman, C. (2011), "Genealogical Pragmatism: How History Matters for Foucault and Dewey," *Journal of the Philosophy of History*, 5 (3): 533–61.

Koopman, C. (2013), *Genealogy as Critique: Foucault and the Problems of Modernity*, Bloomington: Indiana University Press.

MacMullan, T. (2009), *Habits of Whiteness: A Pragmatist Reconstruction*, Bloomington: Indiana University Press.

Marchetti, S. (2011), "James, Nietzsche and Foucault on Ethics and the Self," *Foucault Studies*, 11: 126–55.

McWhorter, L. (1999), *Bodies and Pleasures: Foucault and the Politics of Sexual Normalization*, Bloomington: Indiana University Press.

Medina, J. (2013), *The Epistemology of Resistance: Gender and Racial Oppression, Epistemic Injustice, and Resistant Imaginations*, New York: Oxford University Press.

Mills, C. W. (2007), "White Ignorance," in *Race and Epistemologies of Ignorance*, eds. S. Sullivan and N. Tuana, 11–38, Albany (NY): State University of New York Press.

Sartwell, C. (2005), "'Wigger,'" in *White on White/Black on Black*, ed. G. Yancy, 35–48, Lanham (MD): Rowman & Littlefield.

Shusterman, R. (1992), *Pragmatist Aesthetics: Living Beauty, Rethinking Art*, Cambridge (MA): Blackwell.

Shusterman, R. (1997), *Practicing Philosophy: Pragmatism and the Philosophical Life*, New York: Routledge.

Shusterman, R. (2000a), *Performing Live: Aesthetic Alternatives for the Ends of Art*, Ithaca (NY): Cornell University Press.

Shusterman, R. (2000b), "Somaesthetics and the Care of the Self: The Case of Foucault," *The Monist*, 83 (4): 530–51.

Shusterman, R. (2008), *Body Consciousness: A Philosophy of Mindfulness and Somaesthetics*. New York: Cambridge University Press.

Shusterman, R. (2009), "The Convergence of Ethics and Aesthetics: A Genealogical, Pragmatist Perspective," in *The Hand and the Soul: Ethics and Aesthetics in Architecture and Art*, ed. S. Iliescu, 33–43, Charlottesville (VA): University of Virginia Press.

Shusterman, R. (2011a), "Enhanced Cognition, Ethics, and Some Problems of Self-Knowledge," *Journal of Speculative Philosophy*, 25 (1): 3–21.

Shusterman, R. (2011b), "Somatic Style," *Journal of Aesthetics and Art Criticism*, 69 (2): 147–59.

Shusterman, R. (2014), "Somaesthetics and Politics: Incorporating Pragmatist Aesthetics for Social Action," in *Beauty, Responsibility, and Power: Ethical and Political Consequences of Pragmatist Aesthetics*, eds. L. Koczanowicz and K. Liszka, 5–18, New York: Rodopi.

Shusterman, R. (2019), "Bodies in the Streets: The Soma, the City, and the Art of Living," in *Bodies in the Streets: The Somaesthetics of City Life*, ed. R. Shusterman, 13–37, Boston: Brill.

Shusterman, R. (2021), *Ars Erotica: Sex and Somaesthetics in the Classical Arts of Love*, Cambridge: Cambridge University Press.

Stitzlein, S. M. (2008), *Breaking Bad Habits of Race and Gender: Transforming Identity in Schools*, Lanham, MD: Rowman & Littlefield.

Sullivan, S. (2006), *Revealing Whiteness: The Unconscious Habits of Racial Privilege*, Bloomington: Indiana University Press.

Sullivan, S. (2014a), *Good White People: The Problem with Middle-Class White Anti-Racism*, Albany (NY): State University of New York Press.

Sullivan, S. (2014b), "The Hearts and Guts of White People," *Journal of Religious Ethics*, 42 (4): 591–611.

Sullivan, S. (2019), *White Privilege*, Medford (MA): Polity Press.

Taylor, P. C. (2007), "Race, Ethics, Seduction, Politics: On Shannon Sullivan's Revealing Whiteness," *Journal of Speculative Philosophy*, 21 (3): 201–9.

Taylor, P. C. (2017), "An Aesthetics of Resistance: Deweyan Experimentalism and Epistemic Injustice," in *Pragmatism and Justice*, eds. S. Dieleman, D. Rondel, and C. Voparil, 215–30, New York: Oxford University Press.

Veyne, P. (1993), "The Final Foucault and His Ethics," *Critical Inquiry*, 20 (1): 1–9.

Voparil, C. (forthcoming), "Somaesthetics and the Somatic Experience of White Privilege," in *Bodies of Politics: Explorations in Somaesthetics and Somapower*, ed. L. Koczanowicz, Boston: Brill.

Yancy, G. (2012), *Look, a White! Philosophical Essays on Whiteness*, Philadelphia: Temple University Press.

Yancy, G. (2016), *Black Bodies, White Gazes: The Continuing Significance of Race in America*, Second edition, Lanham (MD): Rowman & Littlefield.

Yancy, G. and T. A. Ryser (2008), "Whiting Up and Blacking Out: White Privilege, Race, and White Chicks," *African American Review*, 42 (3–4): 731–46.

8

Aphrodisia, Eros, Charis: Holistic Bodies and the Stylistic of Reciprocity

Barbara Formis

Soma

The notion of somatics plays a crucial role in philosophy for two reasons: first, it allows the notional and transhistorical rehabilitation of the idea of the body; second, it represents the attempt to overcome the typically Western dualism between physics and metaphysics. From these two reasons, somatics rehabilitates the body as a concept not only from a speculative and theoretical standpoint, but also from a cultural and historical perspective. Somatics overcomes dualisms by *rethinking the body as a whole*. It is this particular aspect of somatics that I propose to study here.

The holistic vision of the body encourages the alliance of the spiritual and the physiological, the aesthetic and the ethical, with the aim of overcoming the dualisms at the core of Eurocentric philosophical thought. In the debate surrounding the body/mind problem, this unifying approach has certain advantages. By bringing together supposedly separate dimensions, such as physiology and psychology, theory and practice, somatics avoids certain pitfalls inherent in Cartesian or Kantian philosophies, notably the intellectual attitude that gives primacy to doubt as a condition for reflection (Descartes), or the posture of distanciation from sense pleasure as a method to be applied in order to achieve aesthetic pleasure (Kant). Cartesian doubt and Kantian disinterestedness are two very different ways of excluding the body. This is not the place to go into details about the prejudices toward somatics, but I would point out that these pitfalls do not seem to me to be peculiar to the philosophies of Descartes and Kant, but they are rather caused by the interpretations of these theories. Indeed, the use and interpretation of theories are often more restrictive and constraining than the philosophies from which they draw their inspiration. More specifically for our purposes, the role of *soma*, as Richard Shusterman teaches us, is indisputable and central to rehabilitating aesthetics as a discipline. In *Pragmatist Aesthetics*, Shusterman puts it this way:

> As the aesthetic was distinguished from the more rational realms of knowledge and action, so it was also firmly differentiated from the more sensate and appetitive gratifications of embodied human nature, aesthetic pleasure rather residing in distanced, disinterested contemplation of formal properties. (PA: 212)

This "hostility" of aesthetics toward the body, in particular, and embodiment, in general, needs to be abandoned in order to reunite aesthetics with the body, or even better, to reunite aesthetics with its own sources and its original sense of *aesthesis*. The etymology of the word "aesthetics" leads us to the Greek *aisthéis, aisthanomai*, which means understanding through sensation but also through the intellect: it refers to a knowledge based on sensations and feelings, analogous to logical and rational knowledge. As a matter of fact, the history of ideas shows that aesthetics has the body as its foundation: from Baumgarten onward, and later with Burke, aesthetics is based on the senses, sensations, and is understood as an intelligent form of sensibility. Aesthetics therefore does not exclude kinesthetics, somatics, embodiment, and lived experience. In the twentieth century, aesthetics has opened up a considerable place for the body, and the conceptualizations derived from the body have become key notions in philosophy, and not just in the discipline of aesthetics.

For instance, in Foucault's work, somatics is linked more to history and politics than to the realms of art or creativity. In the third volume of *L'Histoire de la sexualité*, entitled *Le souci de soi* (*The Care of the Self*), Foucault illustrates not only the link between culture and somatics through the question of subjectivization, but also the problem of desire as a relationship to others. Foucault examines the reevaluation of the body and sexual pleasure as the foundation of the formation of the individual. He does this by analyzing texts that are not often studied, such as those by Artemidorus, Galen, and Pseudo-Lucian. These early texts are decisive in the establishment of the general purpose of culture, that purpose being the emergence of a singular personality, notably a man, capable of making the best use of his body and mind, harmoniously educated, and capable of assuming political functions. Somatics is thus the foundation of politics. Self-concern is not narrow egoism, and through somatics Foucault seeks to re-establish a classical ancient tradition of bodily education as a foundation for politics.

In line with this research into the somatic, Foucault also spoke more generally of "biopower." This notion serves to distinguish between a "traditional" and a "modern" form of power exercised over life, marking an important caesura in the history of techniques of power. Foucault describes two main modalities: the discipline of bodies and the biopolitics of populations. Disciplinary power is implemented in institutions (hospitals, factories, schools, etc.) and consists in investing the body of each individual with techniques for distributing space, breaking down gestures, examining abilities, and using surveillance and sanction mechanisms, in order to extract, finalize, and enhance useful forces.

"Biopolitics," on the other hand—in the narrow sense of one of the two modalities of biopower—consists in the state's power to regulate populations: modifying birth rates, preventing or stopping endemics (as we saw during the Covid-19 pandemic), reducing infirmities or invalidities, controlling the general environment of existence (urban policies), etc. In his 1979 lecture at the Collège de France entitled *La Naissance de la biopolitique*, Foucault seems at times to identify neoliberalism and the concept of biopolitics, as if neoliberalism were another way of defining the state's control over human capital. Taking into account bodily control and biological power, Foucault thus helps us to understand the link between somatics and knowledge.

Taking inspiration from Foucault and Shusterman, what terminology should we choose to describe this philosophical field that specifically investigates somatics as an epistemological field? It is not easy to choose: embodiment, body-ownership, bio-power, proprioception, sensitivity, the concepts seem to abound. In a similar manner to Foucault and Shusterman, I base my intellectual perspective on a conviction that is as simple to formulate as it is rare in the philosophical field: *the body thinks*. The originality of both Shusterman's somaesthetic approach and Foucault's stylistics of existence lies in the reappraisal of "minor" knowledge, at an artistic, cultural, and popular level. Somaesthetics (Shusterman) advocates experience as the guiding principle of research and aims to overcome the old dualisms: theory/practice, action/idea, fact/value, body/mind. The stylistics of existence (Foucault) allows us to define power relationships and methods of emancipation in the routine and collective use of our bodies.

In both cases, for Shusterman and Foucault, it is a question of setting up a philosophy of the body in which the "of" is understood as both an objective and subjective genitive, and this genesis does not exist at a standstill; it takes shape in the movement and multiple interactions of the body, to the point at which the body is rethought in turn. The idea of the body is reshaped in order to distance it from the idea of the object, or an inert corpse, or a defined solid form. The body is in movement and therefore in relation, it models itself and produces meaning through multiple links that are often involuntary and aleatory. In this contribution, I hope to elucidate this idea of relationship through the idea of reciprocity, linked conceptually to the Greek term *charis* that is related to the notion of "consent," but should not be reduced to it.

Aisthesis

Aesthetics, understood as the dimension of the sensible and the senses and a properly sensitive dimension, is a discipline that enables us to undertake a precise analysis of the relationship between practice and theory in the field of philosophy, notably through the notion of "experience." Aesthetics goes beyond the confines of the art world and reunites with bodily sensations. From the point of view of somaesthetics and the stylistics of existence, art, rather than being restricted to an elite of initiates, is instead a way of participating in the world and relating to others. Shusterman's somaesthetics and Foucault's stylistics of existence both consider the body as a means of self-awareness, but also as the seat of transformation, reassessing the importance of material and physical tasks usually excluded from the realm of knowledge.

By considering sensible experience as the foundation of knowledge and power, these two philosophical approaches also reveal an aesthetic dimension in which the body is rehabilitated. It is the case that the concept of the body challenges the classical understanding of aesthetics as a contemplative and distancing experience. It also challenges the traditional classification of the arts, which devalues the arts of the body (such as dance and theater) in favor of the arts that entail physical separation (such as painting and sculpture). But these aesthetic problems are merely a reflection of the devaluation of the body in culture; Foucault and Shusterman help us in counteracting this devaluation.

Shusterman has forged his own philosophy around an innovative concept, the neologism *somaesthetics*, which he coined in 1996. This concept serves to capture the possibility of an aesthetics of the body. In Shusterman's own words, "somaesthetics can be … defined as the critical, meliorative study of the experience and use of one's body as a locus of sensory-aesthetic appreciation *(aisthesis)* and creative self-fashioning" (PA: 267). Shusterman often uses the example of the golfer who can only improve her shot by concentrating on the gesture and not on the goal; bodily introspection and reflective distance being indispensable to the use of the self. Somaesthetics is not foreign to a certain Stoic ethic: the player must concentrate on the shot and not on the target, on the path, and not on the objective. Shusterman's lesson is this: neither art nor philosophy can be reduced to pure theory, since they always emerge from experience. Somaesthetics is founded on movement and a dynamic awareness of the body. It is not simply a question of reflecting on bodily mechanisms or defining the different modalities of organic action, but a whole investigation on the epistemological possibilities of somatic experience.

In this respect, we can clearly see the connection with Foucault's philosophy: for somaesthetics, as for the stylistics of existence, the aim is not simply cognitivist, but *aesthetic* in the broadest sense of the term. It is not simply a question of understanding what knowledge might gain from organic and corporeal knowledge, but rather of putting all intellectual convictions to the test of the *sensible* by recasting their forms of emergence and their modes of expression. So, if Foucault is not directly interested in art, this does not mean that his philosophy is not aesthetic; on the contrary, the stylistics of existence can be understood as an aesthetic discipline, as is the case in the present collective volume.

Somaesthetics and the stylistics of existence both show that aesthetic experience is not restricted to works of art. It is experienced just as much in everyday life. Art is not opposed to life, but builds on it, as Dewey admirably demonstrated in *Art as Experience*. Ordinary experience is made up of gestures, of bodily acts that enable us to move, to grasp objects, and to preserve our organism. Following John Dewey and William James, Shusterman defends a concrete way of looking at philosophy in which aesthetic experience is at the heart of reflection. The aim is to combat what Dewey critically called *the museum conception of art* (Dewey 1934: 6). At the start of his celebrated *Art as Experience*, he writes:

> Many a person who protests against the museum conception of art, still shares the fallacy from which that conception springs. For the popular notion comes from a separation of art from the objects and scenes of ordinary experience that many theorists and critics pride themselves upon holding and even elaborating. (Dewey 1934)

Following Dewey, Shusterman also argues against the idea of the autonomy of art—an idea that is very Eurocentric—and prefers to link aesthetics to the realms of health, therapy, dietetics, sexuality, and, more generally, all those habits and behaviors that make up the art of living. On the contrary, this renewed notion of aesthetics aims to show the porosity of these boundaries, while discerning the specificities of each practice and indicating the cultural and contextual links. Evidently, this anti-dualistic perspective is first and foremost an aim, not a definitive and accomplished method. Dualism is a cognitive bias that has a structuring value within our Western culture, and it would be naive to think that we can get rid of it completely: these theories are anti-dualistic while not being monistic.

Anti-dualism is not necessarily monism, but it could allow a certain form of holism. Ontological differences remain between body and mind, practice and theory, and these differences help to avoid universalism and essentialization, which are dangerous tendencies for the political dimension of scientific research. Comparisons and differences are beneficial if they do not produce sterile antagonisms; they thus serve to maintain effective tensions that reflect the variety of the world in which we are immersed in. Holism could be understood as a specific method of somatic experience and aesthetic knowledge.

Holos

Holism can be understood as a way of creating dynamics within difference. From the point of view of somatic theory, the benefit of maintaining a unifying vision of *soma* is central from a philosophical and aesthetic point of view. Somatics seeks to strike a balance between cognition and sensation. On the one hand, it is important to distance ourselves from Kantian disinterestedness, but on the other, it is important not to fall into hedonism, which would open the door to a passive, even pathological reception of pleasure, ultimately preventing aesthetic experience.

Foucault's notion of self-care is in line with pragmatist aesthetics, even before Shusterman. One of the important lessons from pragmatism, and especially from Dewey's *Art as Experience*, is that aesthetic experience cannot be reduced to an immediate, unconscious, and totally unreflective sensation. Pragmatism is not oriented toward an idea of the practice of a body devoid of consciousness; moreover, it refuses to equate experience with pleasure, and in particular with sensual pleasure. Pragmatism allows to understand aesthetics as a way of undergoing experience that is both sensitive and intellectual.

How can we understand the idea of holism from the perspective of aesthetics? How can we avoid falling into generalization? One objection comes from Shusterman's reading of the notion of biopower. In a text on Foucault

(Shusterman 2000a), Shusterman questions the risks of generalization or universalization that the idea of holism may incur. The problem is philosophical and cultural, according to Shusterman, who writes:

> If Emerson and Nietzsche are right that each self is essentially unique (the unrepeatable product of countless contingencies), shouldn't each self require his or her own special constellation of body disciplines? But, on the other hand, don't our embodied selves share significant commonalities of biological make-up and societal conditioning that would allow some interesting generalizations about the values and risks of different somatic methods? How could philosophy or science (or even practical life) be possible without such generalization? (Shusterman 2000a: 538–9)

This shows that unification cannot be confused with simple generalization. Somatic holism does not have to be monolithic and stable, but must project itself into changing, processual forms and dynamics in which multiple shapes of somatics can unfold into organic, spiritual, cognitive, affective, metaphysical, practical, and theoretical forms. To put it differently, if somatics, as a field of aesthetics, helps us to overcome conventional Western dualisms, it is not in order to impose a forced union erasing all contrasts, but rather in order to maintain a relationship between differences. In somatics, distinctions do not disappear, they are mutualized.

From an etymological point of view, it is interesting to note that the notion of "sexuality," which both Shusterman and Foucault are interested in, is etymologically and conceptually rooted in the idea of segmentation. Indeed, the etymological root of the term *sex* is the idea of division, deriving from the Latin *sexus* and from the root *sec*, which gave *seco*, meaning "to cut," "to separate," or "to divide." Conceptually, sexual difference is understood as a separation and poses the problem of classification. In contrast, the idea of holism as the overcoming of separations thus provides a method of philosophical reflection that does not only valorize discernment and distinction, but rather relationships of power and support.

The question that I would like to ask is the following: What would happen if, instead of applying a dualistic approach, we took a holistic approach to the question of sexuality? It seems important to reiterate that sexuality cannot be scientifically determined by an empirical psychology underpinned by biology, but it can be better understood as based on a complex cultural and social process. Sexuation is only one aspect of a fundamental sexuality that goes beyond the organic and physiological framework. Simone De Beauvoir's famous *incipit* in

The Second Sex, "*on ne naît pas femme, on le devient*" ("one is not born a woman but rather becomes one"), does not only apply to women: everyone goes through phases of transformation and discovery that constitute the formation of their sexual gender, beyond biological assignment at birth and beyond clichés about heterosexuality.

The artificial nature of sexuality as division can be unmasked by the example of hermaphrodites or intersex people, who are unfortunately considered as belonging out of the ordinary, or even monstrosities. In *Les Anormaux*, Foucault recounts the case of Antide Collas, a resident of Dôle, who was denounced as a hermaphrodite, condemned of satanism, and burned alive. The misconception about hermaphroditism is nowadays less brutal, but is still at work in a social process of discrimination and marginalization. In reality, hermaphroditism should not be considered an exception to the norm. As Chantal Jaquet writes:

> Hermaphroditism escapes the sexual alternative of masculine and feminine and cannot be reduced to it, unless we deny the specificity and particularity of a group of human beings. The existence of a sexual dichotomy is therefore not a universal rule. To present it as a law is to consider exceptions as anomalies, or should not be conceived as sexual indeterminacy, but as a sexual determination other than the one we are used to seeing. (Jaquet 2001: 309; my translation)

From this perspective, I would like to take a step further by adding that hermaphroditism not only designates a category in its own right, but could even help us demonstrate that binarism is the result of a process of sexuation based on the separatist, dividing idea of sexuality. In contrast to this binary and heteronormative conception, and similarly to hermaphrodites and intersex, we could add trans and non-binary people to the category of sexual identity that demonstrate the possibility of a holistic approach to the body. As we know, sexuality is not an autonomous biological and cultural cycle, but it is part of a circuit of affects and social relations that transcends the desire for classification and sectorialization. Thus, LGBTQ+ identities clearly demonstrate the broad spectrum of sexuality that contradicts the idea that heterosexuality can be considered a cultural norm and a physical normality. Transexuals and non-binary people, or genderfluid individuals, thus testify to the possibility of a gender identity that maintains the holistic dynamic and reconfigures the notion of sexuality beyond segmentation.

The notion of the holistic body thus helps us to understand that the reduction of otherness to male-female bipolarity is ideologically motivated by the desire to justify the oppressive and normative processes of patriarchy. As Foucault had already elucidated with his idea of biopolitics, there is nothing simple about being normal and ordinary; on the contrary, diversity and difference are the natural form of human identities, and conformism is constituted by disciplinary constraints. Of course, we should be careful and not be creating further confusions: blurring a gender dichotomy is not the same thing as holism. Somebody who is trans could have a sexuality entirely focused on particular organs and acts, not at all holistic with regard to the body and the multiple pleasures that somatic experience provides. The idea of sexuality as a spectrum of practices focuses more on the fluidity of gender than to the sectorization of identities. Rather than exceptional, what we call hermaphroditism is exemplary despite its rarity, and transexuality or non-binarism implement the possibility of sexuality beyond the division produced by the process of sexuation.

Aphrodisia

As we saw earlier, aesthetics is not simply a theory of art, but rather a philosophy of experience and the form of pleasure that emerge from it. We also have seen that the holistic body is not a unified, homogeneous whole; on the contrary, it is made up of heterogeneous qualities that are in continual transformation. It is around this transformation of the sensible that aesthetics can help understand pleasure as a cognitive aspect of somatic experience. Within this research on sensation and cognition, the place of pleasure is key.

As such, both Shusterman and Foucault propose a significant alternative to the Kantian-inspired doctrine of disinterestedness. Contrary to Kant's idea of "pure" pleasure, they propose an approach in which pleasure is "impure" because it is linked to the pleasurable, to a utilitarian form of pleasure close to the Greek idea of *aphrodisia*, studied by Foucault in *L'Usage des plaisirs* and clearly distinct from both *epithumia*, which requires a violent passion, and *orexis*, understood as a sexual appetite close to a physiological need. *Aphrodisia* as a type of pleasure has an aesthetic, even cultural dimension that is different from simple physiology. From the point of view of the pleasurable, on the contrary to Kant, aesthetic experience is engaged and situated in a precise cultural and sociological context. This engagement has its limits: if Shusterman's philosophy has been accused of hedonism, Foucault's has been criticized for advocating violence, through his emancipatory example of sadomasochism.

More generally, what the notion of the pleasurable allows Shusterman and Foucault to work on is the level of passivity in general that is present in the experience of pleasure. How can one experience bodily pleasure without losing one's subjective freedom? How can the sensation of pleasure produce a feeling of beauty without subjugation? How can we use our bodies without becoming objectified? These are the kind of questions Richard Shusterman poses through his analysis of Foucault's somaesthetics (Shusterman 2000a), focusing in particular on the performative aspect of Foucault's somatics, an aspect he understands as being "distinct from actual practice" (Shusterman 2000a: 538). In this text, the main issue that Shusterman investigates via his reading of Foucault is the "malleable" nature of the body: "Foucault's seminal vision of the body as a malleable site for inscribing social power reveals the crucial role somatics can play for political philosophy" (Shusterman 2000a: 534).

The problem Shusterman identifies with Foucault's somatic use of pleasure is the intensity and violence of the somatic inscription, as if this somatic harshness were the condition for instituting power over docile bodies. Norms are presented as natural rules to be followed. Yet it is through norms that biopower is diffused: diffused into habits, usages, and continuous pressures that combine to increase the docility and usefulness of bodies. We should remember, however, that according to Foucault the body is not malleable and docile in itself, but becomes so through the coercion and control of disciplines. In other words, the malleability of bodies is not the condition of possibility of power, but on the contrary its finality.

Another aspect of Shusterman's reading of Foucault is more specifically related to our subject, concerning the multiplication of pleasures. Foucault finds that the harshness of biopower can be countered by equally intense emancipatory practices (such as S/M practices). From Foucault's point of view, then, it seems that the intensity of coercion is harmful if it takes place through the political discipline of power, but it can become beneficial if it enables bodily emancipation, because intense experience is not simply stronger, but also enables a variety of pleasurable experiences. By multiplying pleasures through a spectrum of gradations and intensities, the subject can free himself/herself from biopower. However, this multiplication can mask another form of reduction in the evaluation of the types of pleasure, if a hierarchy of pleasures is instituted. According to Shusterman:

> Here we reach a second objection to Foucault's somaesthetics. By affirming only the most intense pleasures, which he identifies with strong drugs and sex, Foucault again reduces our range of pleasures, thus confounding his explicit aim of rendering us infinitely more susceptible to pleasure through multiple modalities. (Shusterman 2000a: 541)

There may indeed be a reductive aspect in favoring more intense and stronger forms of pleasure, but this reduction is not necessarily a way of giving primacy to sensation and the somatic, rather the opposite, according to Shusterman.

> Though Foucault errs in presuming that intensity of delight requires violent sensory stimuli, his devotion to intense pleasures should be charitably understood in this transcendental connection. The aim is not sensual delectation per se, but the self-transformation that intense pleasure can induce. (Shusterman 2000a: 545)

Shusterman's reading of Foucault helps us notice something quite unexpected: the intensification of pleasures and the emancipation that it allows still present traces of transcendentality. In this interpretation, for Foucault somatic pleasure has a transcendental, if not universal, scope. Herein lies another form of holism to which Shusterman also partially subscribes: the transformation of the self through pleasure, a sensual form of multiple holism.

Eros

As we have seen with the exemplarity of hermaphroditism and non-binary sexual identities, the benefit of somatic holism also has an impact on the idea of sexual difference. This benefit is not only important from a philosophical point of view, but also from a cultural one, since, as Shusterman has shown, and also Foucault or Dewey before him, it is a question of understanding the somatic as a dimension that includes the reflexive and the affective, the spiritual and the practical, and that goes beyond the physical aspect of somatics. Holism can be maintained in a situation of multiplicity such as the complexity and variety of possible pleasures. Eroticism obviously goes beyond sexuality or sex, and is rooted in a dimension that is fundamentally intellectual, even transcendental, as we have seen. This cultural notion would allow us to open our thinking to non-European cultures, notably Asian ones, as demonstrated in Shusterman's recent book *Ars Erotica*, directly inspired by Foucault.

The Greek roots of the term "erotics" can help us in our conceptualization. Etymologically, Eros can be traced back to the Greek word ἔρως ("erōs"), which carries the connotation of desire, longing, or passion. In its original context, Eros was associated with both physical and spiritual aspects of love, encompassing romantic desire, sexual attraction, and a profound yearning for connection. Eros is a half-god, son of the mortal *Penia*—who symbolizes lack and begging—and *Poros*—the God of resourcefulness and expediency.

Eros implies lack and the desire for possession, and its conceptualization associates it with primarily physical love, often associated with the idea of sex, even if the concept itself has spiritual roots. In Plato, especially in the Symposium, eros symbolizes the spiritual ardor that leads to divine love and philosophical wisdom, while also assuming the role of a form of intelligence. There is certainly an instinctual dimension to eroticism, which also functions in the perpetuation of the species by adding a dimension of affectivity. The sensual and affective nature of erotics could be considered as corresponding to an "inferior" form of eroticism, as it is also shown by Aristotle, who poses intelligence against affectivity, and thus "nous" (intellect) against Plato's "eros." However, the demonic and almost divinatory euphoria of the erotic, which Plato inherits from Socrates, is the very foundation of the philosophical concepts of beauty and wisdom, and in this it is in no way inferior.

Shusterman's book *Ars Erotica* bears witness to the philosophical and cultural reasons why erotic arts possess an epistemological value; and this is not just limited to the fields of philosophy and aesthetics, but also includes issues specific to cultural studies, political theory, and moral questioning. It should be stressed straightaway that the classical idea of eroticism is by no means a holistic practice. Particularly in Ancient Greece, the idea of love was founded on the pedagogical practice of educational pederasty (*paideia*), which alone could symbolize the education of beardless young men through the penetration (anal or oral) of their bodies by their masters, notably the Sophists. Thus, pederasty as practiced in Ancient Greece was the opposite of respect and equality; on the contrary, it represented extremely strong, instituted hierarchical relationships in which erotic desire did not go both ways: the master would vehemently express his desire for beardless boys, to the point of physically chasing them down or orchestrating a kidnapping. Moreover, Eros is a demigod who walks around with an arrow—he performs his function with a weapon. We also speak of "falling" in love, which can also be understood as involving a violent loss of control, submission, and passivity.

The pederastic model of captive love is so deeply anchored at a conceptual level that Foucault reminds us there have been residual forms of this type of homosexual relationship within heterosexuality. In Plutarch's *Histories of Love*, for example, Foucault points out that we read of women, especially widows and older women, who pursue young boys and, with the complicity of a few friends, carry out kidnappings—"in part 'real', in part arranged also" (Foucault 1986: 196). Foucault underlines two features of the symmetry between heterosexual classical erotics and Greek pedagogical pederasty: the difference in age—like the Sophists, the ladies were in fact older than the boys they desired—but also the ambiguity in relation to the uses of force and violence, since the abductions were partly arranged, which may suggest that the boy consented to them. Commenting on Charicles, Foucault underlines that "the boy who is passive, hence more or less violated (*hubrismenos*), cannot experience pleasure" (Foucault 1986: 220), which implies that erotic pleasure should not be based on selfish or violent conduct, but should be able to give rise to moral conduct, and thus become exemplary.

Pedagogical and pederastic erotic practice therefore involved a tension between activity and passivity, which in no way included consent. It was in this respect that Socrates played a revolutionary role, arousing the desire of beardless boys with his insolent and politically incorrect imperturbability. Following Foucault's history of sexuality, we understand that the concept of the erotic comes up against a paradox, even a dualism: on the one hand, the pederastic love of boys, which is supposedly violent and non-consensual, and on the other, the love of women, which is an attempt at erotic egalitarianism. Foucault points to a paradox between heterosexual love and the love of boys: "the love of boys or of women is the confrontation of two forms of life, of two ways of stylizing one's pleasure" (Foucault 1986: 218).

In *Le souci de soi*, Foucault repeatedly questions the supposed naturalness of "the love of boys" versus "the love of the woman": it should be noted that pederasty requires multiplicity (boys are plural), whereas conjugal love does not admit plurality. With the end of the primacy of pederastic homosexuality, this paradox of the erotic and the use of pleasures provokes a decline of the erotics of the love of boys. Following Plutarch's and Pseudo-Lucian's texts, Foucault's points out both the "legitimacy" and the "decline as a vital theme in the stylistics of existence" of pederasty and possessive love (Foucault 1986: 192).

One of the great contributions of Foucault's philosophy of the body was to show that boys' love was considered natural, while woman's love was considered artificial. Given that true love did not have any practical purpose, the love for women had to be unmasked in its instrumental nature for the purpose of the reproduction of the species. In the classical framework of erotics, true love is excluded from the male-female relationship. The only true love is the love of boys; this is why, as the history of sexuality shows, the love of women must be framed by a legal framework such as marriage. Historically, Greco-Roman thought has placed women on the side of the artificial, and pederastic love on the side of the natural. We see that the historical texts on sexuality arise to a conceptualization of behaviors and desires only from the masculine point of view. The emerging subjectivity that arises through the history of desires and pleasures is exclusively a male figure related to social hierarchy according to which he evolves.

Over and above the genuine or artificial quality of feminine or masculine forms of love, what is interesting to note, following Foucault, are the power relationships and the uses of pleasure that take the form of violence. This violence is the fruit of the segmentation and dissection that underpins the patriarchal understanding of the notion of sexuality. If history shows a clash between two forms of domination, it is not only because there is, as Foucault writes, a "dualism of *aphrodisia*" (Foucault 1986: 263), but also because the conception of sexuality is necessarily linked to an approach to sexual relations as a form of possessive desire, in which activity is necessarily expressed upon passivity. This type of eroticism draws its meaning from difference and is the very opposite of holism.

Charis

As we have seen, the idea of sexuality suffers from its etymological and conceptual foundation in the idea of segmentarization and difference. This foundation generates an ideology of violence within the European conception of the erotic. The question would then be whether a holistic, egalitarian erotic practice is conceivable. And, in the case it is, would it be possible in the European tradition? How can we overcome the idea of love as an expression of passionate, possessive desire?

Let us be clear: the idea that penetration is the mark of a virile activity imposed upon women—or on young boys—is merely the result of an androcentric perspective. Contrary to this dominating vision of the erotic, an alternative is visible in the concept of *charis*, which Foucault also analyzed. Foucault introduces this concept as a synonym for friendship (*philia*), associating it with a form of consent: "it is the consent that a woman, willingly, grants to a man" (Foucault 1986: 206). As Foucault writes in his passages on Plutarch, *charis* is "kindness" (Foucault 1986: 207), an "acquiescence" that serves "to integrate sexual relations, with their two naturally defined poles of activity and passivity, into reciprocal relations of kindness (*bienveillance*), and to bring physical pleasure into friendship" (Foucault 1986: 207). Again, *charis* becomes "the gentleness of consent" that makes it possible to institute the "affectionate reciprocities" (Foucault 1986: 207) necessary for marriage. *Charis* acts as a counterpoint to the harshness of *eros*. It does not seek to possess or dominate through violence, but proposes a *gentle* relationship. By analyzing the idea of *charis*, Foucault seeks to counteract the "philosophical disinvestment" that the love of boys will undergo after its historical decline (Foucault 1986: 192). Foucault insists upon the feminine nature of *charis* because, if *charis* does occur within a pederastic relationship, then this love is feminized: if the boy is consenting, then he is "effeminate," as Foucault comments on Plutarch. *Charis* thus belongs to the feminine domain.

Foucault's definition of *charis* is still related to an idea of erotics as domination, and does not give *charis* the conceptual autonomy that it deserves. The Greek word *charis* etymologically connotes that which is dear, cherished, lovable, and tender. In French, from the same Greek root comes the word *charité* in the register of value, and the word *caresse* in the register of pleasure. The Greek terms *charis* and *charein* express "the pleasure of being, the satisfaction of fully existing" (Cassin 2004: 945; my translation), more specifically "as harmony with the outside world." Would it be possible to link this "harmony" to the idea of "reciprocity" that Foucault understands from the heterosexual love? The French philosopher reminds us that Pseudo-Lucian in *Les Amours* explains that feminine love involves reciprocity.

Nevertheless, gentleness and consent are not the same thing as reciprocity or gratuitousness, which are the key concepts for understanding *charis*. While consent is the acceptance of an action that is received, gratuitous reciprocity is a dual, dynamic activity whose power can be egalitarian. *Charis* as consent nevertheless enables Foucault to understand the role of *aphrodisia* as akin to softness and malleability; in other words, through consent he grasps the possibility of somatic modalities that produce a non-intense aesthetic pleasure-being. The problem lies in the fact that, in classical eroticism, *aphrodisia* require domination. Foucault recalls that this is the famous dilemma of *the eroneme* explained by Plutarch: the boy, beardless and object of desire, "compelled he feels hatred, and consenting, he becomes and object of contempt" (Cassin 2004: 206).

In contrast to this paradoxical eroticism, the concept of *charis* helps us to understand a holistic sexuality that goes beyond the segmentation and classification inherent in the very idea of sexuality, and seeks to establish the encounter between subjectivities. "Desire," writes Sartre, "is consent to desire" (Sartre 1943: 438); perhaps Foucault was aware of this phrase in *L'Être et le néant* ... Or, to put it another way, *charis* as reciprocity is the encounter between freedoms. In the age of #MeToo, *charis* could enable us to conceive of an erotics of freedom, a sexuality that goes beyond consent. *Charis* as a concept distinguishes itself from appetite (*orekis*) and violent passion (*epithumia*), to give form to "a community of affections (*philetairos koinonia*)," as Foucault writes in his commentary on Pseudo-Lucian. These affections "make good things more pleasant and painful things more bearable" (Sartre 1943: 221). We thereby understand that the fundamental role of *charis* as reciprocity consists in something that mere consent cannot do: namely, an intensification of pleasures (*aphrodisia*) as the community of affections increases the pleasantness of life while diminishing its painfulness.

Affective reciprocity can thus be understood as a stylistic of existence that enables a holistic use of pleasures that goes beyond the possessive individualism of classical eroticism. This notion is interesting for understanding the idea of unity beyond stasis. Bodies are united without identifying with each other; they move toward and away from each other, retaining their difference and freedom. In this way, reciprocity is not to be understood in a normative or essentialist way: it is above all a processual and energizing form, always oscillating and transforming. Aesthetic pleasure is thus renewed in a form of love that is not simply erotic, but exemplary on a political register as a form of equality.

Bibliography

Cassin, B., ed. (2004), *Vocabulaire Européen des Philosophies*, Paris: Seuil/Le Robert.
De Beauvoir, S. (1949), *The Second Sex*, London: Jonathan Cape.
Dewey, J. (1934), *Art as Experience*, New York: Perigee Books.
Formis, B., ed. (2009), *Penser en corps. Soma-esthétique, art et philosophie*, Paris: L'Harmattan.
Foucault, M. (1978), *The History of Sexuality. Vol. 1*, trans. R. Hurley, New York: Pantheon Books.
Foucault, M. (1978–1979), "Naissance de la biopolitique," *Annuaire du Collège de France*, 79: 367–72.
Foucault, M. (1986), *The History of Sexuality. Vol. 3*, trans. R. Hurley, London: Penguin Books.
Jaquet, C. (2001), *Le Corps*, Paris: Presses Universitaires de France.
Plato (1993), *Symposium*, trans. B. Jowett, London: Dover.
Sartre, J.-P. (1943, reed. 1980), *L'Être et le néant. Essai d'ontologie phénoménologique*, Paris: Gallimard.
Shusterman, R. (2000a), "Somaesthetics and Care of the Self: The Case of Foucault," *The Monist*, 83 (4): 530–51.
Shusterman, R. (2000b), *Pragmatist Aesthetics: Living Beauty, Rethinking Art*, 2nd edition, Lanham/Boulder/New York/Oxford: Rowman & Littlefield (cited as PA).

Shusterman, R. (2006), "Thinking through the Body. Educating for the Humanities: A Plea for Somaesthetics," *Journal of Aesthetic Education*, 40 (1): 1–21.

Shusterman, R. (2021a), "Pragmatism and Sex: An Unfulfilled Connection," *Transactions of the Charles S. Peirce Society*, 57 (1): 1–31.

Shusterman, R. (2021b), "Ennobling Love and Erotic Elevation: A Response to Six Readings of Ars Erotica," *Eidos. A Journal for Philosophy of Culture*, 5 (4): 156–70.

Shusterman, R. (2021c), "Sex, Emancipation, and Aesthetics: Ars Erotica and the Cage of Eurocentric Modernity. Response to Botha, Distaso, and Koczanowicz," *Foucault Studies*, 31: 45–61.

Shusterman, R. (2021d), *Ars Erotica: Sex and Somaesthetics in the Classical Arts of Love*, Cambridge/New York: Cambridge University Press.

9

The Body Must Be Defended: Somapower and the Women's Strike in Poland

Leszek Koczanowicz

The Women's Strike

In October 2020, Poland's political scene was rocked by mass demonstrations against the decision of the Constitutional Tribunal that virtually banned abortion. The Tribunal's ruling was then the latest in a series of blows to women's rights, moves that had been reducing and eliminating women's legal capacity to make individual decisions about childbirth.

In the post-1956 communist period, reproductive rights seemed to be a widely accepted standard. The government and its agencies tacitly tolerated sexual minorities, and the opposition had neither the ability nor the intention to stand up for a better treatment of them, with more pressing issues on the agenda. Besides having more urgent socio-political targets to pursue, the opposition was also locked in an alliance with the Catholic Church, and being silent on moral issues was part of the deal. However, the years in which abortion was practically on demand meant that the possibility of banning it was not imagined. Catholic movements that dedicated themselves to the goal of abolishing abortion were generally regarded as a mere reminder of the dogma preached by religion or, at best, as an ethical challenge that reactivated the principles dissipated under communist rule.

As communist rule waned and a new regime emerged, feminist organizations and LGBT movements began to sprout in Poland. This coincided with a considerable change in the conjuncture at hand, as the Catholic Church started vocally campaigning for a ban on abortion and the inclusion of religious instruction in school curricula. Undoubtedly, the Church capitalized on the strong political position it had obtained as a result of its support for the opposition under communism and on the ruling elite's belief that getting through the difficult transition period would be impossible without its further backing. Consequently, the Church had almost all of its demands met: legal abortion was severely restricted, religion classes were introduced in school, and economic privileges were granted to priests and the Church, which also had the property confiscated under communism restored to it.

The powerful position of the Catholic Church discouraged all major political actors from attempting to challenge these developments. As a consequence, the mid-1990s were marked by a tacit consensus on moral issues, which came to be called "a compromise" and soon became an entrenched status quo. Largely stemming from reluctance to antagonize the Church, that status quo was also convenient to all mainstream political parties, which feared that views on these issues were so divisive in Polish society that attempts to change the laws in place would produce a no-win situation for anybody involved. Another prevalent belief was that economic growth, integration with the European Union, and building democratic institutions were more important, and that new supporters had to be sought for these goals. Such a strategy was aligned with the general tendency of politics observable across democracies, where a centrist shift was more and more pronounced. As opposed to this, raising issues such as abortion in Poland would entail positioning oneself at the extremes of the political-cultural spectrum.

The situation changed radically when PiS (Prawo i Sprawiedliwość: Law and Justice) came to power in 2015, having won the presidential and general elections. PiS launched an attack on the values of liberal democracy by undermining the principle of judicial independence, seizing control of the Constitutional Tribunal, and seeking to influence the Supreme Court. These political maneuvers were combined with the fostering of a cultural environment that promoted identity politics.

The package of national and religious values touted by PiS also included moral issues. The party initially continued its strategy of upholding the so-called compromise, but internal pressure from its Church-supported activists and external pressure from increasingly radicalizing nationalist movements gradually caused tensions to escalate. Pro-life movements, affiliated with the Church and also having strong ties with the far right, began collecting signatures for a petition to the Sejm for a total ban on abortion. A fierce dispute erupted soon, as an abortion ban bill drafted by the pro-life movements made its way to Sejm in 2016 and unmistakably gained the support of the ruling party. As a response to the threat of further restrictions on the already very restrictive abortion law, mass demonstrations took place across Poland. Dubbed the "Black Protest," the demonstrations were so widespread and massive that the ruling party decided to withdraw from the bill, but at the same time made all parties aware of the political potential of the moral dispute.

The demonstrations in the wake of the Constitutional Tribunal's ruling of October 22, 2020, marked the next step in this struggle. Entirely controlled by the governing party, the Tribunal drastically curbed the right to abortion. The ensuing protests were much larger than those in 2016, and crucially took place not only in big cities, but also, often for the first time, in small towns in the regions having a reputation of conservatism strongholds. The grassroots nature of the protests also translated into their political clout. The demonstrations, which began as a defense of women's right to decide about their bodies, morphed into a social movement challenging the entire cultural and political organization of the Polish society.

The challenge and critique were directed primarily at the government and the governing party because the demonstrators regarded the Constitutional Tribunal merely as a puppet institution manipulated by power-wielders. Such a political orientation of the protests made it possible to construct a coalition of various political movements and also to draw in several politicians who defended the "abortion compromise," but strongly opposed the governing party.

The protests boosted direct political involvement, but more importantly, perhaps, they buttressed the existing tendencies to defend bodily autonomy. The LGBT/Queer movements were actively engaged in them, resenting the smear campaign which had been a salient part of the election strategy used by the incumbent President Andrzej Duda. In his election rallies, Duda had voiced a range of (in)famous remarks on sexual minorities: "They are trying to make us believe, ladies and gentlemen, that they are people. And this is simply ideology," he said, and added: "If anyone has any doubts about whether it is an ideology or not, then let them look into the pages of history and see what it looked like in the world to build the LGBT movement, see what it looked like to build this ideology, what views were preached by those who built it" (Barejka 2020). Of course, that and similar statements had been calculated to make political gains by winning the conservative electorate. Nevertheless, besides serving that direct aim, they were also informed by an unarticulated belief that the body and our uses of it should be subject to strict norms rooted in a religious worldview.

In a broader sense, the protests were exactly about defending the body against such peremptory claims. This aspect went far beyond current politics and concerned the overall cultural atmosphere in Poland with its dominant patriarchal beliefs about the necessity and legitimacy of political control of the body. In this sense, the Women's Strike was not only a vote of no confidence against the political system as a whole, but also a denouncement of its cultural foundation, which made it possible to institute laws that limited or even nullified corporeal autonomy. Hence, quite unsurprisingly, the body found itself at the center of political discussion and controversy in Poland. A coalition for corporeality formed around the issue of body autonomy. Despite political frictions and differences in their agendas, the movements assembled in this coalition agreed that the autonomy and integrity of the body, and individuals' right to and ownership of their bodies, were the most important determinants of the political front.

Biopolitics, Aesthetics of Existence, and Society

The idea of the body as the center of political discourse has been neglected by political theory and political philosophy. They have primarily explored the realm of disembodied ideas fueling the political action of reform or radical change of political systems. An example of this approach can be found in the otherwise interesting concept of the social imaginary introduced by Charles Taylor and defined as

> something much broader and deeper than the intellectual schemes people may entertain when they think about social reality in a disengaged mode. I am thinking, rather, of the ways people imagine their social existence, how they fit together with others, how things go on between them and their fellows, the expectations that are normally met, and the deeper normative notions and images that underlie these expectations. (Taylor 2004: 23)

Taylor realizes, of course, that philosophical ideas alone do not bear a motivating power, and that they must be fused with the events of everyday life to become part of the psychological mechanism that triggers political behavior. Characteristically, however, the definition of social imaginaries is limited to ideas operating in everyday life, and it fails to accommodate the body and issues of corporeality. This is quite puzzling, seeing that Taylor is familiar with the work of Michel Foucault, on whom he has written interestingly, albeit polemically (Taylor 1984).

Without going into the details of this polemic here, I need to mention one point of it. Specifically, in "Foucault on Freedom and Truth," Taylor reduces

Foucault's thought to the staple themes of political thinking derived from critical theory, such as control, identity, and its potential self-formation, and the grounding of the ethics of political choices. Corporeality as a topical concept in political thinking virtually disappears in Taylor's reading of Foucault. This is evinced by the fundamental questions Taylor poses in the concluding paragraph:

> (1) Can we really step outside the identity we have developed in Western civilization to such a degree that we can repudiate all that comes to us from the Christian understanding of the will? Can we toss aside the whole tradition of Augustinian inwardness? (2) Granted we really can set this aside, is the resulting "aesthetics of existence" all that admirable? These questions are hard to separate and even harder to answer. But they are among the most fundamental raised by the admirable work of Michel Foucault. (Taylor 1984: 181)

Neither of these questions directly addresses corporeality; at best, an implicit reference to it can be gleaned from the remark about the rejection of "Augustinian inwardness." However, the politics of the body, perhaps the most seminal legacy of Foucault's conception, is not mentioned altogether. Of course, such a conspicuous silence may stem from Taylor's narrowed interpretive perspective, but I believe that a deeper problem is at hand. Taylor's interpretation reveals that Foucault's concepts harbor certain ambiguities that make them difficult to apply in analyses of the body politic and its phenomena, such as the Women's Strike in Poland.

To examine this issue, I will briefly analyze three of Foucault's concepts in this context: biopolitics, aesthetics of existence, and technologies of the self. Perhaps the most frequently cited of Foucault's notions, biopolitics is defined in opposition to disciplinary power:

> Now I think we see something new emerging in the second half of the eighteenth century: a new technology of power, but this time it is not disciplinary. This technology of power does not exclude the former, does not exclude disciplinary technology, but it does dovetail into it, integrate it, modify it to some extent, and above all, use it by sort of infiltrating it, embedding itself in existing disciplinary techniques. This new technique does not simply do away with the disciplinary technique, because it exists at a different level, on a different scale, and because it has a different bearing area, and makes use of very different instruments. Unlike discipline, which is addressed to bodies, the new nondisciplinary power is applied not to man-as-body but to the living man, to man-as-living-being; ultimately, if you like, to man-as-species. (Foucault 2003: 242)

While disciplinary power and biopolitics fundamentally differ in range, they primarily seek to shape the body, either a mass body such as a population or an individual body, by the exercise of mechanisms external to it. Foucault meticulously and impressively described the methods and channels utilized for this purpose and the obstacles encountered when we tried to identify this microphysics of power. His tremendous work has furnished us with a new perspective on corporeality and its social embeddedness. However, I believe that Foucault was so preoccupied with the problems of subordination and control that he overlooked other aspect of corporeality. Specifically, he passed over the fact that the body could be active and self-creating, to a degree at least. The one-sidedness of Foucault's focus may (and did) invite interpretations like that offered by Taylor.

Foucault himself appears to have been aware of these limitations, as at a certain moment he exerted himself to vindicate the active side of corporeality as well. This shift is succinctly outlined by Alexander Nehamas:

> In the third and final period of his writing, Foucault turned from the power exercised on, and forming, individuals to the power individuals exercised upon, and through which they formed, themselves. That was part of what he meant by "ethics" … Morality, Foucault argued, is not exhausted by our relations to others, by codes of moral behavior that govern the interaction of various individuals and groups with one another. It also concerns the ways in which individuals relate to and regulate themselves—the ways in which we practice self-government and at the same time constitute ourselves as the moral subjects of our own desires and actions. Ethics is the care of the self. (Nehamas 1998: 179)

In addition to the aesthetics of existence, Foucault introduced and developed the concept of the technologies of the self, which enable "individuals to effect by their own means or with the help of others a certain number of operations on their own bodies and souls, thoughts, conduct, and way of being, so as to transform themselves in order to attain a certain state of happiness, purity, wisdom, perfection, or immortality" (Foucault 1988: 17). While the aesthetics of existence is more concerned with social relations, the technologies of the self are more concerned with the formation of subjectivity. Nevertheless, both are about the appreciation of individuals' resistance to the norms imposed by an oppressive society (in Foucault's conception, a non-oppressive society is hardly imaginable). From my perspective, however, the most important question is whether the concepts help us capture the body as a site of emancipatory and liberation activities, such as the Women's Strike in Poland. In other words, are the aesthetics of existence and the technologies of the self applicable exclusively to personal projects of self-perfection, or can they serve as a scaffolding for collective actions?

If we take the aesthetics of existence as a starting point, it would be difficult to conclude that the protesting women aimed to establish themselves as aesthetic-ethical subjects. Of course, participation in demonstrations often resulted in a radical change of attitude to the self and the world, and bore a considerable potential for the formation of personal subjectivity. A sociological research study conducted shortly after the demonstrations found that two coping strategies had emerged following the failure of the protests. One of them, which the authors call "narrative," involved the creation of stories about the possibilities of personal coping with difficult situations, such as an unwanted pregnancy. The other strategy, a more "activist" one, entailed finding niches where one could act outside the control of the state (Frąckowiak-Sochanska and Zawodna-Stephan 2022: 33). Precious though they might be, these strategies were rather far removed from the aesthetics of existence, if only because they sprang from anger and communal emotions, rather than from personal models of self-improvement. Such attitudes can hardly be considered an enactment of the technology of the self, either; by no stretch of the imagination did the demonstrating women seek to achieve a state of happiness, perfection, wisdom, or immortality. They tried to achieve a specific political goal of overturning the ruling of the Constitutional Tribunal. The defense of the freedom and autonomy of the body was undeniably in the background of this political action, though.

Somaesthetics, Somapower, and Social Action

Corporeality as a philosophical or, more broadly, humanistic concept is at the center of Richard Shusterman's thought. For decades now, Shusterman has been developing somaesthetics as an interdisciplinary field that brings together multiple sciences dealing with the body. Importantly, his somaesthetic framework is not an eclectic combination of various disciplines, but a carefully considered project with consistent theoretical underpinnings and a well-defined goal:

> Beyond reorienting aesthetic inquiry, somaesthetics seeks to transform philosophy in a more general way. By integrating theory and practice through disciplined somatic training, it takes philosophy in a pragmatist meliorist direction, reviving the ancient idea of philosophy as an embodied way of life rather than a mere discursive field of abstract theory. (Shusterman 2012: 3)

Shusterman's project obviously draws on other conceptions of the body in the social sciences and philosophy, most notably on Michel Foucault and Pierre Bourdieu. Shusterman agrees with them that the body is of social nature, but he also shows that it is capable of transforming itself to become better. This capacity of self-transfiguration is intimately premised on an awareness of the body, an awareness of its possibilities and its potential for remodeling. The task of somaesthetics thus lies in "studying the ways we use our soma in perception, performance, and self-fashioning; the ways that physiology and society shape and constrain those uses; and the methods we have developed or can invent to enhance those uses and provide newer and better forms of somatic awareness and functioning" (Shusterman 2012: 188). The normative aspect of somaesthetics, which meaningfully distinguishes it from Foucault's aesthetics of existence, is of paramount relevance in the context of political discourse. While the latter presupposes an unrestricted self-creation, the somaesthetic development of the body aims to constantly increase the possibilities of optimally using the inherent capacity of the body.

Such a normative investment urges passing from an ethical commitment to developing the body's potential to a political commitment. Such a transition comes to the fore when an oppressive regime restricts or suppresses the autonomy of the body and its development opportunities. A collision may then occur that triggers political activity focused on defending the body. In extreme cases, such as in the "Black Lives Matter" movement, it is about the physical defense of the body and its continued existence, but in other cases the protest may be focused on one or another aspect of bodily freedom.

I have called this facet, or moment, of somaesthetics somapower. This term refers to the instances in which the body becomes a vehicle for emancipation or, ultimately, for liberation. The notion builds on Foucault's biopower in that it envisions the body as being shaped by social relations. However, it goes beyond Foucault in believing that the body can actively transform its environment both physically and socially. I have described the conditions under which somapower works elsewhere (see Koczanowicz 2022). Here, let me only restate that somapower is set off by actions that are not political, or at least not consciously so. Rather, they are personal projects for the improvement of corporeality and, with it, of entire personality. Such projects lie at the foundation of what I call the microphysics of emancipation, that is, emancipation in everyday life. When these personal projects become coordinated, niches of emancipation come into being, isolated islands of liberation that often have to defy a hostile environment.

The politicization of somapower occurs when personal emancipation projects, or niches of emancipation, are threatened by oppressive regimes. The Women's Strike perfectly lends itself to being interpreted in these terms. The Constitutional Tribunal's decision that curbed women's reproductive rights threatened the emancipatory projects of corporeality. The movement that formed in defense of bodily autonomy and freedom was precisely a case of the activation of somapower, and in a dual sense, too. First, it grew out of corporeality and, second, it provided bodily means of resistance, such as demonstrations, performances, and other intrinsically corporal practices.

Conclusion

Thus, it seems that somaesthetics, a theoretical perspective developed by Richard Shusterman, offers a greater potential than Michel Foucault's concepts for describing and interpreting social movements that arise in defense of the body or the threatened aspects of its autonomy. This interpretive advantage stems from two key tenets of Shusterman's project. One of them is the tenet of activism founded on a belief that one's awareness of one's body makes it possible to actively transform that body so as to increase one's personal freedom and autonomy. Even if such projects of the body's self-transformation are limited to increasing an individual's cognitive, emotional, and social capacities, their implementation is predicated on a certain "social space" that is free from imposed restrictions. Consequently, they foster actions in defense of the body against restrictions.

This segues into the other tenet, which is anchored in the social meliorism of pragmatism. Pragmatism and somaesthetics as its offshoot insist that any action should be taken not only to promote individual development, but also to contribute to the enrichment of society. This is where the liberalism of pragmatism clearly diverges from the liberalism of Michel Foucault. Foucault was more dedicated to defending the individual against the rules of the modern state than to devising emancipatory social movements. Pragmatist meliorism assumes that there is no fundamental opposition between the individual and society, and that the two can harmoniously interact, provided that society is properly organized. Therefore, going back to the Women's Strike, the defense of bodily autonomy was also a defense of society as a whole against the aspirations of power to exercise total control.

Bibliography

Barejka, P. (2020), "Andrzej Duda o LGBT: Próbuje nam się wmówić, że to ludzie, a to ideologia" ["Andrzej Duda on LGBT: They Are Trying to Make Us Believe That They Are People, and This Is Simply Ideology"]. *Wirtualna Polska*, June 13, 2020. Available online: https://wiadomosci.wp.pl/andrzej-duda-o-lgbt-probuje-nam-sie-wmowic-ze-to-ludzie-a-to-ideologia-6521010473220225a (accessed January 7, 2023).

Foucault, M. (1988), "Technologies of the Self" [1982], in *Technologies of the Self: A Seminar with Michel Foucault*, eds. L. H. Martin, H. Gutman, and P. H. Hutton, 16–49, Amherst (MA): University of Massachusetts Press.

Foucault, M. (2003), *"Society Must Be Defended": Lectures at the Collège de France, 1975–1976*, eds. M. Bertani and A. Fontana, trans. D. Macey, London: Penguin Books.

Frąckowiak-Sochańska, M. and M. Zawodna-Stephan (2022), "Uwięzione między lękiem a gniewem? Powstanie i rozpad wspólnoty buntu w czasie protestów kobiet po wyroku Trybunału Konstytucyjnego" ["Trapped between Fear and Anger? The Emergence and Disintegration of a Community of Rebellion during Women's Protests against the Abortion Ruling of the Constitutional Tribunal"], *Studia Socjologiczne*, 244 (1): 9–35.

Koczanowicz, L. (2022), "Somaesthetics, Somapower, and the Microphysics of Emancipation," in *Shusterman's Somaesthetics: From Hip Hop Philosophy to Politics and Performance Art*, ed. J. J. Abrams, 61–73, Leiden and Boston: Brill.

Nehamas, A. (1998), *The Art of Living: Socratic Reflections from Plato to Foucault*, Berkeley/Los Angeles/London: University of California Press.

Shusterman, R. (2012), *Thinking through the Body: Essays in Somaesthetics*, Cambridge: Cambridge University Press.

Taylor, C. (1984), "Foucault on Freedom and Truth," *Political Theory*, 12 (2): 152–83.

Taylor, C. (2004), *Modern Social Imaginaries*, Durham/London: Duke University Press.

Index

Abrams, J. J. 11
Adorno, Th. W. 13, 91
Agamben, G. 18, 72, 84–6, 88, 90, 94
Alcoff, L. 145–7
Alexander the Great 73
Al-Farabi 78
Allport, G. W. 106, 108
Andrieu, B. 124
Antoniol, V. 1
Applebaum, B. 147, 155–7
Arendt, H. 89
Aristotle 30, 52, 85, 124–5, 176
Artaud, A. 50–1
Augustine of Hippo (Saint Augustine) 187
Austin, J. 53–4

Balibar, E. 52
Barbisan, L. 91, 93
Barejka, P. 185
Barraqué, J. 139
Barthes, R. 107
Bataille, G. 83, 130–2, 134–5, 139
Baudelaire, C. 4–5, 17, 27, 28–37, 74, 114, 124, 129, 139
Baumgarten, A. G. 166
Beauvoir, S. de 13, 55, 171
Benjamin, W. 4, 13, 18, 31, 90–3
Bergson, H. 80
Bernauer, J. 151, 157
Bernstein, R. J. 111
Berry, D. R. 94
Blanchot, M. 130–2, 134–5, 139
Boulez, P. 139
Bourdieu, P. 190
Bratton, B. 86
Burckhardt, J. 4
Burke, E. 166
Burnet, J. 103
Butler, J. 18, 44, 49, 50, 54–7, 85, 89

Canguilhem, G. 154
Cassin, B. 179
Cavell, S. 54

Charicles 177
Christ, Jesus 4–5, 7–8, 14, 27, 36, 63, 67, 69, 82, 84, 109, 127, 139, 149, 187
Colapietro, V. M. 19, 101, 152
Collas, A. 172
Comay, R. 91–3
Confucius 140

Davidson, A. I. 150, 157–9
Davidson, D. 52
Deleuze, G. 50
Demetrius the Cynic 69
Derrida, J. 13, 82–3
Descartes, R. (Cartesius) 54, 56, 79, 81, 104, 115, 165
Dewey, J. 12–13, 105–7, 111–15, 133, 152, 158, 169–70, 175
Dilts, A. 157
Diogenes of Sinope 73, 88, 140
Dreyfus, H. 35
Dubois, W. E. B. 94
Duda, A. 185
Dumm, T. 150, 154–5

Eliot, T. S. 140
Emerson, R. W. 171
Epictetus 65–6, 70–2
Epicurus 6, 64–5, 71, 125–6
Esposito, R. 18, 84–6

Feldenkrais, M. 131
Floyd, G. 94
Fontana, A. 108, 110
Formis, B. 20, 165, 173
Foucault, M. 1
Frąckowiak-Sochanska, M. 189
Frege, G. 122
Freud, S. 53–4

Gadamer, H.-G. 13
Gallie, W. B. 101
Gayman, C. 152
Goulet-Cazé, M.-O. 72–3

Granger, D. A. 146
Gros, F. 9, 72
Guevara, E. "Che" 83
Guilhaumou, J. 55

Hadot, P. 16, 27, 37, 63, 123, 125–30
Haritaworn, J. 86
Harris, J. G. 78
Hayek, F. von 110
Hegel, G. W. F. 18, 82–3, 92
Heidegger, M. 102
Henry, P. 83
Heyes, C. 154, 160
Hobbes, T. 52
Horace 83–4
Hume, D. 52, 115
Husserl, E. 78–9, 91, 104

James, R. 146, 151
James, W. 102, 114, 133
Jaquet, C. 172
Jay, M. 18, 77, 89, 94
John of Salisbury 78
Jolles, M. 147

Kant, I. 9, 30, 139, 165, 170, 173
Kantorowicz, E. 18, 81–2, 92
Kelly, M. G. E. 14
Koczanowicz, L. 20, 183, 190
Kojève, A. 83
Koopman, C. 151, 153–4
Kremer, A. 12
Kunstmann, A. 86

Laqueur, T. 88
Laugier, S. 52
Leder, D. 81
Lefort, C. 82
Lincoln, A. 89
Lorenzini, D. 18, 63, 69
Lovibond, S. 114
Luther, M. 115

MacMullan, T. 147–8
Mahon, M. 151, 157
Maier, H. 103
Małecki, W. P. 131
Marchetti, S. 148, 152
Marcuse, H. 13, 47
Marino, S. 1

Marx, K. 47, 53, 91, 93
Mbembe, A. 18, 84–6
McWhorter, L. 156
Medina, J. 145, 147–8, 152
Mees, M. 27–8
Merleau-Ponty, M. 13, 78–79, 104
Mills, C. 148
Mises, R. von 110
Montaigne, M. de 115, 131
Musonius Rufus 64

Nègre, F. 7, 27
Negri, A. 50
Nehamas, A. 188
Nietzsche, F. 5, 7, 27, 29, 35, 37, 44–6, 49, 102, 106–7, 111, 114–15, 124, 130–1, 134–5, 171

Owen, W. 84

Paul the Apostole (Saul of Tarsus; Saint Paul) 83
Plato 6, 56, 64–5, 71, 101–2, 123–5, 176
Plessner, H. 78–9, 133
Plotinus 128–9
Plutarch 176–9
Posocco, S. 86
Pseudo-Lucian 166, 176, 179, 180

Quine, W. V. O. 122

Rabinow, P. 35
Revel, J. 9
Richter, G. 91
Rorty, R. 133

Sabot, P. 17, 27, 31
Santner, E. 82
Sartre, J.-P. 17, 29, 30–5, 38, 179–80
Sartwell, C. 158
Scheler, M. 78, 91
Schleusener, S. 131
Schmitt, C. 85, 87
Schneewind, J. 52
Schopenhauer, A. 5, 29, 35
Seneca 65
Sforzini, A. 17–18, 43, 50
Short, T. L. 111
Shusterman, R. 1
Smith, P. 52–3

Socrates 6, 28, 37, 70, 101–3, 114, 123–4, 128, 140, 176, 177
Spinoza, B. 50
Stirner, M. 5, 17, 27, 29, 35–9
Stitzlein, S. M. 155
Sullivan, S. 145–8, 152, 155–6

Taylor, A. E. 103
Taylor, C. 186–7, 188
Taylor, P. C. 146, 148, 155
Tedesco, S. 131
Thoreau, H. D. 101, 122, 128–9
Tolstoy, L. 122

Veyne, P. 151
Voparil, C. 19, 145

Wehrle, M. 80
Welton, D. 79–81
Whitehead, A. N. 102
Wittgenstein, L. 102, 122, 131

Yancy, G. 145, 147–8, 155–7, 159

Zawodna-Stephan, M. 189
Zerbib, D. 132

www.ingramcontent.com/pod-product-compliance
Lightning Source LLC
Chambersburg PA
CBHW052118300426
44116CB00010B/1708